Praise for *Inside the Jesuits*

"Robert Blair Kaiser writes with the enthusiasm and insight of one Jesuit for another Jesuit, Pope Francis. A brilliant journalist with immense experience, he explores Jesuit DNA to predict change in the papacy and Church. It excites with surprising revelations and perceptions. This is a must-read for changing times." —**Jane Anderson**, University of Western Australia; author of *Priests in Love*

"I have known Robert Kaiser since we both covered Vatican II back in the 1960s. He had an inside track, having been ten years a Jesuit, and he has now made an eloquent case for the hope that Pope Francis will transform the sclerotic Catholic Church. I hope that he is right." —**Ted Morgan**, author of *Valley of Death*; Pulitzer Prize winner

"It is rare that you can get to know a pope from the 'inside.' Yet that is precisely what Robert Kaiser has done. He has gotten 'inside' Pope Francis by highlighting how the pope's spirituality and training has made being a Jesuit part of his DNA. Francis is a Jesuit to the core of his being, and Kaiser spells out with lucidity and style what this will mean for his papacy. With an insider's eye for detail, Kaiser introduces us to the spirituality and creativity that characterizes the best men in the Jesuit tradition, men who are always out 'on the edge.' He sees Francis as being the first pope for centuries who will challenge the church to move outside its comfort zone, as well as being precisely the style of church leader that Vatican Council II wanted. *Inside the Jesuits* is both provocative and reassuring: 'provocative' when Kaiser outlines just how challenging Francis' approach to being bishop of Rome will be, and 'reassuring' in that Francis is the most Christ-like pope Catholicism has had for centuries." —**Paul Collins**, author of *The Birth of the West*

"A compelling read, if only to hear Robert Kaiser wax rhapsodic about a pope! But there's more, for Kaiser writes from that peculiar twenty-first-century space where a 'former' Jesuit can still profess his enduring affection for the order and the Church." —**Tom Roberts**, editor at large, *National Catholic Reporter*

"Only Robert Blair Kaiser could have pulled this off. *Inside the Jesuits*, an admiring analysis of what makes the Jesuits such extraordinary achievers in the life of the post-Reformation Church, is woven seamlessly into a penetrating, astute, and thoroughly engaging reflection on the promise of the first Jesuit pope. An extraordinary achievement!" —**Donald Cozzens**, John Carroll University; author of *Notes from the Underground*

"At once chatty, insightful, and profound, this part-memoir, part–study of Pope Francis as a Jesuit, written by the doyen of American Catholic religious journalists, will delight and inform a wide audience. Written in an engaging style, it is deeply informative of how and why Cardinal Bergoglio was elected, and what we may and may not expect from his papacy. Kaiser places Pope Francis wisely and well amid his Jesuit peers and the order's history and charism, putting both Kaiser himself and the pope into conversation with major events and movements in the last fifty years of the Catholic Church's history, thus conveying the sense of constructive excitement that Francis's election has brought to the Church." —**Paul Lakeland**, Aloysius P. Kelley, S.J., Professor of Catholic Studies, Fairfield University

"Robert Kaiser has written a spirited defense of the social gospel, with special attention to Pope Francis and his 'Jesuit DNA.' As an ex-Jesuit, I found this enlightening and indeed persuasive at important points. Kaiser's hopes for a curing of the papal curia and his stories of Jesuit theologians' trail-blazing in matters of faith were of special interest." —**Jim Bowman**, author of *Company Man*

INSIDE THE JESUITS

How Pope Francis Is Changing the Church and the World

Robert Blair Kaiser

ROWMAN & LITTLEFIELD
Lanham • Boulder • New York • London

Published by Rowman & Littlefield
A wholly owned subsidiary of The Rowman & Littlefield
Publishing Group, Inc.
4501 Forbes Boulevard, Suite 200, Lanham, Maryland 20706
www.rowman.com

16 Carlisle Street, London W1D 3BT, United Kingdom

British Library Cataloguing in Publication Information Available

Library of Congress Cataloging-in-Publication Data

Kaiser, Robert Blair.
Inside the Jesuits : how Pope Francis is changing the church and the world / Robert Blair Kaiser.
pages cm
Includes bibliographical references and index.
ISBN 978-1-4422-2901-3 (cloth : alk. paper) — ISBN 978-1-4422-2902-0 (electronic)
1. Francis, Pope, 1936– 2. Jesuits—Spiritual life. I. Title.
BX1378.7.K35 2014
282.092—dc23
2014000661

Printed in the United States of America

To the West Coast Compañeros Inc.,
Jesuits-at-heart

President: Robert R. Rahl CALIFORNIA 1963
Vice-President: Jim Donovan CALIFORNIA 1974
Treasurer: David T. Van Etten CALIFORNIA 1958

Board members:
Juanita Cordero SISTERS OF
THE HOLY NAMES 1959
Bob Haslam CALIFORNIA 1962
Bob Kramer ENGLISH CANADA 1953
Doug McFerran CALIFORNIA 1952
Dennis Mulvihill CALIFORNIA 1959
John Suggs CALIFORNIA 1984
David W. Van Etten

And all the rest. . . .

"Jesuits are never content with the status quo, the known, the tried, the already existing. We are constantly driven to rediscover, redefine, and reach out for the magis. For us, frontiers and boundaries are not obstacles or ends, but new challenges to be faced, new opportunities to be welcomed. Indeed, ours is a holy boldness, a certain apostolic aggressivity, typical of our way of proceeding."
—Jesuit General Pedro Arrupe (1974)

"In a higher world it is otherwise, but here below to live is to change, and to be perfect is to have changed often."
—John Henry Cardinal Newman

"To believe in God . . . is to know that all the rules will be fair and that there will be wonderful surprises."
—Sister Corita Kent, IHM

"[T]he missionary joy of sharing life with God's faithful people as we strive to light a fire in the heart of the world."
—Pope Francis in *Evangelii Gaudium*, n. 271

CONTENTS

Preface   xi

1 A Jesuit Pope   1
2 What to Expect of a Jesuit Pope?   9
3 A New Vision   19
4 The Jesuit DNA   31
5 The Interview(s)   67
6 Vatican II   77
7 Other Religions   87
8 Liberation Theology   113
9 Pioneers   123
10 Not Just about Stray Dogs   147
11 Still Jesuits   167
12 The Man in the White Suit   181

Notes   205
Bibliography   211
Index   215

PREFACE

When the College of Cardinals elected the first Jesuit pope in history, my agent, John Loudon, persuaded the editors at Rowman & Littlefield to give me a modest book contract so I could tell readers just exactly what they might expect from a Jesuit pope. I had been a Jesuit myself in the California Province for ten years, and then, after I left the Jesuits for a career in journalism, I had come to know hundreds of Jesuits from all over the world, starting from the time in 1962 when *Time* magazine sent me to Rome to cover the Second Vatican Ecumenical Council. There I found Jesuits (some of them my old classmates finishing up their advanced studies) who were willing guides to the inner workings of the Church in general, and of the Society of Jesus in particular.

During the council, an English Jesuit archbishop from Bombay came to my home for dinner one night and stayed on as my houseguest for two years.[1] After the council, no matter where my reporting assignments took me—Boston, Detroit, Saint Louis, New Orleans, San Francisco, Los Angeles, Jakarta, Singapore, Manila—I always seemed to find Jesuits to help me on my story-of-the-moment. When I visited New York, I often took up residence at *America* magazine's headquarters in midtown Manhattan, attended early evening Mass there with a half-dozen of the Jesuit editors (and their occasional drop-ins), and was always fascinated during cocktails and dinner in getting their takes on the issues of the day. (They knew Church politics, and they knew New York politics.) I was like a brother to them, and they to me, like members of the U.S. Marine Corps (once a Marine, always a Marine).

In 2002 I published a memoir of my life in the Jesuits, a bildungsroman about my efforts to grow up in a remarkable society of all men (no women), most of whom were trying (and sometimes even succeeding in very original ways) to serve God and the people of God. In 1999 Jesuit General Peter Hans Kolvenbach told me I was "still a Jesuit."

Even after I came to ground in Phoenix (not retired, still writing books and occasional magazine pieces), I sought out pioneering Jesuits to come and speak to a club I had cofounded, called the Jesuit Alumni in Arizona. These Jesuit visitors often stayed with me as my houseguests, and, during conversations that went on into the night, they shared stories about their struggles to be of real service (and not just to Catholics, but to anyone in need). I am a board member of an organization made up of (mainly) former Jesuits—more than two hundred of us—called the West Coast Compañeros Inc. Some of us exchange e-mails every day online, and at least sixty of us meet for a weekend every February near Santa Cruz, California. When some three hundred California Jesuits gathered two summers ago at Santa Clara University, I was among a few invited to represent the province's former Jesuits. In the fall of 2012 the Jesuits of Calcutta brought me to India to give eighteen lectures on Vatican II in nine cities. The English Jesuits had me come to speak at Oxford's Campion Hall on October 12, the exact fiftieth anniversary of the beginning of Vatican II.

I may know more Jesuits, and more about the Jesuits, than almost anyone in the writing business today.

Maybe that is why, when Cardinal Jorge Bergoglio became Pope Francis, I found a good many friends asking me, "What's so special about a Jesuit pope? Why should he be any different from the eleven diocesan priest-popes who came before him?" I told them, "Pope Francis has something I call the *Jesuit DNA*, a way of being that Jesuits learn during their seventeen years of formation. They have this inner compulsion to do more." I discussed this with my agent (who was once a Jesuit himself). He said, "Get busy. There's a book here."

Very soon, I was hard at work on my MacBook Pro describing how Jesuits learn this special way of being and then live it. Only one thing nagged me. How could I know whether and how completely Jorge Bergoglio had acquired the Jesuit genes? Not every Jesuit ends up driven "to do more." (Some are only half-vastly driven. Some are born Republicans, and there is not much anyone can do about that.) Pope

Francis gave me one tiny, preliminary clue. On that famous return flight from Brazil back to Rome in July 2013, Pope Francis told the press in his impromptu news conference, "I think like a Jesuit." That gave me a start. All I had to do was tell my readers how a Jesuit thinks. (Not an easy task. Five Jesuits may give you five different views on the meaning of Vatican II.)

At first, I thought it would really help if I could have some face time with Francis so he could spell out for me in more detail how *he* thinks. Could I see the pope? Probably not. I no longer had the power I once had as the *Time* bureau chief in Rome when I landed an interview with Pope John XXIII on the eve of Vatican II. Still, I needed the answers to some questions that only Pope Francis could give me. So what more could I do to back up my feeling that Jorge Bergoglio's Jesuit DNA might compel Pope Francis to try to change the Church—and the world?

Thanks to the Internet and unprecedented, over-the-top reporting by the world's mass media, as well as careful coverage of the Vatican News Service, I found that, over the next nine months, I could see him in action and hear his words on a daily basis. As the philosopher Lawrence of Berra used to say, "Sometimes you can see a lot just by looking." That is all I really needed. To look at him shuck off the trappings of monarchy, to watch him begin a reform of the way they have "always been doing things" in the Vatican, to read his countless, off-the-cuff daily homilies, to smile at his surprisingly candid press interviews and pore over his forty-eight-thousand-word exhortation on the joy of the Gospel confirmed my first feelings about him—that he has been driven by his Jesuit DNA to make changes in the Church that have been up to now unthinkable.

Papa Bergoglio has been a pope of surprises.

I have my own surprise for you. This is not just a book about our first Jesuit pope. In order to explain more about the Jesuit DNA, I have written profiles of some contemporary Jesuits I have known—even some former Jesuits who are still Jesuits at heart—to show you how their Jesuit DNA drives them to get involved in the action and passion of our times. Yes, to change the world.

I

A JESUIT POPE

When I was putting the finishing touches on my *Church in Search of Itself*, a work that culminated in a narrative about the papal conclave of 2005, my editor asked me to send him some pictures of the new pope and the contenders, the men who might have been elected but weren't when Joseph Ratzinger won the final votes that put him over the top. I ended the photo collection with a three-quarter-page portrait of Jorge Mario Bergoglio, S.J., the cardinal archbishop of Buenos Aires. In the caption, I pointed out that he had received the second-most votes in the conclave, and I made a kind of prediction. "If he were elected in the next conclave," I wrote, "he would be the first Latin American pope in history, the first non-European in the last nineteen centuries, and the first Jesuit. We shall see."

I really had no idea then how much the negative leadership of Benedict XVI (and his surprise resignation) would prepare the way for the election of Cardinal Bergoglio in 2013. For the next eight years, we watched Benedict's Church go into a tailspin. We were treated to a succession of stories about one sex or financial scandal after another. The pope made few real moves to do anything about the Church's wayward priests, or about the bishops who covered up for them. In fact, some bishops were rewarded for shielding their villainous clerics from exposure. John Paul II had given Boston's Cardinal Bernard Law a sinecure in Rome (as archpriest of the Basilica of Santa Maria Maggiore) a day ahead of Law's scheduled indictment by criminal prosecutors in Boston. Higher-ups in the Roman Curia were taking bribes to protect the satyr-priest Marcial Maciel Degollado, who founded the Church's fastest-growing order, the Legionaries of Christ. Members of the Curia had split into two factions, and rumors began to spread about a gay lobby inside the Vatican. The Vatican Bank came under investigation by Italian and European Union authorities for money laundering. Papa Ratzinger approved an investigation of U.S. nuns for heresy, to the disgust of many American Catholics who thought these sisters represented the best that the Church had to offer. A kind of blight made its appearance in many places, even in traditional gardens of the faith like Ireland, where 80 percent or more of the Catholics stopped going to Sunday Mass.

This is why, before the conclave of 2013, papal electors told their favorite Vatican reporters they might be ready to vote for a successor who wasn't part of the old guard. They said they might even choose a cardinal from Africa or Latin America. That inspired the Vaticanisti—members of the Vatican press corps—to put three Latin American cardinals high on their lists of popeables. But, forgetting that Cardinal Bergoglio had gotten all but three of the votes withheld from Joseph Ratzinger in the last conclave, none of the experts even mentioned Bergoglio. Why not? Well, he was a Jesuit, and Jesuits, despite their Triple-A rating in most Catholic circles, just didn't become popes, did they?

All the more surprising, then, that the cardinals chose Bergoglio, and that they did it so quickly, crossing up the know-it-alls who were saying that, since every one of the electors had been given their red hat by either John Paul II or Benedict XVI, they would certainly choose someone very much like John Paul or Benedict—that is, men who would give the Church more of the same old, same old.

Some functionary in the office of the Italian bishops' conference was, in fact, so sure of this that, as soon as the white smoke started billowing out of the ancient chimney on the roof above the Sistine Chapel on March 13, 2013, he sent off the conference's congratulations to Angelo Scola, the cardinal archbishop of Milan and a longtime company man in Rome. "A quick decision? It had to be the favorite, Scola, right?"

Wrong. The College of Cardinals picked this Jesuit! Why? Because these cardinal electors were not idiots. They knew that the hierarchical Church, so overconcerned with its own power and its own illusory reputation, was becoming more of a museum than a mission. The cardinals knew they had to come up with someone different. And so Bergoglio.

Even though he was a Jesuit? No. It will take me more than a few pages to make my case here, but I will argue that the cardinals chose Bergoglio *because* he was a Jesuit. As a group, the Jesuits, though roughly half as numerous as they were in 1974, were still, with seventeen thousand members, the largest, brainiest order in the Church in 2013. Once the cardinals realized the Church's need, they had to make a choice—like the coaching staff of any team in the National Football League on draft day—for the best available talent.

George Pell, the right-leaning cardinal archbishop of Sydney, Australia, explained in a *La Stampa* magazine interview, "We got the very best of the traditional Jesuit: faithful to Christ, faithful to the Church, going out to people on the margins. At its best, I don't think there is any tradition in the Church to equal that of the Jesuits." (Pell did not know about the Jesuit DNA or take it much into account, for it was this Jesuit drive to go boldly for the greater glory that prompted Pope Francis to be much more of a reformer than any of the cardinals who voted for him had imagined.)

What Pell and the others saw in Cardinal Bergoglio was a man with leadership experience in the Church's most elite religious order. He'd been tapped to become the Jesuits' provincial in Argentina at the age of thirty-six, and at a very difficult time in his country's history, when, Pell said, "He got mud on his boots." Pell was no doubt referring to Bergoglio's reluctance to give a full endorsement to the forces of liberation theology in Latin America (as most of the continent's other Jesuit provincials had done), marking him as someone prudent enough to stay out of Argentina's messy political world, and pretty much a man who was not afraid to do things his way, no matter how much pressure he felt from his own Jesuit confreres on the left.

If Bergoglio had a bias at all, it was his wish to be in solidarity with the people at large, especially the poor. When John Paul II appointed him the archbishop of Buenos Aires in 1998, Bergoglio won instant admiration for spurning his predecessor's palace to take up residence in a two-room apartment, cooking his own meals, and getting around the city on the subway or in a municipal bus. Soon he started up dozens of storefront churches in the city's poorest neighborhoods. If the poor weren't coming to the priests, he would have his priests going out to the poor.

Before and during the 2013 conclave, the electors also saw something in Bergoglio's words and demeanor that suggested he could help bring 1.2 billion Catholics (and perhaps eight hundred thousand other Christians) closer to their roots in Jesus. He did that in one talk before the conclave when he said the Church was "too self-referential"—which many interpreted as "too much concerned with its own power and not enough interested in serving the people out on the edges" with the Jesus message.

And what was that message? In large part, a message of hope for people who had been overcatechized with a sense of sin as an offense against God. It isn't? No. Fire-and-brimstone preachers (of all denominations) have been scaring us with that story for eons, ignoring the more commonsense opinion of the Church's greatest theologian, Saint Thomas Aquinas, who wrote in the thirteenth century that "God is not offended by us, except by reason of the fact that we act against our own good." Translation: When we sin, we don't hurt God. We hurt ourselves.

Pope Francis made his message of mercy even clearer a few days after his election when he faced his first noontime Sunday audience in Saint Peter's Square and recalled Jesus's "striking attitude" toward the woman taken in adultery as recorded in that day's Gospel, John 8:1–11: "We do not hear words of scorn, we do not hear words of condemnation, but only words of love, of mercy, that invite us to conversion. Neither do I condemn you: go and sin no more! Well, brothers and sisters, the face of God is that of a merciful father, who always has patience. He understands us, he waits for us, he does not weary of forgiving us in his mercy." And that example, Francis implied, has an effect on all of us. "This word *mercy* changes everything. It is the best word we can hear: it changes the world. A little mercy makes the world less cold and more just."

These words echoed around the globe. What we heard Francis telling us was this: "If you miss the mark at times, it's okay. God will forgive you." I sensed 1.2 billion Catholics letting go of their collective breath—a sigh of relief, perhaps, after eight years of tension under a pope who was always more ready to say "No!" to our being human than he was to say "Yes!"

Papal audiences suddenly doubled in size. Robert Mickens, the *Tablet*'s man in Rome, reported that record numbers of people were converging in and around Saint Peter's Square each time Francis held a weekday audience or presided at a Sunday liturgy, that a surge of visitors had started invading the Vatican's various information sites on the Internet, and that the number of visitors to the pope's Twitter account had soared tenfold. What was captivating the people? Mickens had a guess: "It was his direct and effusive way of speaking, his willingness to spend endless hours greeting people, and his eschewing of elaborate attire and protocols."

From that initial public moment on that balcony above Saint Peter's Square, everyone noted this about Papa Bergoglio, even before he began to speak: he was not going to follow in his predecessor's royal footsteps—most especially not in Benedict's red Prada shoes. He wore a pair of ordinary black shoes on his feet and a plain iron cross (not a gold one) around his neck.

His first words were informal. He smiled and said, *"Buona sera"* ("Good evening"), followed by a request to the people below to pray for him and give him their blessing before he blessed them. He didn't, moreover, refer to himself as "the pope" (with all the universal authority that term implied) but as "the bishop of Rome"—a far more modest title. This could mean the new pope wanted the people (and, come to think of it, all of the world's bishops) to regard him as someone who was here to serve them, not dominate over them like a CEO of Christianity, Inc.

Even more important, he did not move into the airy, ten-room Apostolic Palace but established residence in the Holiday Inn–style hotel he had been living in during the conclave, the Casa Santa Marta, and took his meals there with its other permanent residents (mostly priests) in the Casa's modest cafeteria. He did not celebrate his daily 7 a.m. Mass in the confines of his private chapel in the Apostolic Palace, but rather in the Casa Santa Marta's chapel, and there, each morning, he started delivering homilies to a group of about fifty regulars, often using homespun language to put his impromptu glosses on the Gospel of the day. On the morning of May 22, he dared to contradict Papa Ratzinger's repeated thoughts on the Catholic Church as the only door to salvation. Francis said that God "has redeemed all of us, all of us, with the blood of Christ: all of us, not just Catholics. Everyone!" He then added, "Even the atheists."

The very next day, *L'Osservatore Romano* had to correct the pope with a 2,300-word essay by Thomas Rosica, a Basilian priest from Toronto and a Vatican functionary, saying the pope was wrong, and he had the Ratzinger quotes from *Dominus Iesus* to prove it: there is no salvation outside the Catholic Church. James Carroll was quick to write a column in the *Boston Globe* saying just the opposite—that he was astounded but overjoyed to hear Pope Francis saying that "an innate capacity for virtue comes from God and that it lives in the depths of every heart." Carroll, a Paulist priest–turned–fine novelist, hailed Pope Francis for giving an early signal that he would attempt to turn the Church "beyond tolerance toward an authentic pluralism in which the convictions of others are not only allowed but valued."

One of Carroll's readers wondered why, then, we need the Church. Another reader was moved to ask, "Is the pope Catholic?"

You didn't have to dig deep into the *Dictionary of Catholic Jokes* to come up with the answer to that: "No, he's a Jesuit."

However, in this instance, it is no joke. Francis, a slightly wheezy seventy-six (he has one lung[1]), with a wide smile many had never seen before, was making it clear he's a different kind of pope, a Jesuit whom some may not think very "Catholic" (in the narrow, nineteenth-century sectarian sense) at all. For one thing, from the moment of his election, Francis seemed bent on showing the world that he is not "up there" but "down here," demonstrating in little ways that he is not God, not even a god. (Ever since the popes became absolute monarchs, thinking Christians have been fighting an up-to-now losing battle against pope worship. Pope Pius XII didn't help any when he ordered those working in the Vatican to take his phone calls on their knees.)

Furthermore, Francis is daring to tear down the phony walls between the Church's priests and their people that countless churchmen down through the centuries have erected to signal their "holiness"— that is, their apartness.

By now, the *Tablet*'s Robert Mickens was reporting that Francis had "shunned use of the papal coat of arms, which has still not appeared on any of his garments; he routinely stands to shake hands with people rather than sit to have them kiss his ring; and he has largely rejected the use of gold, jewelry, thrones, and costumes that would emphasize that he occupies an exulted, imperial position." He was, Mickens said, "so unremarkably normal." (Francis soon proved how normal he was by trading in the black papal Mercedes limousine for a dark blue four-door Ford Focus.)

I know what Mickens was trying to say, but I would like to amend that word "unremarkably." To me, Pope Francis is "remarkably normal"—otherwise, Mickens and all of Rome's other Vaticanisti would not be reporting the new bishop of Rome's every effort to shuck off the imperial papacy. The real question is this: How did he get to be so normal? I think it has everything to do with his Jesuit DNA.

2

WHAT TO EXPECT OF A JESUIT POPE?

A China-missionary friend, Jeroom Heyndrickx (who is neither a Jesuit nor a Franciscan, but rather a member of the Scheut Missionaries from Belgium), told me in an e-mail how significant it was for him that the new pope chose the name Francis:

- This name (from Saint Francis of Assisi) means simplicity, poverty, humility, and even protection of nature and the environment.
- Saint Francis came from a rich family, but left his riches and lived very simply.
- He was the first to ever try to enter into dialogue with the Muslims, back in the twelfth century.
- He was also famous for his love for animals, plants, and nature in general.
- Never has a pope chosen that name. It is obvious that his name alone implies a whole new spirituality, a whole program of the new pope, different from those who went before him.

At first, my Jesuit friends (and my former-Jesuit friends) didn't know what to think about a Jesuit pope, or, if they did know, they didn't want to say in public what they were thinking. My guess? They felt proud, but, often warned during their early training about the dangers of vainglory, they didn't want to show their pride. "To think that a member of our club has become pope!"

Jesuit Thomas J. Reese, former editor of *America* and now an analyst for the *National Catholic Reporter*, even wondered in print if Papa

Bergoglio was "still a Jesuit." Reese's final verdict? That even if the pope could not participate in specific decision making by the order, he was still a Jesuit. What else would he be? The *Annuario Pontificio*—the Pontifical Yearbook, an annual directory for the Holy See—had no hesitation in identifying cardinal archbishops as Dominicans (Christoph Schönborn of Austria) or Franciscans (Wilfrid Fox Napier of South Africa) or Salesians (Óscar Andrés Rodríguez Maradiaga of Honduras). In the Pontifical Yearbook for 2013, the cardinal archbishop of Buenos Aires was Jorge Mario Bergoglio, S.J.

Soon, however, I overheard Jesuits confessing how good they felt now with a Jesuit at the helm of the Barque of Peter. It wasn't only the identity factor, a warm feeling that the cardinals had chosen "one of Ours." Jesuits who recalled recent covert clashes with John Paul II and Benedict's condemnations of certain Jesuit theologians (when he headed the Holy Office) were saying, "Maybe we'll finally have a pope who understands us." A month after the election, a prominent Jesuit theologian (who asked not to be identified) sent me a short e-mail to hail the election of Bergoglio, which he said "ended thirty-five years of terrorism in the Church."

He was giving voice to his up-to-now private feelings of anguish—felt, I know, by many Jesuits (particularly Jesuit theologians) around the world—that John Paul II and Benedict had all but shut down the Church's research and development arm.

If the Church's deep thinkers were not encouraged to keep recasting the faith in language contemporaries could understand (and they were not encouraged, but investigated to distraction and marginalized[1] and warned not to publish), who would do it? No one except these two pope know-it-alls, surrounded by aides who helped them write abstruse discourses few could understand, if they read them at all. Given their traditional reverence for the pope and the papacy, Jesuit theologians had been able to say very little in criticism of John Paul or Benedict.

It was not just their reverence that held them back, but also fear for their very future. Pope Clement XIV suppressed the Society of Jesus in 1773; in fact, he had the Jesuit general arrested and sent off to die in the dungeon at nearby Castel Sant'Angelo. Another pope could suppress the Jesuits again. John Paul II came close to doing that in 1981, when he put the Jesuits into quasi-receivership. In April 2005, Cardinal Ratzinger told the U.S. Jesuits to remove Tom Reese from his post as editor of *America* magazine—that is, remove the most courageous editor in *America*'s almost-one-hundred-year history. A few days after Ratzinger became Pope Benedict XVI, the Jesuits complied.

Short of suppression, Ratzinger could bash the Jesuits in other ways. He could hand over to Opus Dei management of the Vatican Radio, whose polylingual staff of four hundred has been directed by the Jesuits since Guglielmo Marconi created it in 1931. Or give the Gregorian University, founded by Ignatius Loyola in 1551, to the upstart Legionaries of Christ.

Now, to my theologian friend, it was unthinkable that a Jesuit pope would do anything but offer his blessing to Jesuit theologians (and others with their pioneering spirit) who are trying to find new words and new actions to promote what the Church and its people ought to be doing in the twenty-first century.

Back in the 1940s and 1950s, American Catholics were all about "convert making." (A California Jesuit named John Odou even founded an organization called Convert Makers of America.) Since Vatican II, when we began thinking about ourselves as "a pilgrim people of God" who do not have all the answers but keep making our wandering way through history, looking for new answers to new questions, we do not much aim at convert making anymore (though, somehow, the Holy Spirit is still bringing a good many adults into the Church). Instead, as thoughtful followers of Christ in our own time, we are more likely asking ourselves, "Really, now, what should we be up to?"

American theologian John A. Dick, who has spent most of his teaching career at the University of Louvain, recently criticized Pope Benedict for continually harping on how we might fight back against a "culture of death." In an article on the website *Another Voice*, he proposed instead that we listen to Pope Francis's alternative suggestion to start talking about "a culture of encounter." Dick wrote,

> Certainly a culture of encounter resonates better with our traditional Catholic understanding of the Incarnation: The contemporary world, our daily life events, the people and things around us are the place— the only place—where the Divine-human encounter occurs. God is not "up there," nor "out there," but "in here." We need to unhinge our church talk from a supranaturalistic and mythological worldview that people find totally meaningless; and we need to shift the official rhetoric from fighting phantom evils of birth control, homosexuality,

and women priests and direct our attention instead to signs of the Divine in places like shopping centers, unemployment lines, and shelters for the homeless.

"The encounter" Dr. Dick speaks of is an encounter with others. But how am I, a journalist, to deal with the others I find in, for example, my workplace? If not to convert them, then what?

In the spring of 2013, I gave an interview to Marcia Clemmitt, editor at *CQ Researcher*, a spin-off of the highly respectable *Congressional Quarterly*, for a story she was doing on the "Future of the Catholic Church." On June 7, *CQ Researcher* came out with her twenty-four-page report. It was a thorough job but very unsettling to me, because it gave too much space to a quantitative summary of "Catholic strength," as if we can measure the success of the Church by counting the numbers of new Catholics in Zanzibar (many) or the numbers of new vocations to the priesthood in Ireland (few). Clemmitt is a good reporter, so I could hardly fault her for using a set of old journalistic criteria for her audit. But she is not a Catholic, so how could I tell her about some new post–Vatican II goals (laid down by Jack Dick) that sound quite vague? "A culture of encounter"? What are we supposed to do when we "encounter" someone in our workplace, for example, or at a downtown demonstration against the death penalty or at our neighborhood Starbucks? What words do we use? Or do we use any words at all?

I found one answer to that question just the other day when I was rereading *The Sparrow*, Mary Doria Russell's science-fiction tale about a Jesuit expedition in the year 2050 to the planet Rakhat, where earthlings have found evidence of intelligent life. In her prologue, she wrote, "The Jesuit scientists went to learn, not to proselytize. They went so that they might come to know and to love God's other children."

So what's today's earnest Catholic up to, whether a scribe in the newsroom of the *New York Times* or a housewife and catechist in Dedham, Massachusetts, or a volunteer in Iraq for Doctors Without Borders? "To know and to love God's other children"? Is that enough? Dr. Dick concludes his piece as follows:

> I want to challenge our bishops, our theologians, and all church leaders at every level to move from harangues about the culture of death to the creative openness of a culture of encounter. It's an exciting life journey; but we need people who are trustworthy map-

makers to guide the way. Without good maps, contemporary people cannot travel far without losing direction. If maps are absent or defective, all exploration into God will simply go around and around in circles.

Who are Dick's mapmakers? They are the Church's theologians-on-the-edge, the very men and women who were being slapped around for decades by Cardinal Ratzinger/Benedict XVI for making trouble—that is, for being on the edge of heresy.[2] What's so wrong about that? Maybe nothing. In July 2013, at World Youth Day in Brazil, we heard Pope Francis tell thirty thousand Argentinian kids they should go back to their dioceses and start "making trouble"—or, as one translator put it, "making a mess." Either way, Francesco seemed to be telling the young people to start thinking of new ways to follow Jesus and demanding their rightful voice in the Church.

On November 24, 2013, Pope Francis told the Church's scholars and theologians:

> Proclaiming the Gospel message to different cultures also involves proclaiming it to professional, scientific, and academic circles. This means an encounter between faith, reason, and the sciences with a view to developing new approaches and arguments on the issue of credibility, a creative apologetics that would encourage greater openness to the Gospel on the part of all. When certain categories of reason and the sciences are taken up into the proclamation of the message, these categories then become tools of evangelization—water is changed into wine. Whatever is taken up is not just redeemed but becomes an instrument of the Spirit for enlightening and renewing the world.
>
> It is not enough that evangelizers be concerned to reach each person or that the Gospel be proclaimed to the cultures as a whole. A theology—and not simply a pastoral theology—that is in dialogue with other sciences and human experiences is most important for our discernment on how best to bring the Gospel message to different cultural contexts and groups. The Church, in her commitment to evangelization, appreciates and encourages the charism of theologians and their scholarly efforts to advance dialogue with the world of cultures and sciences. I call on theologians to carry out this service as part of the Church's saving mission.

Papal smiles instead of papal frowns—meaning that theologians can now find their voices, so long muted by John Paul II and Benedict XVI—makes a number of my theologian friends feel optimistic about the future of their work under Papa Bergoglio. In this new open climate, theologians (even, I hope, women theologians) will rediscover and redefine the faith *ad majorem Dei gloriam*. This is the motto given the Society by its founder, Ignatius Loyola. We see it (or the initials AMDG) carved on the cornerstone of many a Jesuit building. It means "for the greater glory of God," but it needs an updated translation. Many of today's Jesuits believe that because God is unchangeable—he already has all the praise, honor, and distinction he will ever need. Perhaps these Jesuits still use the old wording, but, if challenged, they would probably admit they are pursuing something a little more modest: "the greater good of the people of God."

My own fond feelings for Pope Francis stem from the fact that I was a Jesuit. At the age of thirteen, I had become a precocious convert to Catholicism. The catechism says my faith was a gift of God, but from my point of view I became a Catholic because I fell in love with my eighth-grade teacher, a nun, and with the exuberant Catholic kids in my class. At age seventeen, I entered the Society of Jesus, and I left it ten years later, but for the rest of my life I have remained a Jesuit at heart and have made it my business as a journalist to know the Jesuits as well as many of them know themselves. I am still a Catholic because of the Jesuits. They have given me a way of seeing the goodness of the world and my place in it—to help make it better. The Jesuits helped me grow. The Jesuits helped me grow up. They made me a better human being.

Would it be too great a logical leap if I claimed that a Jesuit pope could make a better Church? I will make that claim here, and I base it on something I call the *Jesuit DNA*. There is something special about the Jesuits, their training, their history, their head-and-heart take on the faith, yes, even a joyful take on the faith that can serve as an antidote to the poisonous gloom of our age. (The so-called war on terror, an abstraction, is making us all crazy. As the journalist Scott Raab wrote in the September 2013 issue of *Esquire*, "We are driven beyond all sensible limits by a looming sense of dread we cannot control." Since 9/11, Raab wrote, the United States has spent $1.28 trillion prosecuting the war on terror, "a ludicrous outpouring of resources" to fight a few hundred mentally disturbed jihadists "while all around the world millions go hungry.")

I am encouraged when I see Jesuits (and of course others) make Jesus's mission statement their own: "I have come that you may have life and have it more abundantly." My master of novices once told me Jesus was talking here about "the supernatural life of sanctifying grace." Now I choose to think Jesus was referring to all kinds of life, the so-called secular as well as the sacred, because I tend to think of everything on the face of the earth as a gift of God, something to enjoy across our whole life spectrum—everything from listening to an opera by Verdi to cooking a pot of spaghetti to watching a 49ers game on TV. I was delighted to hear that Pope Francis is a soccer fan.[3] In late July 2013, someone did a statistical analysis of the words Pope Francis used most frequently in his homilies since the election. *Joy* topped the list. Part of his Jesuit DNA? I think so.

The best Jesuits I know are like those poker players I see on TV who never hesitate, when their cards call for it, to go all in—that is, to push all the chips they have into the middle of the table. Jesuits were all in during Vatican II, solidly behind the *aggiornamento* of Pope John XXIII, leaders in the party of change. How, given their history and orientation toward *magis gloriam*, "the greater glory," could they not be among leaders of the updating that John XXIII wanted for his Church? Since the Society of Jesus was founded in 1540, Jesuits have been programmed to rediscover, redefine, and reach out for the *magis*, the greater glory. Who can say that a Jesuit pope will not?

Certainly not the editors of *America* magazine. One day in April 2013, James Martin, an editor at *America*, buttonholed his new editor-in-chief, Matt Malone, and said, "Why don't we try for an interview with the pope?"

Now, you have to know something about Jim Martin. He is not only an editor at *America*, the U.S. weekly Jesuit journal of opinion, but also the author of a best-selling book every year or so (his two latest, both published in 2012, are *The Jesuit Guide to (Almost) Everything: A Spirituality for Real Life* and *Between Heaven and Mirth: Why Joy, Humor, and Laughter Are at the Heart of the Spiritual Life*). He is one of the most media savvy men anywhere. Editors at the Associated Press, National Public Radio, and CBS seek him out for his opinion whenever breaking news involves the Church—because he speaks plain English

(not Church-speak), off-the-cuff and with humor. He has even appeared a half-dozen times on Comedy Central's *Colbert Report* to yuck
it up with Stephen Colbert, and in 2009, Colbert, a Catholic, made
Martin his show's "official chaplain."

So when Martin asked Malone, "Why not aim high?" Malone immediately agreed. Besides, Malone thought, an interview with the pope
would certainly be a journalistic coup for *America*. No pope had ever
done anything like this before. *America* had never done anything like
this before. And the pope was doing a lot of things that no other pope
had done before. There was something embedded in Malone's psyche,
his Jesuit DNA, that told him why the pope was doing what he was
doing: he had this spirit within him, called *magis gloriam*, driving him to
do more. And maybe to do it better than anyone had ever done it
before. Malone said to Martin, "Do you think we could arrange this?"
Martin nodded and said he would start asking around.

After checking with Jesuit officials in the United States and Rome,
Martin followed their suggestion to e-mail Federico Lombardi, the Jesuit who headed the Vatican Press Office, and he got a speedy reply.
Lombardi said the pope didn't do interviews. He suggested that perhaps he (Lombardi) could ask the pope *America*'s questions at a press
conference and then give the magazine the replies. Then *America*'s
editors could publish something that looked very much like an interview.

That option didn't excite Martin. So he e-mailed Antonio Spadaro,
the editor-in-chief at *Civiltà Cattolica*, *America*'s counterpart in Rome,
and asked him if he had any ideas on what to do next.

At that point, Spadaro said that he, too, would be interested in an
interview. He knew that, in Argentina, Jorge Bergoglio had given few
interviews. But if Pope Francis wanted to do this, *Civiltà* would certainly want to get into the act. He promised to follow up with Father
Lombardi. It might help, Spadaro finally told Martin, if *America* and
Civiltà made this a joint project.

For the next two weeks, Martin and Spadaro exchanged a good many
more e-mails. Finally, as Spadaro was headed to a meeting in Lisbon
with editors of all the world's Jesuit journals, he e-mailed Malone and
Martin, saying he would try to get all of them on board with their
ambitious project. "Lombardi can't say no to that." (There are sixteen
Jesuit journals with roughly the same editorial thrust as *America* and

Civiltà—including *Études* in France, *Stimmen der Zeit* in Germany, *Orientierung* in Switzerland, and *Razón y Fe* in Spain, among others.)

And so in June 2013 the Jesuit editors met in Lisbon (Malone could not attend), and there they all agreed to join the plan and submit their questions to Spadaro. If the pope said yes, *Civiltà*'s Antonio Spadaro alone would sit down with the pope, pose the questions, and record the Q & A in Italian. Says Malone, "I remember thinking both Spadaro and the pope would be most comfortable in Italian."

From Lisbon, Spadaro phoned Lombardi at the Vatican Press Office, and Lombardi took the editors' requests to the pope. And, according to Lombardi, the pope said, "Why not?" He said he didn't need to see the questions in advance. (In effect, the pope was making himself accountable. In June 2001 I had asked Cardinal Jan Schotte, who was directing the Synod of Bishops coming to Rome that fall, if the press could sit in on—or at least get a closed-circuit TV feed of—the Synod meetings. He told me and a hundred members of the Vatican Press Corps, "The bishops at that meeting are only accountable to the pope, and the pope is only accountable to God.")

Spadaro and Pope Francis ended up meeting for a total of six hours over a three-day period in mid-July in the pope's own study at his modest digs in the Casa Santa Marta. Spadaro had his recorded conversation with Francis transcribed (in Italian, of course) and then e-mailed copies to all the other editors. He suggested they get some careful translations done in their own languages and then agree on a joint, simultaneous publication date—September 19, 2013.

Martin said the editors at *America* could hardly wait to see the transcript. In effect, the monarch had agreed to subject himself to questions from a group of men who, though Jesuits, were nonetheless journalists. As journalists, they had a primary obligation to serve their readers, not the pope, readers who were informed enough to appreciate good, thoughtful questions and experienced enough to recognize honest answers when they heard them. By this time, four months into Francis's papacy, the editors already had some clues that Francis was not a man to use the kinds of evasions and double-speak that come so naturally to the world's politicians. They prayed that Francis might be ready for something as unprecedented as what they hoped might be a fresh, spontaneous Q & A.

Would they get what they expected? As it turned out, they got even more. Martin recalls, "When we finally received the interview, we were all quite excited. Funny enough, I remember reading it in Italian, and since my Italian isn't that great, I kept saying to Matt, 'Well, he can't really be saying that, can he? I must not understand the Italian all that well.' But then when we got the first English translation, my jaw dropped—he really *was* saying that!"

The other editors at *America*? "They were delighted and very moved," Martin says. "Delighted because the interview actually panned out and moved because of what they were reading. We spent a good deal of the time just shaking our heads and saying, 'I can't believe he said that!' And moved because of the spiritual content of the interview, which was quite profound."

Some of these same editors had been on staff in 2005 when their editor-in-chief, Tom Reese, was sacked by the Jesuit general, under a direct order from Cardinal Ratzinger, for writing things not nearly as subversive as some of the things that Pope Francis was saying in this interview. Martin told me *America*'s editors felt that history itself had its happy surprises: "The change in just a few years—from our editor being removed by the Vatican to our interviewing the pope—was really quite striking. Change does happen."

So I didn't actually need to interview Pope Francis, especially if the Jesuit editors intended to ask him tough questions. If Francis answered them with candor, I would have almost all I needed to analyze the Jesuit DNA as it might be embodied in this first-ever Jesuit pope. Then I could plunge ahead with more confidence to justify my surmise—that the pope's Jesuit DNA will change the Church and the world.

3

A NEW VISION

Íñigo López de Loyola, the founder of the Jesuits, was born into a noble Basque family in the kingdom of Castile in a small town called Loyola. As a youth, he was a ladies' man, but when his people went to war, he lived as a military man, and he almost died as a military man when, on May 20, 1521, he was struck by a cannon ball in the battle of Pamplona. This was a war between the French-backed troops of Navarre (then a kingdom in its own right) against the Crown of Castile, for which Íñigo was fighting. Because the iron ball hit him in the knee rather than in the neck, he was spared a hero's death and forced into retirement while he recuperated for months in his family's castle at Loyola, where he read and reread the only two books in the house, a life of Christ and a volume on the lives of the saints.

One night, he had a vision of the Blessed Virgin Mary, who told him she wanted him to found a new army, recruit others, and fight—not for any earthly prince but for "the glory of God." Íñigo accepted the challenge; took himself to the world's foremost center of learning at the time, the University of Paris; and spent seven years there getting ready for the battle ahead. In Paris, he persuaded some other students, mostly Spaniards, to join him in a new religious order, which would not bear his name (the Benedictines, the Franciscans, and the Dominicans had taken the names of their founders), but that of Jesus himself. And it wouldn't be called an order, but rather "the Company." The term in Spanish, *la compañía*, was a military one, and they say that Íñigo would always think of his men as troops, fighting a new kind of war, standing between two eras: the Middle Ages and the Renaissance. Up until then, many preachers had made Christians feel ashamed of their very sinful humanity. Now Íñigo was a man of his time, the Renaissance, marked by a new world consciousness that celebrated the glories of humankind. Jean Lacouture pointed out in his book *Jesuits: A Multibiography* that "when Íñigo de Loyola came into the world in 1491, Erasmus was twenty-five, Machiavelli twenty-two, Copernicus eighteen, Michelangelo sixteen, Thomas More eleven, and Luther had just turned seven. The very next year . . . Columbus presented the keys of the world to the Catholic sovereigns of Spain." In this new world, Ignatius Loyola felt that no man or woman was excluded or cursed, but rather destined to answer the call of Christ the King and become part of "a daring project." Loyola called this project "the salvation of souls." To him, that probably meant "getting into heaven." After Vatican II, however, most Jesuits I know call salvation "being all we can be in this life" (and let heaven—which we know so little about—be what heaven will be). The new meaning comes out of the council's reevaluation of celestial cosmology as laid down in its crowning document, *Gaudium et Spes*. We are no longer here simply "to get to heaven" but to make a difference in the lives of everyone on the planet.

In 1540, Pope Paul III gave Loyola his approval for a small "company"—no more than sixty professed fathers. Sixteen years later, in 1556, Loyola could say as he lay dying that he had followed the pope's orders. He had held the number of professed fathers in the Society of Jesus down to fifty. In fact, at the time, he actually had more than a thousand Jesuits at work in seventy-four countries.

How did he do that? Ingenuity. He wrote new rules. He set up two classes of Jesuits, *professed* and *coadjutors*. Only the professed were full-fledged Jesuits. The spiritual coadjutors, a class unheard of in any order until then, were priests but not professed. Loyola also recruited temporal coadjutors, called brothers, to do much of the heavy lifting. And he set up a fourth class of Jesuit, whom he called the scholastics, to be men in training teaching in the new Jesuit colleges springing up all over the place. (This Jesuit idea was obviously an idea whose time had come. One hundred years after the founding of the Society, in 1640, the Jesuits had 15,683 members in 868 houses.)

Unlike all the other religious orders up to the time of Ignatius Loyola, Jesuits didn't sing the daily office at stated times of the day; rather, they said it out loud privately, whenever they could find time. They weren't attached to a particular monastery for life but "made the whole world their house." They had a conviction that most problems have solutions and that they should try to solve them with imagination, perseverance, and an openness to new ideas. As stated in John O'Malley's *The First Jesuits*, they became "all things to all men so they could win all men to Christ." They didn't just do good. They did the *greater* good.

In the early history of the order, this free-swinging, nonformalistic, nonclerical approach (Loyola had prescribed no uniform and urged his men to dress like the people they were working with) took the Jesuits into a newly emerging world of science, into the courts and governments and universities of Europe, into the vanguard of exploration into Asia, Africa, and the New World.

Spanish Jesuits built a utopian society—the famous Jesuit Reductions, forty different communities that became homes to as many as a hundred fifty thousand Indians in the jungles of four Latin American nations. French Jesuits became strong, expert canoeists, paddling the Saint Lawrence Seaway and the Great Lakes region to bring Jesus to the Iroquois and the Hurons, and later, in the Pacific Northwest, to the Flatheads, the Coeur d'Alenes, and the Blackfeet. The meticulous diaries of their missions now fill seventy-six volumes. Italian Jesuit Matteo Ricci brought Western astronomy to the court of Beijing (where he himself imbibed a good deal of Chinese learning), and he might have made China a Catholic country had Rome not vetoed his ingenious adaptations of Catholic liturgy for the Chinese culture. European Jesuits of the eighteenth century plunged into the so-called secular sciences and made so many advances in astronomy, physics, and math that thirty-five moon craters have been named in their honor. In hundreds of prep schools around the world they became superadept teachers of Greek and Latin classics.

In sum, the Jesuits—as a group—became learned clergy, doing things their way, sometimes in startlingly idiosyncratic ways. An eighteenth-century French Jesuit helped codify and name all the steps in classical ballet. Nineteenth-century Jesuit Gerard Manley Hopkins became one of England's most celebrated poets—with no encouragement at all from his superiors. In fact, when Hopkins died, his father minister burned most of his work. We only have "Pied Beauty" and "God's Grandeur" because Hopkins had mailed copies to his friend Robert Bridges, then England's poet laureate. I knew one Detroit Province Jesuit named Jack Lucal who was a Quiz Kid on the radio in the 1940s before he became a Jesuit; he spent years in a college classroom and then decided to become a missionary in Kazakhstan, at which point he learned the language from scratch at the age of seventy-five. I also know a California Jesuit, Nick Weber, who became a full-time clown with his own traveling circus. His mission: to bring people closer to Jesus by making them laugh. Superiors encouraged him—even bought him a van and some trucks; the province treasurer, a former U.S. Marine, foreseeing the liability involved in having a donkey and an elephant in the show, took out insurance on all the circus livestock.

In 1773, after more than two hundred years on the Church's frontiers, the Company of Jesus skidded into disgrace when Pope Clement XIV suppressed the order. *Suppressed* has a gentle sound to it, maybe like a kindergarten teacher calming her noisy kids down after recess. But the termination of the Society shuttered hundreds of Jesuit communities around the world and sent thousands of Jesuits into exile.

A small band of Jesuits hung together when Catherine the Great of Russia did not allow promulgation of the pope's decree in her kingdom. (The Jesuits were running the best schools in Saint Petersburg, and she couldn't bear to see them leave.) So Russia nurtured a remnant of the order for some forty years until another pope, Pius VII, needing good men, found it expedient to restore the order in 1814. In fact, during the suppression, forty-seven former Jesuits, including John Carroll of Baltimore, had become bishops.

The restored Society represented a step backward. Still suffering from the aftereffects of the suppression, they feared what would happen to them if they didn't kowtow to the pope's notions, no matter how crazy. So they pitched right in, helping shore up the papacy during its period of deepest paranoia, cutting itself off from "the world" (which was evil), affirming its absolute power, nailing down a division in the Church that bedevils it to this day, its clergy riding on the upper deck of the Barque of Peter and the laymen in second class. (Laywomen? They rode in steerage.)

Pope Leo XII (1823–1829) removed laymen from administration of his territory and replaced them with members of the clergy or the Roman nobility. Gregory XVI (1831–1846) banned street lights in his kingdom because he was sure those large lamps would give those who were plotting against him an ideal place to hold their meetings. Pius IX (1846–1878), in an attempt to keep his Papal States, went to the extraordinary length of forcing 593 bishop delegates to declare him infallible at the First Vatican Council. According to Bernard Hasler's *How the Pope Became Infallible*, when one of his aides told the pope that infallibility was not in the tradition of the Church, Pio Nono uttered the most self-referential statement of all time: *Traditio sono io; io sono la chiesa* ("I am tradition; I am the Church").

Two popes following Pius IX had their bad days, too. A few years before he promulgated the socially progressive *Rerum Novarum*, Leo XIII condemned Americanism (fearing democracy in the United States might lead to democracy in the Church). Pius X wrote one of the dumbest encyclicals of all time, *Pascendi Dominici Gregis*, which was soon followed by his Oath against Modernism, condemning human progress.

Pascendi singled out George Tyrrell, a brilliant English Jesuit, as one of the leaders of the Modernist heresy. Rather than defend Tyrrell (who had the backing of most of his Jesuit confreres in England), Jesuit superior general Luis Martín forced Tyrrell out of the Society and had him formally excommunicated. Tyrrell died of heartbreak at forty-eight and was buried in "unconsecrated ground" (as they then called it). Tyrrell had offended Pius X by urging modern preachers and theologians to learn to recast the faith into language people could understand. In composing his Oath against Modernism, Pius X made sure everyone understood that dogmas cannot change their meaning from one generation to the next, and that the Church has men who have "full and perfect powers for ruling, teaching, and judging"—these words from another of his encyclicals, *Vehementer Nos*. In it Pius X laid down a classic definition of the Church that gave Vatican II reformers fifty-six-odd years later a sitting target:

> The Church is essentially an *unequal* society—that is, a society comprising two categories of persons, the Pastors and the flock, those who occupy a rank in the different degrees of the hierarchy and the multitude of the faithful. So distinct are these categories that with the pastoral body only rests the necessary right and authority for promoting the end of the society and directing all its members towards that end; the one duty of the multitude is to allow themselves to be led and, like a docile flock, to follow the Pastors.

In 1930, the Anglican Church's seventh Lambeth Conference gave its tentative approval to birth control. (The Anglicans hadn't said contraception was good, although they would, later, in 1958.) They insisted that "the primary and obvious method [of limiting offspring] is complete abstinence (as far as may be necessary) in a life of discipline and self-control lived in the power of the Holy Spirit." But they allowed that contraception was permitted in special cases. The reaction of Pius X's successor, Pius XI, was ponderous. He said he saw himself "standing in the midst of moral ruin" and compelled to condemn contraception as "an offense against the law of God and of nature," and to brand those who indulged in it "with the guilt of a grave sin." His successor, Pope Pius XII, referred to this pronouncement more than once and ratified it (he thought) for all time: "This precept is as valid today as it was yesterday, and it will be the same always, because it does not imply a precept of human law but is the expression of a law which is natural and divine."

Where were the Jesuits during all of this? Aiding and abetting. A Jesuit teaching at the Gregorian University in Rome wrote Pius IX's definition of infallibility, another Jesuit at the Gregorian wrote Leo XIII's diatribe against Americanism, a Jesuit helped write Pius X's encyclical *Pascendi*, another Jesuit wrote Pius XI's *Casti Connubii*, and still another Jesuit professor from the Gregorian guided Pius XII's pronouncements on birth control. The Jesuits were the pope's "shock troops," defending the Church from the world.

But not long after, contemplating the ruins of World War II, some of the Church's best minds felt they needed to reevaluate the split between the Church that prayed and the world that sinned. Cardinal Emmanuel Célestin Suhard of Paris was something of a spokesman for a group of deep thinkers in postwar France who were beginning to see that Christianity had marginalized itself by getting all wrapped up in an otherworldliness that ignored what men and women needed in this world. Suhard wrote that capitalism puts humankind at its service. He proposed turning that system upside down and replacing it with an economic system "at the service of men, and not just of some men but of all men." Suhard said that Christians had to roll up their sleeves and start helping to change the world; his famous pastoral letter *Growth or Decline?* won respectful attention, even in Rome. He wrote that God took on our humanity so we could take on his divinity and carry on in the world as other Christs "to complete creation."

The Jesuit superior general chimed in. In letters to the whole Society, read in my novitiate refectory more than once, Jean-Baptiste Janssens outlined a new Jesuit approach to the worldly work of advancing "the Kingdom." The Jesuits had not only to preach the Gospel and "win souls" but also to do something for people's earthly needs—help feed the hungry and, moreover, figure out why people were hungry. Janssens also encouraged every province to send some of their best men to higher studies: Men with ideas were reshaping the postwar world. Jesuits would have to be among them.

Soon after came Vatican II and its crowning document, *Gaudium et Spes*, urging the faithful to bring joy and hope to the world. Toward the end of the council, the Jesuits elected a new joy-and-hope general, Pedro Arrupe, a Basque missionary in Japan who had survived the atom bomb dropped on Hiroshima in 1945. He was soon pushing his men to trim their sails in the direction the council seemed set upon. In 1974, he gathered 223 Jesuit delegates to the order's thirty-second General Congregation and told them that the overriding purpose of the Society of Jesus—namely, "the service of faith"—must now also include "the promotion of justice." This new commitment was to be "a concern of our whole life and a dimension of all our apostolic endeavours." He said:

> Jesuits are never content with the status quo, the known, the tried, the already existing. We are constantly driven to rediscover, redefine, and reach out for the magis. For us, frontiers and boundaries are not obstacles or ends but new challenges to be faced, new opportunities to be welcomed. Indeed, ours is a holy boldness, a certain apostolic aggressivity, typical of our way of proceeding.

The order's promotion of justice was a strategy that would lead the Jesuits into social and political arenas that would incur the wrath of the rich and the powerful—and, in certain countries, the military goons they employed. "Some of us," warned Arrupe, "will find martyrdom."

The delegates—including a young Father Jorge Bergoglio, there in Rome as a provincial from Argentina—spent a good deal of prayer and discussion over Arrupe's charge. They finally endorsed the order's new direction in Decree 4 of the thirty-second General Congregation.

Father Bergoglio may have had his reservations about this new direction, and particularly about his social-action Jesuits in Argentina who had joined with others in the movement called *liberation theology*. Or maybe he simply feared for the safety of his men who had been targeted by Argentina's military junta. When two of them were arrested and tortured, he made no public protest, but he did help free them and have them quietly deported.

Did Father Bergoglio tremble in the face of Argentina's ruling junta? Probably. Made the head (or provincial) of the Argentine Province at the age of thirty-six, he was too unsure of himself to oppose those in power, and he was a lousy leader. Paul Vallely, a British journalist who came out with one of the first early books on Pope Francis, quotes a number of Jesuits in Latin America who knew Bergoglio. One of them, a former provincial, told Vallely, "He left the Society of Jesus in Argentina destroyed, with Jesuits divided and institutions destroyed and financially broken. We have spent two decades trying to fix the chaos that the man left us."

Vallely described Bergoglio as, then, an authoritarian figure who tried to reverse the policies of his liberal predecessor, Ricardo O'Farrell. As one former student recalled, "He tried to make us more like a religious order, wearing surplices and singing the office." He introduced a fixed schedule for the students and insisted on integrating manual labor into their formation. O'Farrell had allowed students and priests to wear nonclerical clothing; Bergoglio insisted on clerical collars instead. He himself wore a cassock. Bergoglio instructed the teachers of moral theology appointed by O'Farrell to revert to a textbook in Latin, even though many of the novices now had no Latin. He brought in conservative lay professors to replace teachers he considered too progressive. He sacked the theology lecturer Orlando Yorio, his own former teacher and one of the Jesuits kidnapped by the military in 1976. He also purged books by the other kidnapped Jesuit, Franz Jalics, from reading lists and withdrew them from the college library. "Liberation theology was actually forbidden," said another student, Father Rafael Velasco, who is now the rector of the Catholic University of Córdoba.

As we shall see below, Papa Bergoglio repented that move. Vallely reports that Father Bergoglio went through a radical conversion when he was transferred to a low-status position as spiritual father to the scholastics in a Jesuit house of studies in Córdoba. There Bergoglio, no longer a superior, lost his lordly (or maybe just fearful) ways. And when he was made a bishop, and then archbishop, of Buenos Aires, he began to look more like Fathers Yorio and Jalics, a liberation theologian working the city slums. And now his election as pope has given him a new boldness. "The man who is now pope," says Vallely, "remains a work in progress."

To those following the almost-daily newsbreaks out of the Vatican these days, that seems delightfully obvious. Pope Francis is now a poster boy for Cardinal Newman's observation that "to live is to change, and to be perfect is to have changed often."

One month into his papacy, Pope Francis appointed an eight-man international panel of cardinals to advise him on the governance of the universal Church and the reform of the Roman Curia. His predecessors had talked about a reform of the Roman Curia but confessed that they were afraid to attempt it. Francis could hardly wait to do it. Looking for a better way was in his Jesuit DNA, and so was his leaning on the wisdom of his colleagues in order to choose the best way.

As a young Jesuit superior in Argentina, he had been a one-man band. Most Jesuit superiors seek input on major decisions from their formally appointed advisors, or *house consultors*. Every provincial has a team, too, composed of *province consultors*. The general of the Jesuits has his own team—nine *general assistants*, one from each of the nine Jesuit assistancies—Africa, Asia and the Pacific, India, Latin America (North and South), Central Europe, Western Europe, Southern Europe, and the United States. The more input the general gets (that is, the more information and the more varied perspectives), the better decisions he will make. (Information theorists say they can prove this phenomenon mathematically.)

But it wasn't only information the Jesuits share. It was love. They program themselves to love God by loving others, starting with their own Jesuit brothers. If it sounds strange to list love as something that sets virile-but-celibate young men apart, think for a moment about the men of the U.S. Marine Corps who have fought and died for one another in all their nation's many wars. Their machismo may have prevented them from uttering the only word to describe their closeness—love. They loved one another.

Love is what often happens when men live and work together under the same banner. We see it happen on winning prep football teams. Decades after their championship seasons, the men will gather to remember how they struggled together and how, without using any words at all, they loved one another. In the case of the Jesuits, add the *ad majorem Dei gloriam* element to the equation (a "We're playing on God's team" mentality), and you have another marker that sets Jesuits apart—the Jesuit DNA.

My group of former Jesuits, the West Coast Compañeros Inc., comes together for an annual reunion because we have a high regard (yes, love) for one another. Like Marines, we have a special identity. We fought in the same cause together, and maybe that's enough to explain why we stay close. In our daily listserv conversations, we worry about the future of the Church and the future of the world. We cheer one another in our personal victories and commiserate in our defeats. We pass on the latest Internet joke. We trade health tips and haikus. We ask for prayers. We keep one another honest.

Ignatius Loyola wanted his men to make themselves "indifferent," a term that did not mean "I don't care." It meant that a Jesuit was supposed to put aside his "attachments" (or his "affections") so he could devote all of his energies to the project at hand. How did that play out? We see the Jesuit DNA at work in the annals of the order, in the lives of their saints (more than two hundred of them), and in the strivings of many who were never canonized. Jesuits remember their heroes, and the memory of their exploits is a big part of their Jesuit DNA. In fact, the only formal prayer that brings Jesuit communities together, usually before bedtime, is the Litany of the Saints.

Take, for example, a now largely forgotten Portuguese Jesuit named Benedetto de Goes. In the fall of 1602, young Goes set out on foot from the kingdom of Agra in northern India to see if he could find an overland route to China, a place his Portuguese Jesuit companions were determined to missionize. His three-thousand-mile journey was supposed to take six months. It took Goes four years of incredible hardship through the Himalayas, walking through parts of what is now India, Pakistan, Afghanistan, Russia, and Mongolia, before he ended up in Xuzhou—in China, to be sure, but a thousand miles short of his goal. He died all but alone, physically broken and exhausted, with nothing to show for it all but his diary accounts, which were later found and delivered to Matteo Ricci in Beijing. Was he a failure? "One need not make a big, visible, self-aggrandizing 'win' to be successful," says Christopher Lowney. "Sometimes success comes in the form of a contribution that helps the *team* to win. In Goes's case, leadership was proven by something as unremarkable—yet arduous—as exploring a blind alley so that future colleagues wouldn't have to."

Lowney spent seven years in the New York Province of the Society of Jesus before he left to make a career on Wall Street. Upon retiring from J. P. Morgan, he wrote a thoughtful work called *Heroic Leadership: Best Practices from a 450-Year-Old Company that Changed the World* to show his contemporaries in the world of business how they could profit from the very things he had learned as a Jesuit: self-awareness, ingenuity, love, heroism, and the daring to think and act outside the box.

Lowney tells Benedetto de Goes's story to show how an early Jesuit could fail in one sense and triumph in another: "Like so many explorers who discovered what's not out there, he helped others realize they had to head in different directions." Goes and other explorers had one thing in common—they dared to push back the frontiers.

As Lowney saw it, Goes could push these frontiers because he was a Jesuit. With no monastery walls to hold them in, and no attachments, the Jesuits were free to innovate, remain flexible, adapt constantly, set ambitious goals, think globally, move quickly, take risks, make mistakes.

I won't try to tell you that all Jesuits are heroes. The Jesuits ain't perfect. Often enough, Jesuit superiors are too craven to stand up to their bishops. Some Jesuits, loath to offend their rich benefactors, tend to diss their brother Jesuits who not only want to eliminate hunger but are also looking for ways to cure the causes of hunger in the world. For men vowed to poverty, many U.S. Jesuits live (and eat) too well. (By contrast, I discovered on a visit to India in September 2012 that my hosts, the Jesuit community in Calcutta, dined mainly on rice and gravy and had no hot water in the house for showers.) Some Jesuits I have known, like the Second Vatican Council theologian John Courtney Murray, are too proud of themselves. Murray took credit for crafting the council's Declaration on Religious Liberty. But he was only one of the declaration's many authors.

Some Jesuits still cover up for one another. The Oregon Province went bankrupt in 2010 after paying out millions to Alaskan Indians who had been used sexually decades ago as kids by a number of the Jesuits who came north to win their hearts for Christ. For forty years, a half-dozen Chicago provincials knew about the sexual predations of Donald McGuire and covered up for their Jesuit buddy while he was roaming the world, often in the company of beautiful young men, extracting money from rich widows and turning some of the loot over to Mother Teresa—which prompted Mother Teresa to make McGuire her order's chaplain. (He kept the job until Mother Teresa's death in 1997 and was later imprisoned in Wisconsin for raping one young man.)

The Jesuits also covered up the skullduggery of the Irish Jesuit Malachi Martin, who had operated as a secret, paid lobbyist at Vatican II for the American Jewish Committee. (He specialized in disinformation, planting false tales about "the Jewish schema" in the international press to make it appear as if anti-Semitic Catholic bishops were trying to scuttle a project that had the enthusiastic backing of John XXIII and Paul VI and 95 percent of the council fathers.)

I can say of the Jesuits, however, pleading guilty to a kind of Henry Higgins–like pride, that "by and large they are a marvelous lot." Very few of them are scoundrels, and more than a few of them are saints. As for the rest, they preach and teach and write books and do research and run missions—and play an occasional round of golf—"for the greater glory of God."

4

THE JESUIT DNA

There is no sensible way of summing up the Society of Jesus. For five hundred years its members have taken different positions on every issue imaginable, and this, surely, is what we should expect (even demand) from a multifaceted, global religious order.

—Jonathan Wright, *The Jesuits: Missions, Myths, and Histories*

Wright misses the point. Members of the Society can do almost anything they want to do—if it is "for the greater glory of God." Some Jesuits are scholars. Some are not. At one time not long ago, some twenty-two of them were also Buddhist monks. One Jesuit who founded a monastery near Damascus calls himself "a Jesuit Muslim."

This is the beautiful thing about the Society of Jesus: its men (sadly not *yet* any women in the order) have many faces, with differing politics, different passions, and decidedly different natural gifts that few of them ever want to change. This only makes the order itself more able to be (as Ignatius Loyola once hoped) "all things to all men."

The truth? Jesuit history and the Jesuit tradition tell us that all Jesuits, no matter how different they may be in their various ministries and their varied talents, have the same DNA. They were not born with it. They acquired it during the longest, most intense training period ever devised for men anywhere, even by the U.S. Navy Seals. It takes seven years after high school to become a diocesan priest. From novitiate to final profession, it takes a Jesuit seventeen (and sometimes more), a course that begins and ends with a thirty-day-long retreat according to a work of genius written by the order's founder called the Spiritual Exercises.

According to my longtime mentor, Australian Jesuit theologian Gerald O'Collins, those Spiritual Exercises of Saint Ignatius "make Jesuits what they are." A book can do that? No. In a half hour, one can flip through the terse set of meditations, instructions, and considerations that Saint Ignatius put together in his exercises and get very little out of it. The exercises are not a book to be read but a series of things to do—that's why they're called *exercises*, a kind of spiritual callisthenic that can help anyone with a wish to serve others make himself (or herself) into a principal actor in the Christian drama.

The exercises make Jesuits into men who are self-aware, with a confidence and a sense of freedom that compels them to risk whatever any situation calls for out of a love for God and humankind.

In the exercises, they fuel that love with the stories from the Gospels of Matthew, Mark, Luke, and John, which Ignatius set in a matrix of meditations meant to stir them (and stay with them) for a lifetime of generous service. I found a kind of poetry in these key meditations—on the Incarnation, the Call of the Kingdom, the Two Standards, the Three Classes of Persons, the Three Degrees of Humility, and the Contemplation for Obtaining Love—that appealed to the romantic in me and, I suspect, to millions of others over the past five hundred years who have immersed themselves in the exercises (they are often called *retreats*) and then (after they ask themselves, "What have I done for Christ? What am I doing for Christ? What will I do for Christ?") dedicated themselves to the ever greater glory of God or, as I prefer to translate the Jesuit motto, "the greater good of the people of God." What does that mean? It does not mean that Jesuits all march in lockstep. Instead, it means that they are constantly engaged in a discernment process, asking themselves in each particular instance, "What will work for the greater good of the people of God?"

Rather than give you an abstract account of the Jesuit training, I choose to tell you my story with as much concrete detail as space allows—this so that you can feel you are "inside the Jesuits." (In Pope Francis's celebrated interview with the Jesuit editors, I was pleased to hear him say, possibly in response to a question about his training as a Jesuit, that "the Society of Jesus can be described only in narrative form." I think he meant that the best way to understand the Jesuit training—and the Jesuit DNA—is to sit back and listen to one Jesuit's story.)

Here is my story (adapted from my 2003 memoir, *Clerical Error*).

I was a seventeen-year-old in August 1948, barely shaving when I entered the novitiate of Los Gatos in the grapevine-covered foothills of the Santa Cruz Mountains in California. When Jorge Bergoglio entered the Company six years later in Argentina, he went through the same training, marked most particularly by a month engaged in the Exercises of Saint Ignatius—thirty days of silence, meditation, prayer, and penance.

Why the exercises? Ignatius Loyola made that clear right on the first page of his manual: "To overcome oneself, and to order one's life, without reaching a decision through some disordered affection."

"Disordered affection"? Well, affections were the things we loved. If we were human, we all had our loves. But if our loves controlled us— love for our jobs, our learning, our books, our institutions of higher learning, or (one of the more dangerous loves) our power—if they led us away from what we were created for, then they were "disordered." And what were we created for? In Loyola's view, "human beings are created to praise, reverence, and serve God and by means of this to save their souls." Then Ignatius laid down his famous *tantum quantum* rule:

> From this it follows that I should use these things *to the extent* [*tantum*, in Latin] that they help me toward my end and rid myself of them *to the extent* [*quantum*] that they hinder me. To do this, I must make myself "indifferent" to all created things, in regard to everything that is left to my freedom of will and is not forbidden.

Tantum quantum was a ruthless rule. It was a piece of common sense that Ignatius Loyola no doubt picked up from the exploits of every leader in the history of the world in their single-minded battles for power. Why not use this rule to train his men in their strivings for the advancement of Christ's kingdom? Why not use it to help his men maintain their freedom to exercise whatever tactics were called for in their battle for the greater good of the people of God?

In the exercises, Jorge Bergoglio and I were given thirty days to figure out where we were heading and how we were going to get there. We were not given a checklist. We were given a compass. Our compass was Jesus. The exercises taught us how to become more like Jesus (*Jesu-ita*, in Latin, means "like Jesus"), so that we could be men for others.

Under the direction of my master of novices, I spent most of my thirty-day retreat getting on intimate terms with Jesus by immersing myself in scenes from his life in a special kind of "Ignatian meditation." I took myself back in time as if I were actually there in the Holy Land, casting myself as an extra, for example, in the Bethlehem stable where Jesus was born. I was encouraged to have fond conversations with the principals—the infant Jesus, his radiant mother, his proud father, the shepherds who had come to see what was going on, maybe even the Wise Men from the East who had brought gifts of gold and incense and expensive oils. If I was so moved, the master suggested I might even choose to scratch the ears of the donkeys in attendance there in that stable.

In his exercises, Íñigo demonstrated his own vivid imagination. In the first of his key meditations—on the Incarnation—he asked me to see the scene:

> [T]he Three Divine Persons looking down upon the whole expanse or circuit of all the earth, filled with human beings, some white, some black, some at peace, and some at war, some weeping, some laughing, some well, some sick, some coming into the world, some dying . . . all nations in great blindness, going down to death and descending into hell.

It was in this context that Ignatius saw (and bid me see, too) the Three Divine Persons determining to work the salvation of the human race and then making their dramatic move—sending an angel to tell a young Jewish girl that God had singled her out for Something Special.

After observing all the details of this drama in my mind's eye, I was invited to reflect on all of it and to close the meditation conversing with any or all of the actors—"the Three Divine Persons, the eternal Word incarnate, or his Mother, our Lady"—and then, "according to the light received, beg for grace to follow and imitate more closely our Lord, who has just become man for me." God wanted me to be a follower and an imitator of Christ, like Jesus? *Jesu-ita*? That was an offer I couldn't refuse. I said this prayer every day:

Lord, teach me to be generous.
Teach me to serve you as you deserve;
to give and not to count the cost,
to fight and not to heed the wounds,
to toil and not to seek for rest,
to labor and not to ask for reward,
save that of knowing that I am doing your will.

The charm of this approach, for me, lay in the fact that this call made me into something of a major historical figure, at least in my own mind. Kneeling there in my little cubicle, I let my fertile fancy go. I panned over the whole face of the Earth, zeroed in on the intimate little scene "in the city of Nazareth in the province of Galilee," and then put myself in the middle of the entire Jesus scenario.

For three weeks, I was trekking with Jesus and the men and women of the Gospel along the Sea of Galilee, helping them gather up twelve full baskets of leftovers after he fed the multitude on a few loaves and fishes, eating the Pascal Lamb with them in an upper room in Jerusalem, and watching Judas leave the gathering to go out and sell my Lord. I helped Jesus carry his cross to Golgotha, listened to his seven last words, and, roused by Mary Magdalene and the other Mary, ran to the tomb on the first Easter morning alongside John, while Peter came puffing up behind, and found it empty. Afterward, on the road to a place called Emmaus, I stumbled along with two disciples whose hopes had been dashed—until a stranger fell in step with us and showed us how it was fitting that Jesus should suffer, die, and rise again. The stranger shared a meal with us and made us know when he broke bread with us that he was the Christ. "Were not our hearts burning within us when he spoke?" one disciple said after the stranger had disappeared. Uh huh, I said. My heart was burning, too.

On the thirtieth and final day of the retreat, I dedicated myself to this Arsonist of the heart with words suggested by Saint Ignatius in the last of the key meditations in the exercises, the Contemplation for Obtaining Love. I nodded my assent when Ignatius told me about the sacredness of everything in the universe, and I thanked God for this gift (Everything in the universe for me? Wow!), and I flashed on the kind of response God wanted me to make: the service of others. I made my own a key line: "Love is shown in deeds." And I repeated this prayer:

Take, Lord, and receive all my liberty,
my memory, my understanding, and my entire
    will, all that I have and possess.
You have given it to me.
To You, Lord, I return it.
All is Yours.
Dispose of it wholly according to Your will.
Give me Your love and Your grace.
This is enough for me.

To sum up, I acquired a new way of looking at the world and my place in it. The world I saw had been redeemed by God-become-flesh and charged with God's grandeur. It was a world in which I could see God in all things and all things in God, a world that I could love and enjoy and help make a better place—if I cared to be a "saving" presence in my own time and place.

I think I (and most of my Jesuit peers) understood "salvation" in earthly, not heavenly, terms. I could be a saving presence if I set out to be all I could be—in this life. The next life? Well, that would take care of itself. Like most Christians, I was pretty sure I would go to heaven. But I didn't daydream about heaven or rev myself up on the heavenly reward theory. I was too busy being all I could be (through reading, study, conferences with my master of novices, and meditation) and developing my own self-awareness (through a twice-daily, fifteen-minute review—called an *examen*—of what I had done, or not done, in the past dozen hours or so).

The examen had five points, three minutes a point. (Boy, were we organized!) (1) I thanked God for all the blessings I had received in the past twelve hours. (2) I asked God for "the grace to know how I had missed the mark" during that time. (3) I ran through the past hours since my last examen, reviewing my thoughts, words, and deeds to see where I had missed the mark. (4) I asked God's pardon for my slips. (5) I resolved, with God's grace, to do better.

I did this examen twice a day for four years until it became a habit for my next six years in the order. By then, I knew who I was and what I was—a sinner—but not the kind of sinner who sees himself as some kind of outcast. I knew I was just being human and, being human, as prone as the next man to err. As a result, I became more of a mensch, easier on others, more ready to give them a hand up, more able to feel compassion for everyone I encountered.[1] That was the theory, anyway. I wasn't always able to summon up compassion for the occasional fool or scoundrel who crossed my path—more material for my next examen.

I also became skilled in a variety of ascetical practices. I avoided pleasure and sought pain. In the privacy of my cubicle, at the burst of an electric bell, I chastised my bare back with a small whip, and then stopped when the bell rang a second time. I fastened sharp, tight metal chains around a bicep and a thigh during my morning, one-hour meditation. Fridays I fasted, and on certain holidays, such as Christmas or Easter, I feasted on elaborate seven-course dinners. Most of the time, I didn't speak at table but listened while a lector read to the whole community "so that, while eating, the soul might also have her food."

This is a quotation from our Common Rules, which also told me I could not touch anyone of my brothers, "not even in jest." (That was Rule 32, observed so strictly in the novitiate that we played touchless touch football. Strictly a pass-catch game, no running after the catch.) Those rules even listed those things my fellow novices and I could talk about during times of recreation. We could talk about the Ten Commandments, for example, except the Sixth and the Ninth. We could not talk about sex or food or worldly things. Better to talk about the lives of the saints, whom we learned about from a huge library of biographies, often of canonized Jesuit saints (more numerous than the saints from other orders).

We devoured books on the life of Christ and books about Saint Ignatius of Loyola.

We spent fifteen minutes every day reading the Bible (we called it *Scripture*, because "Bible" was a Protestant term) and another fifteen minutes reading *The Imitation of Christ* by Thomas à Kempis. In retrospect, I don't know why we made so much of Thomas, a medieval monk whose philosophy could hardly help us become the do-everything guys envisioned by the order's founder. Thomas believed that every time he went out among men, he returned to his cell "less a man." Saint Ignatius liked going out among men.

In the master's exhortations, he tried to give us the benefit of everything he knew and everything he thought he knew. I now think his barrel full of certainties was too full—of beliefs about the nature of God, the Trinity, the angels and the creation of the world, and the necessity of always having Mass in Latin. But my master had some solid wisdom, which made sense to me then and still makes sense today. He explained the difference between true and false spirituality, and true and false religion, and he warned us about "the human element in the Church of God."

The master tried to teach us self-discipline by showing us how to live a penitential life, according to the principle that "if it gives pleasure, reject it; if it gives pain, embrace it." I suspect that this wasn't the master's idea: as the master, he had to pass on this particular perversion. During our thirty-day retreat, we spent a whole day meditating on hell "so that, if by our faults, we forget the love of God, the thoughts of hell will deter us from sin."

How many different ways could I meditate on hell? My master found five ways, culminating, finally, in an "application of the senses," bidding me to imagine what hell looked like, sounded like, smelled like, tasted like, and felt like as I was being roasted on a spit or boiled in oil. The master seemed to take great glee in hell. I didn't find much joy in thinking about it at the time, but now I can smile about it, too.

I am not sure that, then, I believed in hell, and I do not believe in it now (and neither do many thinking Catholics today). To me, stories about hell are metaphors or myths, not "articles of faith." In fact, the Church says that, while there may be a hell, it cannot say that anyone is in residence there. As for Lucifer, the fallen angel and devil-in-chief, well, the catechism still gives him a mention. And he plays an occasional role in the homilies of Papa Bergoglio—a holdover, no doubt, from his own vivid meditations on hell in his novitiate days.

After we were given a full day in hell, we also got a more solid, three-week grounding in what it meant to be a follower of the Jesus who had said, "I am come that you may have life and have it more abundantly."

"Life is to enjoy," said the master. "God made the peach taste good so you'd enjoy eating it." And living that life didn't mean going around grimacing all the time and spreading gloom, much less "embracing pain." This wasn't just his opinion, said the master. It was the opinion of the official Church, which, for centuries, had taught (against reformers like Savonarola who were "always holier than the Church") that Christians never had to opt for the more difficult way just because it was more difficult. The Church had marginalized those moral theologians, he said, who had taught a doctrine called *probabiliorism*—which held that anyone faced with a moral dilemma always had to choose the more probably moral course. Whenever there was a real doubt, our master assured us, we were free to opt even for the less probable moral alternative. The principle was formulated in the Latin, *Lex dubia non obligat*—"a doubtful law does not oblige." Otherwise, life would be too gloomy, too Calvinistic, and a far cry from the freedom of the sons and daughters of God that Jesus had come to proclaim.

We laughed a lot during recreation. I remember one day escorting a visitor past our novitiate courtyard when my brothers were "in recreation." He asked me, "What are they all laughing about?

I said, "We're always laughing. I guess it is just the joy of being together—and a relief from our rigid schedule." It *was* rigid.

In my novitiate, and in young Jorge Bergoglio's novitiate, we spoke only Latin, except during "recreation"—that is, for a half hour or so after our noonday dinner and another after our evening supper. They split us up during our times of recreation into assigned companies of three so we couldn't gravitate to our favorites, a practice that, in retrospect, trained us to be able to speak to almost everyone, no matter how dull or crazy they were. (It was a skill I used later in my life when I was interviewing Sirhan Sirhan almost every day for six months before, during, and after his trial for the assassination of Robert F. Kennedy.)

We also followed another ancient, monkish principle, *deny yourself*, and often went to absurd lengths to shun pleasure, even a dish of ice cream, a drink of cold milk, the smell of a garden rose, or the nighttime view of the twinkling Santa Clara Valley below.

We denied our own will. At the sound of bells every fifteen minutes or so, we jumped through all the myriad exercises of each day, instantly, "even to the letter unended." (That is, on the upswing of the letter *E*, we dropped our pen and moved on—in silence.) If we had something necessary to say, we said it in Latin. We had drinking fountains in the hall outside our cubicles, but we could not use them unless we asked permission of the beadle. *Licetne bibere?* we asked him. "May I get a drink?" *Certe*, he would always reply—"Certainly." But we had to ask. Obedience, the master kept reiterating, was the preeminent virtue of a good Jesuit, as poverty was for a Franciscan or recollection for a Trappist.

Of course, there were other virtues, too. Each of us tried to select one to work on each month, even kept count on a pocket abacus of the number of times we "practiced" that virtue, or slipped into a repetition of its opposite. I was born and bred into an impatient and irascible family. (My grandfather, Charlie Blair, used to heave decks of cards across the room during heated poker games.) And so, for the entire two years of my novitiate, I worked on patience. I never learned patience, but my impatient nature gave me something to think about during my examens. And I learned, at least, to suppress many of my impatient nature's outward manifestations, which made life a bit easier on those around me.

I never thought that losing my temper on the basketball court hurt God—it hurt me. And it hurt my team. During one game that I have never forgotten, I was called for committing my fourth foul. At that, I protested so bitterly (because I hadn't charged Louis Peinado—I still remember his name—he had charged me). For my too-bitter protest, I drew a fifth foul that sent me to the bench. That meant my team had to play the rest of the game (and lose) with four men. Recalling the incident during my examen that evening, I told myself I never would have made such a scene except for my "inordinate affection"—wanting to win too much.

I have always wanted to win too much. I suspect it's in my genes. My mother, who was captain of her basketball team at Hollywood High in Los Angeles in 1927, and my father, who was a captain of his football, basketball, and baseball teams at Highland Park High in Detroit in 1925, both loved winning at everything and would do almost anything to win. I can recall my mom's typical MO at the racetrack: she would surreptitiously buy four win tickets on four different horses in the same race so that, after the race, back at the family table in the clubhouse, she could pull the winning ticket out of her purse, wave it, and announce to all, "I had that one!" Was she hurting God? I don't think he gave a damn. She was hurting herself.

Learning how to get along with my fellow novices, each of them with their own (sometimes annoying) ways, was also part of my training. But then, my quick tongue and my competitive nature must have seemed pretty annoying to my fellow novices, too. During my twice-daily examens, I came to be more and more aware of my failings. And where I failed to see for myself, my brothers told me.

They told me so on a dull gray afternoon in March of my second year in something called an *Exercitium Caritatis*, or "Exercise of Charity." These were truth sessions—something like those the Communists imposed on every village and hamlet in China soon after the party take-over in China during the late 1940s and early 1950s. With them, the Red Chinese could gain group control over individuals who were different (and therefore subversive). I assume now that our Exercises of Charity had the same rationale—to help us conform to the others, though they were ostensibly "for our own good."

The *Exercitium Caritatis* worked like this: All the novices sat in folding metal chairs arranged in a large oval in our common room. On a given day in each week, the master would call out a novice to go to the center, make the sign of the cross, kneel, kiss the floor, fold his hands, and listen as each man around the circle stood and told the master what defects they had noticed in Brother So-and-So. Generally, the circle had time to examine two men during each session, giving each of them a half-hour's rundown on their defects.

"Father," I would say, "it seems to me that Brother Hombach is supercilious. He doesn't listen to the opinions of others. And sometimes he goes on reading *America* at the bulletin board after the bell has rung calling us to something else." Then I would sit down, and the man next to me would stand and deliver his analysis. And so on, until everyone had had his say. Then the master would invite the next victim to go kneel in the middle.

When my day came, most of my brothers had a lot to say—so much, in fact, that they needed the whole hour to detail their observations. I took a perverse enjoyment in this. I am probably an Enneagram 4: I liked being noticed, and I rather enjoyed the attention—and the discovery that my brothers couldn't put me in neat pigeonholes, couldn't even agree which of my ways were defects and which were virtues.

Brother Wolf said I was too naïve, and Brother Blake said I was too knowing. Brother Wagner said I was too familiar, and Brother Smith said I was standoffish. Brother Ryan said, "Father, it seems to me that Brother is too loose. Why, one day after we had put the refectory back together after a big feast, he just lay right down in the middle of the floor." "Father," said Brother Brill, "it seems to me that Brother is too tense. As scullery boss, he's such a driving force."

Many others had scullery stories to tell. It was obvious that in my role as field marshal of the kitchens and dining room I had nettled many of the troops. Brother Maher was the only one who tried to defend me. He pointed out that I had to give a thousand orders a day—

in Latin. "And it isn't always easy to take some of the orders he has to give. It's hard to go into that scullery line after a big feast when you know there's a ton of dirty pots downstairs and hear him say *Muta vestimenta et adjuva in ollis.*" Everyone in the circle knew what that meant: "Go down to the change room, take off your cassock, and don rubber boots, a Levi jacket, and a big black rubber apron, because you're going to scrub huge metal cauldrons." They roared, because they knew that Brother Maher was right, and they also knew how much he hated working in that steamy dungeon called "pots." He sat down soberly, and out of the corner of my eye I could see that he seemed pleased that he had made his point so well; he burst right out laughing.

Though my mind was telling me that I was enjoying all of this, too, and that I would earnestly try to reform my ways according to the manifest wishes of my brethren, I found, to my surprise, that my body was giving me a different message. During the closing prayer, after I had risen from my knees and returned to my place in the circle, I found that all the valves in my stomach were opening and closing in peculiar, uncomfortable ways.

Hiccupping after this exercise, I went to the master's room and told him I was sick. He said, "Yes, I can see. Your stomach is backing up. I can smell your breath way over here." He clapped a hand over his mouth, pulled on his bulbous nose, squeezed his cheeks, and then said, finally, "Go lie down. Skip dinner. If you feel like it, go down later and eat at second table with the waiters."

Lying on the narrow bed in my cubicle, I reviewed my brothers' remarks. I found some consolation in the fact that their observations were all so contradictory. They couldn't all be right, I said. Therefore, I reasoned fallaciously, none of them were right. *Strange*, I thought to myself, *no one mentioned my overly competitive nature. Anyone who watched me play my fiery brand of basketball could see that.*

I had grateful thoughts about Brother Maher's intervention on my behalf. In the ethos of the novitiate, however, I couldn't show my gratitude. I even had to demonstrate the opposite. The very next day, we had a big feast, and I had completely forgotten that I needed an extra man to scrub pots that night—until Brother Maher appeared before me in line. The sight of him reminded me. And, once I was reminded, I couldn't play favorites by skipping him and condemning the next man in line to the dungeon of the greasy cauldrons.

Muta vestimenta, I said without a smile, *et adjuva in ollis*.

"Jeez!" he cried, and crumpled like a man who'd just been socked in the stomach. He recovered and hurried off toward the change room, muttering—not in Latin, for he was talking to himself—"Try to stick up for a guy and what do you get for it? Jeez! Try to stick up for a guy!"[2]

Chris Lowney makes much of "the Jesuit ingenuity" (stemming from the self-confidence produced during the exercises) that led to such outstanding results in the order's earliest years. Within a decade of their founding, after deciding to make the education of poor young men a priority, the Jesuits had opened more than thirty colleges. Xavier himself beat Loyola to the draw; in Portuguese Goa in 1550, without consulting headquarters, he opened the first Jesuit-operated school of its kind anywhere in the world, this to educate native children and those of the Portuguese colonists. In a letter back to Rome, he suggested the order think about going into the education business.

How could Xavier be so sure that opening a school was the right thing to do? Obviously, he saw an opportunity and took it. But what made him decide to go with that opportunity, in addition to a number of other efforts he undertook? (He had a Jesuit printing press—another first—operating in Goa that same year.) My guess is that Loyola's Rules for the Discernment of Spirits were already second nature to Francis Xavier, who, as one of Íñigo's original companions at the University of Paris, had been doing the exercises under Loyola's direction for fourteen years. You had an inspiration. You asked yourself if it came from "the good spirit or the bad" and if it was for "the greater" glory. And then you went into action. If you by chance failed, you didn't beat up on yourself; you said, "Hey, that wasn't a hot idea after all. Must have been the devil made me do it, ha ha." And then you went on to your next apostolic adventure.

Loyola had always talked about his men on the move "with one foot raised." By the time Xavier was finished, he had set up Jesuit outposts in what are today India, Malaysia, Indonesia, Japan, and the Persian Gulf port of Hormuz. Within a few years of landing in Goa, he had thirty Jesuits working there. By the time of his death, he had more than seventy European and Indian Jesuits laboring across Asia.

Even though I didn't believe in the devil, I found it fascinating to see how the minds of Loyola and Xavier worked. They had this mental picture of Lucifer, the fallen angel of high intelligence, working on their psyches day and night to lead them astray, tempting them to do evil under the guise of good. This is because they were men of their time, when everyone believed in the devil. But if you understand how the human mind works, you don't need to posit a devil who tempts you to "do evil" under the guise of good. Whoever "does evil" under the guise of evil? You do what you do because it seems like a good idea at the time—or, as Bill Clinton once explained when asked why he did what he did with Monica Lewinsky, "because I could."

Satan did not tempt Eve with an old, brownish, wormy, wrinkled-up apple. My guess is that he presented her with a big, crisp, red, round, juicy, overwhelmingly sweet-smelling, glossy, shining apple. Naturally enough, Eve reached for the apple and took it to Adam. It wasn't until—Shazam!—Adam and Eve were standing there in Eden, suddenly aware that they were naked, that they realized they had made A Big Mistake, a mistake according to the original sin myth created by Saint Augustine that "stained" the whole human race forever.

I do not believe in original sin—the very idea that I am not worthy to enter heaven because Adam ate the apple when God warned him not to—or in the up-to-now generally accepted doctrine of redemption—that no one will get to heaven unless "washed in the blood of the Lamb." (God sent Jesus down so he could have his son crucified on a cross to "save" poor little me?)

I do believe in my own natural ability to err on a wide variety of fronts. If the great Babe Ruth struck out sometimes, so can I. I am heartened when Pope Francis tells me it's only human to strike out and that I should cast myself on God's mercy and move on.

I find it interesting and worth a comment that in his Rules for the Discernment of Spirits Ignatius Loyola never blames us for striking out (or missing the mark), much less does he try to scare us with the thought we are headed for hell when we do so. Rather, he suggests we take a look at ourselves and consult our own feelings. If we feel sad, we know we've struck out. If we feel happy, we know we've gotten a base hit—or maybe even a home run. If we've hit a home run, great—we go on hitting more home runs. If we've struck out, we've learned something more about ourselves. This lesson, too, is part of the Jesuit DNA.

This mindset, Jesuit historians tell us, made it possible for the most intrepid Jesuits to keep attempting new things, even after they'd tried something new and failed. If they didn't risk, they (and the order and the Church) would never see any reward. Of course, the most risk-taking Jesuits didn't always see the reward; over their 473-year history, exactly ninety-four Jesuits have found martyrdom, including the six social-justice Jesuits in El Salvador who were pulled from their beds at dawn one morning in November 1989 and executed by military goons. (You say martyrdom is another kind of reward? Yes, we see that, if we have the eyes of faith.)

In looking for a case to illustrate how a Jesuit of our own time might pursue this Ignatian inclination to take risks (indifferent to success or failure), I don't think I can find a better example than Daniel Berrigan, the Jesuit poet and peace activist who in the late 1960s felt duty-bound to make highly provocative demonstrations against the U.S. war in Vietnam. In June 1968, in the company of eight others, he broke into a U.S. Army recruiting office in Catonsville, Maryland, removed a file of draft records, and incinerated them in a parking lot outside. The act made headlines across the world; that's why Berrigan did it—to get his fellow citizens to think critically about what their government was doing in the name of the idol "America." He and his eight companions were indicted, tried, and convicted, quite "indifferent" to the consequences, which, as it turned out for Berrigan, was a stay in the federal prison at Danbury, Connecticut.

There, he wrote *No Bars to Manhood* and *The Trial of the Catonsville Nine*, giving testimony to the fact that he chose his action (and its consequences) as a "contribution to the poetic liberation of the American conscience." In this, he was a true son of Ignatius Loyola, who wrote in the exercises that a man with a mission had to be "indifferent" to the consequences and should prefer "neither a long life nor a short one." Berrigan spent a short twenty months in Danbury, but as of this writing he's ninety-two and still living out a long life. While he was in Danbury, his father general Pedro Arrupe made it clear that Berrigan was a good Jesuit by calling a news conference to announce that "if a defense of freedom meant incarceration, a Jesuit had to take that risk."

What does all this have to do with Pope Francis and his Jesuit DNA? Simply this: that the pope's Jesuit DNA will help him make the right, courageous decisions at this crucial moment in the Church's history. What if Pope Francis should decide to take away the Roman Curia's egregious power "for the greater good of the people of God"? And what if he is flooded with complaints from a half-dozen curial cardinals making public charges that his move will destroy the (imperial) papacy? What would he, as a good Jesuit, do then? Could he hold his ground and assert his freedom to act for the good of the whole Church? Or would he pull back, more attached to his own good repute with the cardinals who elected him than to the greater good of the people of God?

Almost every move that Francis made during his first nine months as bishop of Rome tells me he will answer that question with a *No*. He will go for Loyola's *magis gloriam*. In the words of Ignatius, he would be "indifferent" to his "success" in the eyes of some Roman cardinals. He would simply dare to rediscover, redefine, and reach out for the *magis*. Part of his Jesuit DNA.

I made my first profession in the Society on August 15, 1950, along with thirty-eight others in my class, each of us vowing in turn *paupertatem castitatem et obedientiam perpetuam in Societate Jesu*—"poverty, chastity, and perpetual obedience in the Society of Jesus." I wandered around in something of a rosy cloud, hardly able to believe that I had made it through the novitiate, unwilling to take off my new tailored cassock or my new white linen collar or that stiff medieval hat called a biretta, even for a moment.

I still have a picture of myself taken that day. It shows a tanned young man with a far-off gaze in his eye and a serious set to his jaw, his biretta at an important tilt. The entire look said this young man knew what he was about—and that it was all business, God's business.

The serious business ahead was called *juniorate*, an entirely new phase of training. If the novitiate had been boot camp, then the juniorate was no less than Officer Candidate School. The novitiate had helped me establish my pieties, my dedication to "the Kingdom." But I had learned that a Jesuit had to have more than piety and dedication— he had to acquire an expertise that would make him an outstanding officer in Christ's army, whom Íñigo had enlisted not to conquer but to serve.

Jesuits weren't Trappists, who would serve the world simply by praying for it and making a better liqueur. They were men who followed in the footsteps of those learned Jesuit missionaries who did not go off to Brazil and India and China and Japan and become fluent in their languages so they could tell people how to resign themselves to the miseries of this world in order to win some bliss in the next. Jesuits tried, instead, to help these people use their wits to make this world a gentler, happier place, a place that people could live, and love, in.

The eighteenth-century Jesuits in Europe decided they could make a difference in the world by getting involved in politics, and they did such a good job of it that they made powerful enemies who put pressure on Pope Clement XIV to suppress the order (which he did in 1773). I know some contemporary Jesuits who argue that those politically minded Jesuits did the right thing; suppression of the Society of Jesus was the price they had to pay for their courage. As my esteemed former California Jesuit contemporary Robert Brophy (who specialized in his later years at getting arrested in peace demonstrations) once said so well:

> The Gospel is totally political. What use is "love as I have loved you" if we think nothing, pray nothing, and do nothing about making that love real? Politics moves love from charity to justice. Yes, we have different gifts, different vocations. But politics is a dimension of all of us.

I was in the juniorate in 1950 when Pius XII came out with *Humani Generis*, an encyclical that condemned the work of contemporary Catholic scholars who, with their writings about evolution, threatened to "undermine the foundation of Catholic doctrine." (They were carefully unnamed, but everyone knew he was referring to Pierre Teilhard de Chardin.)

We didn't read Teilhard in the juniorate. We did read another French visionary of the time—or, rather, we had his pastoral letter *Growth or Decline?* read to us in the refectory. He was Emmanuel Suhard, the cardinal archbishop of Paris, a quiet, do-nothing prelate during the war who'd undergone a profound conversion when he stepped into the ruin of post–World War II France and discovered that his country, nominally Catholic, was not even Christian any longer. What to do? I can still remember the core of Suhard's message: *Roll up your sleeves, and get out to work in the real world.* His actual words were stirring:

> Being an apostle means taking on everything and penetrating everything belonging to man and the world he has made . . . to extend the benefits of the Redemption to the whole created world. The Chris-

tian has not only the right but the duty to complete creation and then make of that an offering to the Creator. To convert the world, it is not enough to be a saint and to preach the Gospel; or rather, it is not possible to be a saint and invoke the Gospel we preach without doing all we can to assure for all men conditions of work, housing, food, rest, and human culture without which life ceases to be human.

"Completing creation." Such a task, said Cardinal Suhard, would not be easy, nor could it be done in a generation or two. It would have to be done by men with talent and intelligence who loved a challenge.

This was a high-minded global vision, a piece of idealism in stark contrast to the vision of many of my American contemporaries in the 1950s, which was pretty much zeroed in on a new home in the suburbs with a wife in the kitchen and two kids in the backyard swimming pool. I bought into Suhard's ideal, completing creation. I would try to develop the critical tools necessary to helping remake society, to helping the world's movers and shakers make life more human. It was a vision that would gradually lead me out of the Society, when I would finally come to the dreamy, youthful conclusion that I could "complete creation" more effectively out of the order than I could in it.

The irony was that my Jesuit education itself was the thing that would give me the critical tools to make this independent judgment.

The critical tools would come first from my classical schooling. The fathers at Los Gatos didn't teach us clumsy Church Latin and New Testament Greek, but rather the elegances of the Latin historian Livy, of the orator Cicero, of the poets Virgil and Horace, and the Homeric Greek of the *Iliad* and the *Odyssey*.

They told us we weren't studying the classics as mere tools that would help us get through philosophy and theology but in order to develop the "perfect eloquence" of the Renaissance man, which, they hoped, would be just as valid in the twentieth century as it had been in the seventeenth when the Jesuit *Ratio Studiorum* (or plan of studies) was written.

As part of that plan, I read Dante and Shakespeare and Molière and Tolstoy. I listened to Bach and Brahms and Beethoven. I tried to appreciate the genius of Michelangelo and Da Vinci, El Greco and Reubens. I analyzed the poetry of Pope and Dryden, Wordsworth and Byron, and tried to emulate the prose style of Dickens and Thackeray and Robert

Louis Stevenson. I wrote speeches by imitating the rhetorical style of Edmund Burke and Winston Churchill and Franklin D. Roosevelt.

I got a marvelous education, one that probably had no equal in the English-speaking world of 1950 (if for no other reason than that I worked at it about twelve hours a day, with hardly any distractions—certainly not the distractions of dating and drinking that characterized collegiate life in the 1950s). I did well. I learned to speed read. I learned to write. I learned to think (if not feel). And superiors told me that if I kept on doing well, I could also look forward to getting my doctorate in some other field—in sociology or history or economics or political science—and at one of the best universities in the world to boot. My rector, John F. X. Connolly, wondered if I wanted to go to Harvard. To Berkeley or Cal Tech? To Oxford or the Sorbonne?

I didn't know yet. It's okay, he told me. I would have three or six or ten years to decide—no hurry. He said I could proceed on my course, just like most of my other classmates: three years philosophy at Mount Saint Michael's in Spokane, three years regency in one of our province's high schools, then four years theology, probably at Alma College in the Santa Cruz Mountains. After this I could begin special studies. I should have appreciated the leisurely pace of it all, an academic free ride enjoyed by only the richest, most privileged young Americans in the 1950s, but I believe the trip gave me guilt pangs. I was vowed to poverty but lived as if I were rich; I dined on filet mignon, I was learning to drink cabernet, I read Horatian odes, I listened to Bach.

There was little scullery, little manual labor. I never had to wash a sock, shop for food, or wonder if I could afford a haircut. I was a gentleman.

The studies at Mount Saint Michael's in Spokane, during the next three-year phase of our training, called philosophy, were pretty much a bore. I studied Aristotle and Saint Thomas Aquinas, and I took some survey courses on ancient and modern philosophy and some seminars on Hegel and Marx, but I found it hard to keep bearing down on them with the intensity and drive that I had learned in the novitiate and juniorate. I found more juice and more joy in politics and history and discovered that none of the faculty seemed to mind that I spent more time on these than I did on Aquinas. My first week at the Mount, I came upon a copy of a current bestseller, *Witness* by Whittaker Chambers, a former Communist. I stayed away from classes for several days while I raced through the narrative, fascinated by the tale of a man who had given his life for a faith that had failed. I was grateful to Chambers; he brought me up to date on some of the current American history that I'd missed while reading Thomas à Kempis.

And so, though I earned an MA in philosophy, as my California superiors expected me to, I also won approval to do my thesis on "Journalism and Prudence"—a study of the virtue of practical wisdom according to Aristotle and Aquinas as it applies to the problems of interpretive reporting in a democratic society.

My thesis was a first step in my own master plan—to develop my expertise in a new academic field called "the mass media." If the Jesuits were going to have a moral influence on the world, I could not imagine any better place than the fields of news and entertainment. I wasn't exactly sure how I could get involved in either of these areas, as a Jesuit, but I wanted to prepare myself so I could make some new things happen in the media world. As far as I knew, no California Jesuit had ever set serious foot in this world (forgetting that in 1946 George Dunne, a California Jesuit way ahead of his time, had written and produced the anti-segregationist play *Trial by Fire*).

I liked the Mount because I found some encouragement there to be more human, more spontaneous. At least half the men in the house, mostly the men from the Oregon Province, were a down-to-earth, no-bullshit bunch. They ignored some rules, like the rule of silence, and they insisted, along with the spiritual father at the Mount, who had been their superior during their novitiate, that they were serving God even when they were "just having fun." This, to me, was a more real approach, more akin to the Jesuit life I had seen lived when I boarded with the Jesuits at Loyola High in Los Angeles. I enjoyed every fun minute at the Mount.

I studied hard, at least nine hours a day, after classes, but I played hard, too. I played touch football every afternoon, even when the rains (and then the snows) came, this time real two-hands-below-the-waist touch football. I played hockey, too, something I hadn't done since I'd left Detroit at the age of twelve.

For almost a month in the summer, the whole community pitched tents on the southeastern shore of Lake Pend Oreille in Idaho. On our first day at Pend Oreille, everyone in the community received $10,000 in play money. We set up a casino in our refectory and played bridge, pinochle, blackjack, and poker on into the night. Some of the Brethren of the Strict Pious Observance refrained, calling the games "very secular" (that is, worldly). I found it all very exhilarating. Playing for money (even play money, which we used in an auction for candy bars and gum at vacation's end) only made it more so. Poker games were always an event when my family got together on holidays; I can remember learning the game sitting on my mother's lap at age seven and playing penny ante with my cousins at a fourth of a cent a white chip. (When my grandmother, Nanny Blair, died at the age of eighty-eight, we included in her casket a poker deck and some poker chips—and a second deck, in case someone in the long night demanded new cards.) It was fun to play poker again.

And to see movies once more, after a four-year hiatus. We had first-class sound projectors at the Mount, and a friend of the rector who owned a movie theater in downtown Spokane sent current flicks up to us whenever we wanted them. We wanted them mainly on big feast days; the choice was made by the rector, in consultation with the house beadle, who had access to the movie reviews in *Time* magazine.

In my opinion (I never discussed it with others), they goofed one night when they ordered up an Academy Award winner, *From Here to Eternity*, with Burt Lancaster and Deborah Kerr. Did we see the famous beach scene, when these two embraced in the surf? Well, no. Better. The projectionist had orders to block out that beach scene: too sexy for us. So he just let the damn projector run in silence for five minutes or so, while we sat there in the dark and let our imaginations provide a sexier scene than MGM could have gotten by the censors in 1953. I had a wet dream that night, and I confessed it first thing the next morning. No, technically speaking it was not a matter for confession—that is, a sin. But it was considered a good ascetic practice to confess it anyway.

The whole experience told me that, as far as the virtue of chastity was concerned, a total blackout of women from my life, according to the novitiate way, was the most effective way to go. If I didn't see women, in the flesh or on the silver screen, I didn't have images of them troubling me at night. Eventually, of course, I would be out among men (and women). I would have to learn how to deal with temptation. I told myself I'd deal with that when the time came.

And so at the Mount, I learned how to flip by the pages of a sexy layout in *Life* magazine and how to avert my eyes when, say, on a trip to the dentist in Spokane I spied a pretty woman coming up the street. Now I wonder: What damage did I do to myself by learning to think of women primarily as temptations?

Since Jorge Bergoglio had the same training in Argentina that I had in California, I can imagine how puzzled and inadequate he must feel even today when he is confronted by smart, sassy women who are demanding a voice, a vote, and citizenship in the Church. Pope Francis seemed to have the best will in the world when he said in his celebrated interview with the Jesuit editors that there ought to be "more space" for women's contribution to the work of the Church in the world. But it was obvious that he wasn't at all sure how he would give women "more space" in a Church that has, up to now, been such an exclusive, male preserve. The Church's all-male society tends to produce men who do not think of women very much or wonder why women have always been given third-class status in the Church. But I have reason to hope Pope Francis will wonder before he is finished making his contribution to Church reform. He has to learn what he must do to encourage women to be all they can be.

Why will he? Because of his Jesuit DNA, pushing for the *magis*, in new ways, now that he is pope of all the people. And because he may well try to make up for the Society of Jesus's longtime marginalization of women, which is also part of the Jesuit DNA. It wasn't that the Jesuits throughout their history have just decided to be misogynists; they simply ignored women and have not, up to this point, included them in any grand plan for the "christification of the universe" (a Teilhard expression). Talk about crazy. Women comprise half of the human race and half of the Church's membership, as well as, in my opinion, three quarters of its common sense and 90 percent of its zeal, energy, and commitment—and the men in charge continue to think of them as third-class citizens. If they think of them at all.

So there I was at the Mount, a red-blooded young man of twenty-four, trying not to think about women. The Jesuit rule said, "What concerns the vow of chastity needs no explanation, since it is plain how perfectly it ought to be kept, endeavoring to imitate angelic purity in cleanness of both body and mind." But of course I was a man, not an angel. My manhood was telling me that—more and more strongly every day.

One villa day, my classmate Tom Williams and I were headed to Gonzaga University to pick up some books from the library. Father Ed Lindekugel, the minister of the house, or second-in-command, asked if, on our way, we would mind delivering a package to an address in Hill-yard.

We found the address, a little white cottage next door to a church, and Tom rang the bell. The sweetest young woman I had ever seen— dressed in the habit of the Sisters of the Holy Names, fair, freckled— came to the door and shone a dazzling smile at us.

I did not exactly sink to my knees. But for what seemed like an hour or more (it was probably just a matter of a few seconds) I was paralyzed with—what? Wonder? Longing? Passion? I cannot say. Finally, I was aware that Tom was clearing his throat, because, though I was holding the package, I was making no move to hand it over. I gulped, shook my head with a dopey grin, and gave this gorgeous creature the bundle. For a moment, our eyes met, and an instant of understanding passed be-tween us. She blushed.

That was too much. I lowered my eyes, literally closing the windows of my soul. She turned to Tom and thanked him, perhaps not trusting herself to talk to me, because I had made my feelings so very, very obvious—and more, had elicited an instinctive (and no doubt unset-tling) response in kind from her. She disappeared into the house, and the door swung shut as if by itself.

I stood staring at the door, and then cursed my own clumsiness: no one should see me like this. Tom pretended he hadn't seen anything and engaged me in a discussion about Seattle U's chances in the up-coming NCAA playoffs.

I never learned who this nameless sister was, and I never saw her again, except in my mind's eye, where she made unexpected and unbid-den appearances for months to follow. For the first time since my earliest days in the novitiate, I started asking myself the key question: What am I doing in the Jesuits?

My next stop was something they called regency, a three-year teach-ing phase, during which I was to gain some more maturity before mov-ing on to theology, the last stage before ordination. During my regency, I matured right out of the order.

I was assigned to Saint Ignatius Prep, on a windy hill in San Francisco, along with ten others of my class. Other scholastics reported to one or another of the province's three other high schools, and a few of the older men wound up teaching on the college level at the University of San Francisco, Santa Clara, or Loyola in Los Angeles.

Now I had a supercharged life of my own, in a Jesuit prep school at last. The hurly-burly of the scholastics' life at Loyola High was one of the things that had attracted me to the Society in the first place, and one of my heroes then was Robert Leonard, a husky scholastic who taught math and coached football and swimming. Now I would be a scholastic, too, at a school very much like Loyola, with a student body of a thousand boys, and working under the direction of Robert Leonard, who was now a priest and the principal of Saint Ignatius, which we called SI ("Ess Eye"). Father Leonard proposed that I teach English and Latin and run a spiritual program for freshman, monitor the yards at noon, coach baseball, and publish the school paper, too. It was a job, he joked, that I could do easily in my twenty-hour workdays.

I liked the idea, because I needed to be busy, needed exhaustion at the end of every day as a sign to myself that I was giving my all "for the Kingdom." In order to make the sacrifice called for by the vows, particularly the vow of chastity, I had to feel that I was doing something special, and doing it as well as, or better than, anyone had ever done it before. I gave my young men 200 percent of me, teaching Shakespeare and Virgil in the classrooms and coaching football and baseball on the playing fields. In doing so, I was trying to show them that their religion, fully lived, was something that could make them more human, happier individuals, with a humanity and a happiness that would bring joy to those around them. I wanted to destroy the image of religion as something that made people less human, less joyful, less real.

In the classroom, I did this mainly by creating a sense of excitement about learning. "Nobody gets bored here," I announced right from the beginning. "If you're bored in any of my classes, you can get up and leave. If you're bored, I'm not doing my job." No one ever walked out. They wouldn't dare miss the fun and laughter that has always marked a lit class that deals more with life than letters. One day, I had our varsity quarterback on his feet, reading Chaucer.

I stopped him. "What does that mean, Gaffney?"

"Huh? What?"

"You just read that the prioress was 'nat undergrowe.'"

"Yeah."

"What's that mean?"

"I don't know."

"Well, it must mean something. Don't you have a clue?"

"'Nat undergrowe.' Hmm." He squirmed.

I moved in on his Irish Jansenism. Smiling, I said, "Well, if you were describing one of the girls from Mercy and you said she was 'nat undergrowe,' what would it mean?"

My scholar-athlete said he didn't know.

"Well, Gaffney," I said, "wouldn't it mean that she was well stacked?"

That was in 1955, eons ago, before the so-called sexual revolution, a year so puritanical that a harmless comedy called *The Moon Is Blue* would not win the Seal of the Hollywood Production Code. Cardinal Spellman would even condemn it because someone in the picture used the altogether shocking word *virgin*. Gaffney turned beet red. The class roared, delighted that a Jesuit scholastic would dare use one of their own off-scene expressions. *Well stacked*. Not bad. The word went around the schoolyard: some of these misters were pretty cool. (And, in retrospect, pretty dumb, too. Living in an all-male world for the past eight years or so, I didn't have a clue about women. I didn't know how I could help my young students have more than a clue either. And I didn't.)

I did the best I could. Outside the classroom, I was not sad, not pious, and that, too, served to make me—and the Jesuits—something real, something of the world of my kids. I did this in a bold way by encouraging my young journalists to put out a magazine that took an independent, sometimes even critical, view of SI's administration. And, to his credit, Father Leonard let me get away with it. "We believe in freedom of the press here," he told me. My editors (who still stay in touch with me more than fifty years later) were impressed.

I also plunged into some serious coaching. We had a high school that was hooked on sports, with city championship contenders almost every year in every sport except football. SI had no football tradition, and a poor varsity coach, and so I could only cheer toward the end of my first year when Father Leonard hired Pat Malley, an SI alumnus by way of the University of Santa Clara and the U.S. Army, to remake the football program.

Malley had a face like a sunrise and a high enthusiasm. He wasn't there long in the spring of 1956 before he asked me to help coach football, and together we started recruiting the hitherto overlooked talent in our own student body. By the next fall, we had a good turnout of terrific young athletes; with them Pat took the varsity to the city playoffs, and my junior varsity team ended up with eight victories, one defeat, and one tie.

By the end of my next, second, year of teaching, however, I was exhausted by the frenetic pace and getting more and more disaffected with the formalism that seemed to dominate the Jesuit Order in California. The father minister, Norton Herrold, didn't seem to care whether and how I was doing the job I had been sent here to do but only whether I was following "the Rule."

For him, this came down to getting up at five in the morning and going to bed at ten at night, and I never saw him in the hallways, or met his nervous gray eyes, without feeling that he was trying to catch me in some heinous transgression—serious things like not getting up at reveille or going to bed at taps. Sometimes I could do neither, but I had already had one run-in with him that taught me he was not the kind who would understand if I told him that my work sometimes demanded irregular hours. He would have simply said to drop the work, because "the Rule" came first, not the work. God didn't need my work.

No, God didn't need my work. But I thought the school—and the kids—did. I had transformed the school newspaper, which had been an unsightly bore, into a newsmagazine called *Inside S.I.*, done *Time*-style. Naturally enough, a slick magazine demanded much more time and energy than a pulpy tabloid. Sometimes it would be two in the morning when the kids and I would be putting the finishing touches on the magazine down at SI. Then I'd have to make my way up to the faculty residence and climb the fire escape to my room (the minister locked the front and back doors at ten) for three hours' sleep before I had to appear for a 5:30 Mass and be ready for another long day. I couldn't keep going like that forever. To survive, I just stopped showing up for 5:30 Mass. Lazy lout, I'd sleep in until six so I could make the 6:30 Mass. When the minister caught me doing that, he told me I was "not a good Religious."

The minister's disapproval bothered me, but I went right ahead do-ing what I was doing because I got a good deal of support from the other priests and scholastics at the high school, and even from the Jesuits on the faculty of the university, who, unwittingly, helped me think hard about what I was doing there. More and more, my manhood was speaking to me. Was the sacrifice of that manhood really worth it if all I caught from my superiors was disapproval?

Many of the young university priests were brilliant, innovative teach-ers, but I soon found that the more these men did, the less the superiors liked it. It was almost as if the superiors rewarded mediocrity and squelched excellence. Father Eugene Schallert was one who excelled. He had an idea that was years ahead of his time. In order to survive in a world that was coming of age, the Church would have to start declleri-calizing itself and begin training laymen and laywomen to do jobs that priests had been doing for centuries.

One of his colleagues, Father Eugene Zimmers, began the process by establishing something called the Institute of Lay Theology, which trained laymen to serve as parish professionals, most especially in what then had the unfortunate term *convert making*. He was disciplined for his zeal by the university president and accused of being a troublemaker by the university's chief fund-raiser, who shouted, "What the hell are all my Jewish contributors gonna think about this—this convert making?"

Gene Zimmers would later go on to win plaudits all over the world for founding the institute (and making it work). In the middle of the battle, however, the university's president seemed to agree with his fund-raiser, which caused Zimmers to invite the president to go soak his head. Not good. They delayed Zimmers's final vows, and the provincial told him he would not become a professed father (that is, one of the order's elite) but a simple coadjutor (literally, a helper). In reality, no one cared very much then whether a man was a professed father, but the unfairness of the whole thing bugged all of us who knew what had happened.

I remember being part of a bull session with Zimmers and a number of the younger Jesuit priests at USF where they puzzled over Zimmers's "demotion." Bud Schallert developed a theory to explain it all. He main-tained that what we had here was "a metaphysical problem" that seemed endemic to the order in California, and he cast the problem in the form of a question: How could there be more horses' asses in the province than horses? And how, moreover, could all the horses' asses be in the saddle? It was a humorous analysis, and Bud Schallert used humor in order to keep on living the life, and fighting off the horses' asses. But I didn't have his sense of humor, and there didn't seem to be any way around the conclusion that those who wanted to do anything creative in the Society would run into trouble.

I started studying the older priests around me and decided that many of them were embittered old men. I didn't think I wanted to be like them, or like Gerard Manley Hopkins, the late nineteenth-century English Jesuit who so completely accepted the order's Eleventh Rule ("better to be accounted as nothing and a fool in order to be more like our Lord") that he didn't think he should publish his poetry. That would bring him fame, something he'd been told was decidedly "not in the spirit of the Society." He once wrote to a poet friend, R. W. Dixon, "It is the holier lot to be unknown than to be known." Hopkins was a product of the "deny thyself" school of Jesuit spirituality, to the everlasting sorrow of some modern Jesuits, who could have given him plenty of good, unselfish reasons to go on creating some of the finest poems in the English language—like this one, "Pied Beauty," published posthumously, as was most of Hopkins's poetry that survived:

> Glory be to God for dappled things—
> For skies of couple-color as a brinded cow;
> For rose-moles all in stipple upon trout that swim;
> Fresh-firecoal chestnut-falls; finches wings;
> Landscape plotted and pieced—fold, fallow and plough;
> And all trades, their gear and tackle and trim.
> All things counter, original, spare, strange;
> Whatever is fickle, freckled (who knows how?)
> With swift, slow; sweet, sour; adazzle, dim;
> He fathers-forth whose beauty is past change;
> Praise him.

In 1888, a little more than a year before his death at age forty-five, Father Hopkins wrote to the poet Robert Bridges of the desolation that resulted from his self-denial: "I can give myself no sufficient reasons for going on [writing poetry]. Nothing comes. I am a eunuch—but it is for the kingdom of heaven's sake."

After two years at SI, I could see that superiors still demanded that subjects be eunuchs, and I said to hell with it. Eunuchs don't "complete creation" (Cardinal Suhard's words), much less do a good job teaching high school boys in San Francisco, if they have to fight off superiors in order to do so. And if I couldn't do a good job, then the sacrifices demanded by the three vows didn't make any sense.

During the summer, I got an appointment to see the provincial, Carroll O'Sullivan. I told him I wanted to leave. "Why, mister," he said, "you're one of the best scholastics we have." He tried to draw me out. He found that I wasn't leaving because I didn't want to serve but because I did. I told him how disappointed I was with the order's General Congregation that had met in Rome that year to update the Society. The only creative thing it did was issue an order for Jesuits to stop smoking (an order that was almost universally ignored).[3]

The provincial smiled and surprised me by agreeing with me, telling me that he was impressed by my obvious zeal. He said that, no matter what Norton Herrold thought, I was a good Jesuit. I nodded. I knew that I was. The only question was, could I serve God in the order? The provincial was trying to tell me that I could. I said, "I'd like to think so."

He had a suggestion: "Let me go ahead and ask Rome for a dispensation from your vows. But you're not out 'til you sign the papers. If you don't want to leave, you just don't sign them."

That seemed like a good move. I went back to SI, back to my English classes, back to my football team. As a third-year regent, I sailed with the wind at my back. I needed far less time to prepare my classes and could take more time correcting my precocious students' essays and short stories. (Thanks to the Internet, I still correspond with some of them, who express their gratitude to me for helping them be all they could be.)

I gave up the magazine to C. M. Buckley, another scholastic. And, with one season of coaching behind me, I put together a football team that was disciplined, proud, enthusiastic, and all-winning. Everyone on the squad played in every game, and, up until our last game against Lincoln, we had scored 192 points to our opponents' 18.

Austin Morris was my assistant coach, a husky crew-cut guy from Piedmont, California. He had been a P-51 pilot in World War II, came home to graduate from Berkeley and Boalt Hall, passed the bar, and then joined the Society. Audie coached the line, I coached the backs. I coached the offense, he the defense. And soon we were drawing big crowds from the university community on Thursday afternoons to see our kids play their swarming, stunting defenses and execute a high-scoring belly-option offense, with a lot of passing.

Friday nights, Audie and I would generally celebrate a successful week by borrowing the old Ford pickup they used for a garbage truck on the USF campus and rattle on downtown to see a movie, laughing at our daring, because the gas gauge usually said empty and we only had $2 each in our pockets. We drew $2 a week for "bus fare," whether we were going to take a bus or not, and that $2 a week was our effective salary.

Our Wildcat JVs won the big game of the season against Lincoln, the only other unbeaten team in the league, 19–12, but Father Tom Reed, our new principal, took that victory away from us. The refs had tossed one of my halfbacks out of the game in the first quarter when he threw a punch at a kid who was trying to gouge his eye in a pileup. I thought nothing of putting him back in later on (I had this inordinate attachment to winning, you see). But, after the game, the opposing coach protested to the league office. According to the rules, putting an ineligible player back in a game draws a fifteen-yard penalty. It doesn't call for a team to forfeit the game. But that's what happened here.

"We had a league meeting yesterday," our new principal, Father Tom Reed, told me as I was heading out to practice. "I forfeited the game to Lincoln. And I cancelled your last game against Sacred Heart, too."

"Just like that, huh?" I said. "Without even talking to me or anything? Well, that makes you look good with the principals of the other schools, but how do you suppose my kids are going to feel? Why don't you go and tell them you're taking the championship away from them? I'm not going to do it."

Father Reed's eyes narrowed. "Why, you goddamn son of a bitch."

That did it. At SI, I had felt that, no matter what Norton Herrold thought of me, the principal, the vice principal, and my colleagues at the high school who knew me were with me. Now, for the principal to call me a goddamn son of a bitch!

I said, "God love ya, Tom," and walked—no, ran—to the nearest phone and dialed the provincial's residence. "My papers still there?" I said to the provincial's socius. "Good. I'd like to come over and sign 'em." Which I did without much regret, more a feeling of triumph—making the first adult decision of my life. I was leaving because Tom

Reed had helped me see that there would be a good many horses' asses (Father Schallert's horses' asses, who were all in the saddle) lying in wait for me in the years ahead.

That night, I told as many of the scholastics as were assembled in our recreation room for our Friday night pour—usually port wine—that I was going to make my exit from the Society. I'd teach until the Christmas vacation started. Then they wouldn't see me anymore. They were shocked. When others had left the Society, they didn't tell anyone or even say goodbye. They just quietly disappeared. Those who knew me best and liked me anyway said they were sorry. They'd miss me, but they understood.

So, there you have it, a concrete narrative description of how the young Jesuits in my time (including Jorge Bergoglio in Argentina) got their DNA. Contemporary Jesuits receive the same training I did—the Spiritual Exercises and the daily examens and the *Exercitia Caritatises* and the rigorous course of studies and the camaraderie and the closeness of like minds and willing hearts (minus some of the nonsense, including the whips and chains and the dopey superiors insisting on blind obedience). They are members of a religious order, but they do not parade their piety, and they have a winning worldliness that inspires admiration and trust in their students.

A majority of U.S. Jesuits teach in the order's forty-seven prep schools and twenty-eight colleges and universities, but their numbers are dwindling fast, and the up-to-now eight U.S. provinces are in the process of consolidating into three. There's a vitality in their schools, largely because the Jesuits in charge have done such a good job of recruiting lay faculty (men and women) who share the Jesuit vision. Some say this is good enough. I do not.

The fact is that the order is dying. In 1974 there were 29,436 Jesuits worldwide. As of October 9, 2013, that number had dropped 40 percent to 17,036. Some died, not to be replaced by a dwindling number of novices. Potential recruits, not anxious to pledge the rest of their lives to celibacy, were finding other outlets for their high ambitions. After Vatican II, a good many formed Jesuits also left, unwilling to remain in an order that was too resistant to change (even the changes suggested by Vatican II). In parts of the Third World, the number of Jesuits soared. Jesuits in India's fourteen provinces now number 4,014, almost double the number of Jesuits in the United States. The median age of U.S.

Jesuits is sixty-five (versus a median age of forty-four in India), and there are more ex-Jesuits in the United States than there are Jesuits (2,404). This is not necessarily a negative; later, I will tell you about some outstanding former Jesuits who are still going for the *magis*, including Jerry Brown, the governor of California.

The Jesuits have known about their impending decline for more than thirty years, but they haven't done much hard thinking about it and have taken very little action.

In 1995, the Jesuits' thirty-fourth General Congregation poked around on the fringes of the Church's biggest scandal, its marginalization of women. Many were the discussions over what to do about it, and the congregation ended up endorsing an experiment in lay collaboration that had begun a year before by Bert Thelen, the Wisconsin provincial. He had recruited men and women, married and unmarried, many of them already working in Jesuit ministries or teaching at Marquette, into something called Ignatian Associates, setting up chapters in Milwaukee, Minneapolis, and Omaha. Those chapters (each of them made up of a dozen or more, singles and married couples) did their Jesuit thing, taking a form of the vows, hoping to provide a model for other such experiments around the world—men and women for others gathered in community (though not necessarily living under the same roof), going for the *magis*, each in their own creative ways.

The fathers of the congregation liked the idea but stopped short of saying these collaborators could or should become a new kind of Jesuit. In fact, they said explicitly that these collaborators "will not be admitted into the body of the Society."

Why not? Bert Thelen told me some members of the congregation wanted to do just that. But they were ignored by others who said specifically that they did not want to "blur the line between lay and religious." I told Thelen I wondered how helpful that distinction was to the mission of this General Congregation—"to meet the challenges and opportunities of the modern world." I didn't think the Society could meet its challenges as long as it kept drawing that line between lay and religious—which I suspect are code words for *celibate* and *noncelibate*. "Who drew that line?" I asked him. "God? Or men? And if men drew it, then why can't men undraw it?"

Thelen said he was amazed at me. But he seemed to enjoy my frankness when I said the Jesuits ought to consider taking the kind of bold risks suggested by Father Joseph Conwell of the Oregon Province. "We must set aside fear," Conwell wrote in the conclusion of *Impelling Spirit*, a brilliant work published in 1997. "Have no fear of the future, fear of change. The call is to listen, listen to the Spirit within, listen to one another, listen to events outside, listen to the sights and sounds of the times, listen to the needs of God's people and God's world."

I would ask now whether the order has been listening enough to prophetic voices like Father Conwell's. In *Impelling Spirit*, Conwell tells about his discovery in the Jesuit archives in Rome of a radical new paradigm for the Society of Jesus. He found this new paradigm in a seminal document called *Cum ex Plurimum*, written by Saint Ignatius and his original six companions for the signature of Pope Paul III, then laid aside and lost in the archives for centuries. That document, says Conwell, erases our old view of Ignatius as the soldier-saint, a man of steely will, a coldly rational, orderly administrator. Conwell says that view "betrayed Ignatius and his first companions and has long pervaded both the practical application of the Spiritual Exercises and the practical living out of the constitutions of the Society of Jesus." Conwell's "impelling spirit" was the Holy Spirit.

Under John Paul II and Benedict XVI it was more than likely that the Jesuit Curia in Rome would bury or burn Conwell, or at least his book, if they thought any contemporary Jesuit would ever take him seriously. But now that we have a Jesuit pope, I wonder what is stopping the Society of Jesus from acting in new ways to save the Ignatian vision, AMDG—not for the greater glory of God but for the greater good of all the peoples on the face of the earth?

Here is a one-word answer to that question: *inertia*. Some far thinkers in the Society may have the most keen ideas for change. But how do they get through what has become the Jesuits' play-it-safe bureaucracy?

In 2008, thirteen years later, the delegates at the next General Congregation, GC 35, terminated the Ignatian Associates' experiment without any explanation. Bert Thelen wasn't there, and his successor, another Wisconsin provincial, had no wish to sponsor the experiment any longer. Rumor had it that no one else at GC 35 had much enthusiasm for blurring the lines between lay and religious. Jesuits were special; why hybridize the breed? And why bring women into the mix? One member of Thelen's experiment, Stephanie Russell, who is now vice president of mission and ministry at Marquette University in Milwau-

kee, commented sadly, "We gave them our best selves, and they rejected us. They don't know what they lost."

There is still a bit of male chauvinism in the order—maybe more
than a little—that has to change if the Society doesn't want to end up a
relic. The chauvinism will not disappear, however, as long as the Society
remains a male redoubt. I could say the same thing about the Church at
large, still run as it is by male celibates. Time, of course, will solve that
problem as more and more intelligent, articulate women demand (and
get) a voice in the Church.

The Jesuits could accelerate that process right now by admitting
women into the Society of Jesus as perpetual scholastics. There is no
Church law that would stop the order from having a woman take vows
as a Jesuit scholastic. In fact, on October 26, 1554, Ignatius Loyola
accepted into the Society a twenty-year-old widow, Princess Juana, regent of Spain, daughter of Charles V, and sister of Philip II. He gave
Juana a code name, Matteo Sanchez, and had her working as a secret
Jesuit, AMDG, from her position of great influence in the Spanish
court. She wasn't headed for the priesthood. But she was, and would
be, a Jesuit until the day she died.

I submit that the Ignatius-Juana model could be a way forward in
the future for the modern Society. The Jesuits taught us a theorem in
minor logic: *esse ad posse valet illatio.* "If it has been done, it can be
done." The Jesuits could put shoes on that theorem now and walk it into
the twenty-first century. I would suggest they do that best and most
practically by recruiting married couples, who would not join old-fashioned Jesuit communities but continue to live as they have been living,
as couples, and work, AMDG, in the real world—in academia (either in
Jesuit universities or in other private universities or state universities),
in the world of government and business, in social work, in the media,
in law and medicine and science and engineering—while they find spiritual sustenance and the occasional companionship and moral support
of men and women with like minds and the same willing hearts. Married Jesuit couples, perpetual scholastics, with the three vows? Why
not? The vows would have to be adapted for married couples, of course,
but they would still apply. Chastity does not necessarily mean "no sex."
Married couples are chaste when they remain faithful to each other.

I am sure that any reform of the Society along the lines I am propos-
ing will meet with opposition from traditionalists in the Society who

fear change and so do nothing, and from some in the Roman Curia (if there's still a Roman Curia two years from now!) whose fear of change leads them to fight this novelty with all their might. But these are political problems. Politics is people, and, as the biography of Ignatius Loyola tells us and the history of the Church demonstrates, almost anything is possible for those who have the political skills and the patience.

I am also convinced that the Holy Spirit has already had a say in this evolution by inspiring the College of Cardinals to elect a Jesuit pope who may be more ready than even he knows to acknowledge full citizenship to women in the Church. He could make a start by encouraging new kinds of Jesuits—married men and women scholastics who are (in Father Conwell's words) "passionate, creative, innovative, propelling, driving, pushing, blowing like an untamed hurricane" for the greater good of the people of God.

In his first three hundred days, Pope Francis set a new, joyful style for the Church. Because of his Jesuit DNA, I have already seen him "going for the *magis*," encouraging the whole Church to push back the frontiers. He knows what the Church needs to do, and, in the spirit of the ruthless *tantum quantum* rule, he will shove aside whatever stands in the way of our having life and having it more abundantly. This will mean less doom-and-gloom spirituality, more laughter, more joy in just being human. Will anyone say that this new joy is not for the greater good of the people of God?

5

THE INTERVIEW(S)

On September 19, 2013, the *America/Civiltà* interview with Pope Francis made the Internet. It flashed around the world in milliseconds. And the world, the whole world, not just the Catholic world, was as stunned as the editors of *America* were when they first read it.

Father Spadaro's first question startled the pope. "Who is Jorge Mario Bergoglio?"

Francis stared at him in silence. Spadaro quailed, giving himself away as a rookie interviewer. An old hand at the interview game asks a hard question and waits to see how his poor fish of a subject tries to wiggle off the hook. Spadaro didn't wait. In the silence, he asked the pope, "May I ask you this question?" Wrong move. He was scared. What if Francis had said, "No"? Spadaro might have had to skip over half of his questions or, worst-case scenario, turn off his recorder, pick up his briefcase, and depart.

Fortunately, Francis was setting his own surprising rules for this interview: no question was out of bounds. He wanted to give an honest account of himself and to tell the world what he had in mind for the future of the Church in a medium the world would pay attention to. He'd learned that an impromptu news conference aboard the plane on his return flight from Brazil in July drew a thousand times more press attention than any formal papal statement might have received.

Now, thanks to his media-savvy U.S. Jesuit brothers, he was experimenting with a new kind of papal communication, potentially more effective than an encyclical or other stiff doctrinal pronouncement. He plunged right in with an answer that was just as startling as Spadaro's question: "I am a sinner. This is the most accurate definition. It is not a figure of speech, a literary genre. I am a sinner."

He went on to give the most honest accounting of himself, his Church, and his place in the Church than any of the 265 popes who preceded him. He didn't waffle with his answers. He not only said he was a sinner (as we all are), but he was also quite specific about some of the sins he had committed when he was provincial of the Jesuits in Argentina. "I was thirty-six," he exclaimed. "It was crazy."

Crazy for the general in Rome to make him a major superior at the age of thirty-six, or crazy to think he could keep the Jesuits in Argentina afloat during a time (in the early 1970s, when nearly half of the men in the province were leaving the Society), or crazy to expect him to take an openly critical stance against the military junta that had seized power in his country and kidnapped its critics and made them "disappear"? He did not say. Whichever it was, he confessed he hadn't done a very good job of it. He made a passing reference to his assignment in Córdoba after he had finished the standard six years as provincial. The Jesuits had a house of studies there, and his job in Córdoba (as a spiritual father for the scholastics) was a humbling comedown, but, in any event, a time for his own conversion. His brother Jesuits in Argentina say he underwent a radical change in Córdoba, so that, when the Vatican tapped him to become an auxiliary bishop in Buenos Aires, he plunged into doing the very work in the city's slums that he had objected to when it had been undertaken by the two young Jesuits who had gotten into so much trouble with the junta. (What was he doing in those slums? Nothing special, except "being present" to the poor and down-trodden so that he, like the fictional Jesuits in Mary Doria Russell's novel, might "come to know and to love God's other children.")

And then, in the *America/Civiltà* interview, he turned a critical eye on "the Church." He meant the Church's central administration in Rome (that is, the popes and the Roman Curia and some of the world's bishops who, he said, had become "obsessed" with peripheral moral issues—abortion, gay marriage, and contraception) for putting dogma before love and for prioritizing moral doctrines over serving the poor and marginalized. They were obscuring the primary reason for the Church's existence: to bring people closer to Jesus and his saving mes-sage. "It is not necessary to talk about these issues all the time. The dogmatic and moral teachings of the Church are not all equivalent. The church's pastoral ministry cannot be obsessed with the transmission of a disjointed multitude of doctrines to be imposed insistently."

> Those who today always look for disciplinarian solutions, those who long for an exaggerated doctrinal "security," those who stubbornly try to recover a past that no longer exists—they have a static and inward-directed view of things. In this way, faith becomes an ideology among other ideologies.

Instead, Francis wanted us all to embark on a new way of thinking. It turned out not to be so new at all. His exact words were a pretty good summary of how the fathers of Vatican II had redefined the Church, a Church Francis did not want to dominate over but simply be a part of. He was no more infallible than the people of God:

> The Church is the people of God on the journey through history, with joys and sorrows. Thinking with the Church, therefore, is my way of being part of this people. And all the faithful, considered as a whole, are infallible in matters of belief, and the people display this *infallibilitas in credendo*, this infallibility in believing, through a supernatural sense of the faith of all the people walking together. The Church sometimes has locked itself up in small things, small-minded rules. The most important thing is the first proclamation: Jesus Christ has saved you. And the ministers of the Church must be ministers of mercy above all.

Francis goes even further: "The risk in seeking and finding God in all things, then, is the willingness to explain too much, to say with human certainty and arrogance: 'God is here.' We will then find only a god that fits our measure. The correct attitude is that of St. Augustine: Seek God to find him, and find God to keep searching for God forever."

Richard Rohr, the Franciscan out of New Mexico who has been campaigning for a dozen years in his lectures and books against rigid, either-or thinking in the Church, could hardly resist pointing out that Pope Francis was only saying what he, Rohr, had been saying all along—that we have to embark on a new way of thinking that is deeply formed by the Gospel:

Up to now, Catholicism has largely emphasized metaphysics ("what we think we know") and has severely neglected epistemology ("Exactly how do we know what we think we know?"). Francis is not so much telling us *what* to see (which our dualistic minds will merely fight and resist) nearly as much as teaching us *how* to see and what to pay attention to. Somehow he is telling us that true seeing is first seeing through the eyes of love and mercy. And this is Christianity itself.

Rohr summed up as follows: "Francis has become a living and happy invitation to all of humanity, even beyond the too-tight boundaries of Christianity, instead of an exclusionary bouncer standing at the always-open gates of heaven. In that alone, he has changed the papacy—perhaps forever. It will be very hard to go completely backward again."

In his column in the *Boston Globe*, James Carroll, the Paulist priest–turned–novelist, hailed the pope for zeroing in on "the centrality of global poverty as the overriding moral issue of our age."

The pope aims to start "a long-run, historical process" on behalf of the poor. No one denies his seriousness on this issue—from the choice of his name, to the place where he lives, to his witness in Brazil. But the pope knows as well as anyone that the single-most powerful engine drawing people out of poverty is improvement in the economic status of women, which can only occur within a larger cultural transformation. Education. Participation. Power. Reproductive freedom. Yes, women's liberation. There can be no other strategy for ending poverty.

It was not too clear to Mary Hunt, a feminist theologian who is cofounder and codirector of the Women's Alliance for Theology, Ethics and Ritual (WATER) in Silver Spring, Maryland, that the pope did know what James Carroll said he knew—that women's liberation was the cure for world poverty. Hunt knew that the pope had not thought nearly enough about women. In an article titled "The Trouble with Francis," she made light of his references to women's motherhood, Mary as more important than bishops, the institutional Church as Mother, and so forth: "I had a fine mother, and I try to be a good mother, but enough is enough on mothers. What about seeing women as persons, human beings, agents of their own lives?" She went on to say,

It is intellectually embarrassing to hear a man who is so conversant with music, literature, and poetry have such a paltry vocabulary when it comes to women. Thus far, Francis has not had any public conversation with a woman church leader of any sort. The continued oppression of U.S. women religious, allegedly approved by him, is a negative sign as well. But maybe it will fall into the category of small things to which he will pay little attention.

I think Dr. Hunt's prediction may be mistaken. The pope is beginning to realize (if for no other reason than that he may be starting to read commentaries by the likes of Dr. Hunt) that he has a lot of catching up to do with regard to half the human race. In the *America/Civiltà* interview, he acknowledged as much when he said it is necessary "to widen the space for a more incisive feminine presence in the Church"—a line that was unaccountably omitted from the English translation of the interview but not the Italian and Spanish versions.

The fact is that Francis did say it: *non c'è spazio qui*—"there's no space here" for women. If he meant those words, then I say we'd better stay tuned. With his Jesuit DNA clicking away, he must start making more space for women in the Church. His very manner of speaking in the interview ("sweet and meek" is how the *New York Times*'s Frank Bruni describes it) tells us Francis will be a listening pope. Here's what Bruni wrote:

> It's about time. The leader of the Roman Catholic Church has surveyed the haughty scolds in its ranks, noted their fixation on matters of sexual morality above all others, and said enough is enough. I'm not being cheeky with this one-word response. Hallelujah.
>
> But it wasn't the particulars of Pope [Francis's] groundbreaking message in an interview published last week that stopped me in my tracks, gave fresh hope to many embittered Catholics, and caused hardened commentators to perk up.
>
> It was the sweetness in his timbre, the meekness of his posture. It was the revelation that a man can wear the loftiest of miters without having his head swell to fit it and can hold an office to which the term *infallible* is often attached without forgetting his failings. In the interview, Francis called himself naïve, worried that he'd been rash in the past, and made clear that the flock harbored as much wisdom as the shepherds. Instead of commanding people to follow him, he invited them to join him. And did so gently, in what felt like a whisper.

What a surprising portrait of modesty in a church that had lost touch with it.

And what a refreshing example of humility in a world with too little of it.

A prelate who has given few examples of humility ever since he started climbing the clerical ladder, Timothy Dolan, the cardinal archbishop of New York, pretended that he didn't even notice that the pope, in speaking about the "obsession" of some with abortion, contraception, and gay marriage, had given him a figurative slap in the face. Dolan went on NBC's *Today Show* to tell the world that he agreed with the pope, just as if he were not a leader of the U.S. bishops in their fight against the Obama administration's plan to assure American women of their right to exercise responsible parenthood. And he gave a disingenuous interview to *America* that took my breath away:

> We bishops welcome and applaud [the pope's] remarks. If the Church is perceived as crabby, nagging, hung-up on a few "pet peeves," or judgmental, *as unjust and inaccurate as that perception might be* [emphasis mine], we can't evangelize very well. What Pope Francis has done is popped the blister of that perception, and we bishops cheer him on.

Only four days after Francis's *America/Civiltà* interview had flashed around the Internet, Eugenio Scalfari, the founder and editor emeritus of Italy's *La Repubblica*, had his own private interview with the pope that made the pope's reservations about his papal predecessors and the Curia even clearer.

"Heads of the church have often been narcissists, flattered and thrilled by their courtiers," the pope said in his interview with Scalfari on September 24, 2013. "The court is the leprosy of the papacy." Scalfari, a professed atheist, had written a friendly letter to the pope asking for a meeting with him but was surprised when he picked up the phone a few days later to hear the pope on the other end of the line, inviting him to come over "on Tuesday at three o'clock, if it is convenient."

Francis said his Church should not be a clerical Church but a people's Church—my paraphrase. His exact words according to Scalfari: he wanted to see "a community" of people, priests, and bishops who "are at the service of the people of God," especially the poor, the old, and the young "crushed" by unemployment.

In her report on the Scalfari interview, Laurie Goodstein of the *New York Times* compared Pope Francis's concern about real people—specifically people without jobs—to Pope Benedict's frequent focus on two abstractions: "the great evils of secularism and relativism."

Scalfari's interview came on the eve of the pope's scheduled series of meetings with his Commission of Eight, men he had asked to help him to (among other things) overhaul the Curia, sitting at the apex of the clerical pyramid. The pope told Scalfari, "Clericalism should not have anything to do with Christianity."

The Curia had been running the Church, but Francis said he hoped he could end that. The Curia should be more like a "quartermaster's office" in the army, meant to provide "the services that serve the Holy See," not make policy or (my gloss here) micromanage bishops from Toledo to Toowoomba. Francis told Scalfari that the Curia pays too much attention to itself (he said it has a "Vatican-centric" view) and not enough to the world around us. "I do not share this view," the pope said, "and I'll do everything I can to change it."

Francis also confessed to Scalfari that he was redefining the papacy. In appointing eight cardinals to advise him, he explained, he was ignoring men in the Curia (whom he called "courtiers") in favor of some "wise people who share my own feelings." The move, he said, "is the beginning of a Church with an organization that is not just top-down but also horizontal."

Laurie Goodstein wrote, "This second interview leaves no doubts that he is in a hurry to further the stalled work of the Second Vatican Council: to open the church to modern culture and to have a dialogue with other religions and nonbelievers." Francis had told Scalfari that after Vatican II was held in the early 1960s, "very little was done in that direction. I have the humility and the ambition to want to do something."

At the end of the interview, Francis suggested that he and Mr. Scalfari meet again to discuss "the role of women in the church." I suspect that here the pope already realized he hadn't addressed the women's issue nearly enough and was admitting as much by sending a subtle message to critics like Mary Hunt, who had complained about the pope's "paltry vocabulary when it comes to women." Judging from the plain humility of the man as revealed in the *America/Civiltà* interview, I would say he'd be quite ready to plead guilty to Dr. Hunt's charge that he hasn't given women much thought at all.

Needless to say, the pope's two interviews upset Catholic conservatives. They'd never heard a pope talk like this—so candidly, so off the cuff. Past popes had been like gods. They conveyed their ideas in encylicals or papal bulls or *allocutios* or *motu proprios*, always in the most authoritative tones and in a kind of Church-speak that most people could not understand, assuming they bothered to read the pronouncements at all.

William Donohue, director of the Catholic League—a defense organization modeled on the Anti-Defamation League—advised in a news release that the media had mispresented what the pope was saying. Commenters at the conservative Catholic blog *Angel Queen* resorted to some old-fashioned name-calling. One referred to the pope's offerings as "loose-cannon interviews." Another said the pope was giving interviews because he was "functionally illiterate." A third commenter said he could only regard the pope's remarks as "professions of idiocy—call them f-bombs." Germain Grisez, an American moral theologian, accused the pope of "being self-indugent enough" to use unconventional methods (for a pope) of giving interviews "with as little care as he might unburden himself with friends after a good dinner and plenty of wine." A columnist in Italy accused Pope Francis of "trying to found a new Church."

Jeff Mirus, editor at CatholicCulture.org, advised his readers to calm down. "We are under no obligation to follow the pope's every word; we are obliged to pay close attention only when he is exercising his Petrine ministry in relation to ourselves." Mirus added:

> I have already suggested a number of keys to understanding the broader initiatives of this pope. He does give us plenty to think about. But it will not be fruitful to tie ourselves in knots every time Pope Francis makes a personal comment or addresses himself directly to this or that person. So the pact I suggest is this: let us take this interview in stride more rapidly than we did the last.

Francis X. Rocca, a columnist for the Catholic News Service, owned and operated by the U.S. bishops, also tried to soothe his readers. "For many Catholics," he wrote, "it will take time to get used to a pope speaking not only as priest, prophet, and king but also as a fellow member of the 'people of God,' voicing personal priorities and views that do not have the status of church teaching."

It's probable that at that moment, Pope Francis had already begun writing a more formal discourse—not an encyclical, but rather an apostolic exhortation called *Evangelii Gaudium* ("The Joy of the Gospel")—that would meet the criteria of conservative papalators like Donohue, Grisez, and Rocca when it was published on November 24, 2013. Even that piece of papal prose may have been too slangy, however, for those who were offended by the pope's informality—for example, Francis's use of the word "sourpusses" (which may even have described some of his critics).

Richard Gaillardetz, one of America's best new theologians, a professor at Boston College, also tried to reassure the Church's conservatives in the *National Catholic Reporter*:

> Will this pope rewrite controversial Church doctrines? No, but that isn't how doctrine changes. Doctrine changes when pastoral contexts shift and new insights emerge such that particular doctrinal formulations no longer mediate the saving message of God's transforming love. Doctrine changes when the Church has leaders and teachers who are not afraid to take note of new contexts and emerging insights. It changes when the Church has pastors who do what Francis has been insisting on for the last six months: Leave the security of your chanceries, rectories, parish offices, and episcopal residences. Set aside the "small-minded rules" that keep you locked up and shielded from the world. Go meet the people where they are.

Federico Lombardi, the pope's press spokesman, likewise attempted to soothe the Vatican Press Corps. Some Vaticanisti, so accustomed to doctrinal pronouncements coming out of the Roman Curia (sometimes on a daily basis), were wondering what "authority" they could give the pope's rambling remarks to a Jesuit editor or to an editor of *La Repubblica*. Father Lombardi told the reporters they were covering a new kind of ball game:

> The pope feels free to express himself in different ways, trusting the public to understand there are differences when he is speaking in different venues, from homilies to interviews to official teachings. I think the pope's charisma is obvious, as is his desire to communicate

directly with people. This is a very clear message of the pope's interest in dialogue without prejudice.

Some commenters on the Internet said the papal interview was a new kind of message. These included Ralph Coelho, who observed vis-à-vis a news report by John Allen in *NCR* on October 6, 2013, that this Jesuit pope was looking a lot like Jesus:

> The phenomenon of Pope Francis is his confident return to the style of Jesus who confounded all the "authentic" scholars of the time by ignoring the recognized religious leaders and going down, at every opportunity, to the poor, the sick, the sinners in their own lives. He did not reject the company or the invitations of the authentic alders, but he did tell them that their ways were not the ways of his Father.

Within the *National Catholic Reporter* Tom Reese explained to his friends in the media what the pope was doing: "It is no surprise that Pope Francis has made some people in the Church nervous, just as the council made some people nervous. Francis is simply bringing to fruition what was started at the Second Vatican Council."

Bravo to William Portier, writing in *Commonweal* on October 7, 2013, for saying what my theologian friends had been thinking all along but had not been able to say nearly as well: that Francis has found a way to take the Gospel back to the people.

> In response to a journalist on the flight back from Brazil, [the pope] described himself as "a street priest" who feels somewhat "caged" in the Vatican. With the papal news-media interview, Pope Francis has found a way to pop the bubble that seemed to isolate his predecessor during his last days in office. He has, in a real sense, made it back to the streets. This new genre of papal pronouncement dodges grasping handlers and bureaucrats who would brand the pope restrictively, frustrate his wishes, and control his access. Pope Francis is now an anticipated part of the news cycle. The papal news-media interview takes him directly to the people, all the people.

6

VATICAN II

Religion does not originate; it reacts. It does not denounce; it adapts. It does not set forth new models of conduct and sensibility; it imitates. Its rhetoric is without deep appeal; the worship it organizes is without piety. It has become less a revitalization of the spirit in permanent tension with the world than a respectable distraction from the sourness of life.

—C. Wright Mills, "A Pagan Sermon to the Christian Clergy," 1958

Here, Mills wrote what amounted to the Church's obituary. Imagine Mills's surprise when, in the fall of 1962, Pope John XXIII launched Vatican II. He brought in some twenty-five hundred bishops from around the world to help him "revitalize the spirit" within his own Church, and, incidentally, in most of the world's other religions. John XXIII came up with new models of friendship. "I am Joseph, your brother," he told a group of visiting rabbis, and if Professor Mills had shown up, the pope would have chuckled at Mills's own self-description as "a Wobbly"—*someone who wants to be, and wants everyone else to be, his own boss at all times, under all conditions, and for any purposes they may want to follow up.* At the council, Pope John encouraged the bishops to be their own men and to speak freely, which they did and continued to do during the four years of the council.

For too many centuries, churchmen talked about the world as an evil place and the Church as a thing apart from that world: we had the Church over here *and* the world over there. The council's great theologians (the greatest collection of theologians in the history of the Church) worked out something entirely new. The Church was in the world, inspired by a God who chose to enter human history and start his pilgrim people on a march through that history, learning as the world learned, changing as the world changed. Other Christians were there to see the changes in thinking happen before their eyes, and the mass media were present as well, to chronicle the revolution. At the end of the council's first session, even before the council fathers had had a chance to nail down the Church's new approach, *Time* magazine hailed John XXIII as the planet's Man of the Year.

> By launching a reform whose goal is to make the Catholic Church *sine macula et ruga* (without spot or wrinkle), John set out to adapt his Church's whole life and stance to the revolutionary changes in science, economics, morals, and politics that have swept the modern world: to make it, in short, more Catholic and less Roman.

Up until the council, the Church had made much of the fact that it never changed, that its truths were eternal, and that they were most unambiguously understood in Latin. Cardinal Ottaviani, the prefect of the Holy Office during Vatican II, had the words *Semper Idem* emblazoned on his coat of arms. Vatican II turned that assertion upside down. During the council's four sessions, the world's bishops, who had long thought of themselves as "the teaching Church" (as opposed to the rest of us, "the learning Church"), suddenly found they were part of the learning Church, compelled out of their own self-respect to update much of the theology they had learned in their sleepy seminaries. They learned by keeping their ears open inside the conciliar aula, they learned at afternoon and evening seminars all over Rome, they learned at conversations that went on during dinners at Roman trattorias and on into the night.

They learned from (among others) the twentieth-century Jesuits at the council who were there to atone for the wrong-headedness of the Jesuits of the nineteenth. At Vatican II, a good many order priests (most notably the Dominicans and, among them, at the top of the list, Yves Congar) took a huge role in Pope John's *aggiornamento*. But the Jesuits took a leading role on many of the council's key issues. German Jesuit Cardinal Bea assumed control of the all-important conciliar commission, the Secretariat for Promoting Christian Unity, which helped the council end the Counter-Reformation and establish a new era of good-will and cooperation among all Christians. Karl Rahner, a German Jesuit, helped free the Church from its entirely self-serving notion that it had a monopoly on salvation. In helping draft the schema on the Church, Rahner moved the council fathers to redefine the Church as "the people of God," a reformulation that allowed the bishops to assign themselves a more modest place as the servants of the people, not their lords. Gustave Weigel, the Jesuit ecumenist from Woodstock, Maryland, made "the separated brethren" feel comfortable enough at the council to offer amendments to many of the council documents (the *schemata*); he made the observers into collaborators so that mainline Protestant bodies now started thinking of themselves as members of the family. John Courtney Murray, a U.S. Jesuit, spearheaded what amounted to new Church doctrine on religious liberty—which had been condemned as "a delirium" less than a hundred years before by Pope Pius IX. Italian Jesuit Roberto Tucci helped craft the council's crowning document, *Gaudium et Spes*, which offered a new definition for salvation—namely, being all we can be in this life—and putting to rest the long-traditional Catholic fear and hatred of the world as something evil. The preconciliar scholarship of French Jesuits Henri de Lubac and Jean Daniélou helped the council zero in on the primitive sources of our faith, Scripture, and the writings of the early Church fathers. "A people's Church"? That phrase came from de Lubac, who had stashed his cassock to go fight (and suffer serious wounds) with the French Underground during World War II.

On the eve of Vatican II, in early October 1962, I met Thomas K. Gorman, the bishop of Dallas, at an outdoor dinner party given by *Newsweek*'s Curtis Pepper at his hilltop estate overlooking Rome. Gorman listened patiently when I complained to him about the Vatican's meager press arrangements. "You're a former chairman of the American bishops' press committee," I said. "Can't you do something?"

He lit a foot-long cigar and said that he couldn't help me and laughed at my naivete. He said, "You won't see many headlines coming out of this council," explaining that the Roman Curia had a lock on everything and that many American bishops were saying they were there in Rome to approve what had been prepared for them in advance by the Curia and then go home "in about three or four weeks." He was echoing Arnaldo Cortesi, the veteran Rome bureau chief at the *New*

York Times, who'd told his readers that he expected "no great changes" (and hence little news) out of the council. Poor man, he was only reflecting what his sources inside the Curia had told him.

The council ended up changing the very way we thought about God, ourselves, our spouses, our Protestant cousins, Buddhists, Hindus, Muslims, and Jews—even the way we thought about the Russians. When a handful of bishops kept pushing for conciliar condemnation of Communism, John XXIII kept insisting that kind of talk would only blow up the world. Pope John and his council also made some preliminary moves that helped end the Cold War.

The Jews? The council reversed the Church's long-standing anti-Semitism. Until that time, Catholics had believed that if Jews didn't convert to Catholicism, there was something wrong with them. The council fathers took another look at that idea and decided that Jews were still living their ancient covenant with God. We decided there was nothing wrong with the Jews; they became our brothers and sisters.

Before the council, we'd thought we were miserable sinners when, really, we were being nothing but human. After the council, we had a new view of ourselves. We learned to put a greater importance on finding and following Jesus as "the way" (as opposed to what we said in the Creed, simply giving voice to a set of doctrines we may or may not have understood). What mattered was what we *did*: helping to feed the hungry, clothe the naked, and find shelter for the homeless. That's what made us followers of Jesus.

Before the council, we were told we were excommunicated if we set foot in a Protestant church. After the council (at which Protestant observers were welcomed, given seats of honor, and spoken of no longer as *Protestants* but rather as "separated brethren"), we stopped fighting the Methodists and the Presbyterians and conspired with them in the fight for justice and peace and marched with them to Selma.

Before the council, we thought only Protestants read the Bible. Since the council, we've seen a new Catholic appreciation for the Scriptures; they've been given a more prominent place at Mass, and in many parishes we now have groups gathering every week for Bible study.

Before the council, we took pride in knowing that we were the only people on earth who could expect salvation, according to the centuries-long mantra that "there is no salvation outside the Church." After the council, we began to see there was something good and something great in all religions. And we didn't think we had all the answers. After Vatican II, we started thinking of ourselves not as "the one, true Church." Instead, we were "a pilgrim people." It was a phrase that summoned an image of a band of humble travelers on a journey who, though subject to rain and snow and high wind and hurricane, to thirst and starvation and pestilence and disease and attacks by leopards and locusts, keep on plodding ahead with a hope and a prayer that we will someday reach our destination. The image was calculated to counter an old self-concept that hadn't stood up to scrutiny—of a triumphal Church that knew it all, lording it over humankind.

Before the council, we identified *salvation* as "getting to heaven." After the council, we knew that we had a duty to bring justice and peace to the world in our own contemporary society, understanding in a new way the words that Jesus had given us when he'd taught us to pray "thy Kingdom come, thy will be done *on earth* as it is in heaven." By the end, among the most influential figures at the council we encountered two humble souls—one a woman, Dorothy Day, founder of the Catholic Worker movement, who wasn't allowed to speak to the assembled bishops at Vatican II (no woman was), and the other a birdlike figure, Dom Hélder Câmara, the archbishop of Recife, in Brazil. Both of them went around Rome begging individual bishops and those who were putting together the council's crowning document, *Gaudium et Spes*, "please do not forget the poor." The council did not forget the poor. And neither did the popes who came after the council; for all their wanting to turn the clock back on Vatican II, they kept allying the Church with the world's have-nots. And neither has Pope Francis. As *Time* magazine noted when it made Francis its Man of the Year in December 2013, "You could argue that he is simply saying what popes before him have said, that Jesus calls us to care for the least among us—only he is saying it in a way that people seem to be hearing it differently."

Before the council, we were sin-obsessed. It was even a sin to eat a hamburger on Friday night after the game. After the council, we had a new sense of sin. We didn't hurt God when we sinned. We sinned when we hurt somebody else. Or ourselves. After the council, we had a new holy, hopeful view of ourselves, redefining holiness as the famous Trappist monk Thomas Merton defined it: to be holy is to be human.

Before the council, we were told we were condemned to hell if we made love to our spouses without at the same time making babies. After the council, we knew we had a duty (and the God-approved pleasure) to make love even if we could not afford to have another baby.

Before the council, we thought God spoke directly to the pope, who then passed the word down the ecclesiastical pyramid to the bishops, then to the priests, then the nuns, and, properly filtered, to us. After the council, we learned a new geometry. The Church wasn't a pyramid. It was more like a circle, in which we are all encouraged to have a voice. We are the Church. We have a right and a duty to speak out about the kind of Church we want.

Most of these changes did not come about because the fathers of Vatican II revamped what we had already professed believing in the Apostles' Creed. They didn't change our faith; they didn't come up with a new understanding of God. Still one God, two natures in Jesus, three persons. For that reason, Papa Ratzinger kept saying that the council didn't come up with anything new. No, no new dogmas. (And thank God for that. The last thing modern, thinking Catholics want are dogmas of any kind. *Dogma* and *dogmatic* are words that don't have much resonance with us. When I think of dogma, I think of the hundreds of anathemas laid down by the Council of Trent: "believe these dogmatic propositions, or be damned.")

The council fathers tried to re-create what the faith had been in its primitive beginnings. To rediscover the beauty of that faith, they said we have to take a deeper look at sacred Scripture and study the fathers of the Church. And only then would the council speak to the world in language it can understand.

And not just words. They also struck new attitudes. They eased up on the certainties that had been codified at the Council of Trent and dispelled the gloom that had overtaken the Church of the Piuses (Ninth, Tenth, Eleventh, and Twelfth), and they made a happier Church. They pointed out that when Jesus addressed the multitude on that hillside overlooking the lake, he did not enlighten their minds by reading them the Ten Commandments. He enkindled their hearts by telling them what would make them happy. (We translate his words as "Blessed are the poor . . ." But *beatus* means "happy" as well as "blessed.")

The council fathers did not follow the example of Trent. They followed the example of Jesus. They did not anathematize anyone or anything. They established a new style of thinking about ourselves as followers of the guy who told us how we could have life and have it more abundantly.

We make a mistake if we comb through the sixteen documents of Vatican II and hope to find explicit warrants for the Church we want to see take shape in the future. We can only capture the real, revolutionary meaning of the council by looking at the new kind of language that permeated all those documents. It was not the kind of juridical language Cardinal Ottaviani loved. Jesuit John W. O'Malley, author of the most authoritative work on the council, *What Happened at Vatican II*, says the council's message was hidden in plain sight. Father O'Malley describes it by contrasting the old language with the new:

> At stake were almost two different visions of Catholicism: from commands to invitations, from laws to ideals, from definition to mystery, from threats to persuasion, from coercion to conscience, from monologue to dialogue, from ruling to service, from withdrawn to integrated, from vertical to horizontal, from exclusion to inclusion, from hostility to friendship, from rivalry to partnership, from suspicion to trust, from static to ongoing, from passive acceptance to active engagement, from fault finding to appreciation, from prescriptive to principled, from behavior modification to inner appropriation.

Mere words? I don't think so. They underline my thesis—that the council helped us all be more real, more human, and more loving. The council helped us realize that the world was a good place. It was good because God made it, and he made it because he loves us (and loves the world, too).

This is precisely the language Pope Francis is using today. He is a living example of what the fathers of the council wanted—leaders who could help us all be more real, more human, and more loving. It is because Pope Francis has imbibed the spirit of the council that he has surprised the world as he has, mostly with his informal interviews, his off-the-cuff homilies, and his impromptu asides when he drops his prepared remarks and speaks to audiences from his heart. Francis has not been *telling* us what the council means. He has been *showing* us what it means by his actions.

Twentieth-century popes went through all kinds of contortions to avoid contradicting popes who'd gone before them. The most heated debates at Vatican II revolved around papal infallibility: one on religious liberty (condemned by Pope Pius IX in his *Syllabus of Errors*, published in 1864), and the other on birth control (condemned by Pope Pius XI in 1930). At Vatican II, it only seemed like common sense for the council fathers to revisit and revise both teachings, but how could the council contradict the solemn, infallible teachings of previous popes? For four years, on and off during Vatican II, members of the no-change party, led by Cardinal Ottaviani, said that no matter how much sense it made to revise the Church's traditional teachings on religious liberty, the council could not do it. Otherwise, what would happen to papal primacy? Those who were writing the council's statements on religious liberty had to convince themselves with an argument from past history—that the Church had "always taught" that everyone had to follow their own consciences in religious matters—and with an argument from current history—that the world at large had largely bought into the United Nations' Universal Declaration of Human Rights, among them the people's right to worship according to the dictates of their own consciences. Jesuit Cardinal Bea admitted that the council's declaration on religious liberty "is not traditional teaching. But life today is not traditional."

In the speeches and applause during the council's debates on the ends of marriage (as close as they could come to a debate on birth control), we could see that the council fathers were all in favor of couples making love even when they couldn't make a baby. So were all but seven members of the seventy-nine-member papal birth-control commission, who came to the satisfying conclusion that the Church shouldn't be telling couples how to practice responsible parenthood. But even they had to battle back against the contention of the seven: If we change the Church's teaching, what will happen to papal infallibility? Even then, those writing the commission's final report had to figure out how to say that Pius XI had been wrong without actually saying he'd been wrong. Fifty years ago, those council fathers could not come right out and say papal infallibility was A Big Mistake. In their debates on collegiality, they came close, but no cigar. Paul VI, fearing he would lose his primacy, terminated the debate. Even so, I know of no reputable Catholic theologian today who believes in the pope's infallibility as defined at Vatican I—that the pope is infallible in himself and not with the consensus of the Church.

The major issue in the Church is change. In the Church's cultural war that has been raging for at least two centuries, we have divided into two factions: the party of change versus the party of no change. The change party wanted to update the Church. The no-change party despised the word *update* and its sister word *reform*. The no-change people clung to the notion of the pope as monarch. The change people wanted to see a pope who would not only listen to people but also heed their words, so he could serve them with what they said they needed rather than what he thought they ought to have. The overwhelming majority at Vatican II—usually twenty-three hundred votes to two hundred on a few issues, but more like twenty-four hundred to fifty or so on most of the others—were in the party of change.

By now, there is little doubt as to where Pope Francis stands. He believes the Holy Spirit was with the council, and he has given at least one public (though gentle) rebuke to his predecessors for downplaying the council's deepest implications. On April 16, 2013, he asked in one of his "off-the-cuff" homilies "whether we have done everything the Holy Spirit was asking us to do during the council."

"No," Francis answered his own question bluntly. "We celebrate this anniversary, we put up a monument, but we don't want it to upset us. We don't want to change, and, what's more, there are those who wish to turn the clock back." This, he went on, "is called stubbornness and wanting to tame the Holy Spirit."

Exactly right. John Paul II and Benedict tried to take us back to our embattled, keep-the-world-at-arm's-length posture that characterized the Church before Vatican II. In one of his last synods, Benedict was asking the bishops to figure out ways of doing battle with an abstraction he called *secularism*. By that I thought he meant that the world was getting more worldly. If there is anything wrong with that (and I am not sure there is), then the Catholic cure for it is not to withdraw from that world, but rather to celebrate its goodness, thank God for it, and try (in the spirit of Vatican II) to make it better. Which is what Pope Francis is trying to do. It is in his Jesuit DNA.

7

OTHER RELIGIONS

For centuries, the Christ of the missionaries was a foreigner. The Spanish and Portuguese and Belgian traders brought with them colonial soldiers, a colonial government, and a colonial Church. Vatican II's charter, as contained in *Lumen Gentium, Gaudium et Spes*, and *Ad Gentes*, the document on the missions, repudiated this colonial Church. If Christ came for all men, then Christ's message and Christ's meaning had to be for all cultures. Jesus didn't need a passport. He had to be African. He had to be Asian. The new postconciliar Church had to plant itself in other cultures. It had to become a Church that was homegrown, homespun, homemade—a process they called *enculturation*.

Some of the best thinking on enculturation has come from the Indian Jesuit Samuel Rayan, who said he and his confreres in India had to "decolonialize theology" itself. As stated in my *A Church in Search of Itself*, he wrote, "Colonial theology can only reflect the colonizers' interests, use the Gospel to justify oppression, and to call for submission and resignation. It cannot nurse us into freedom fighters, cannot suckle a spirituality for combat. It easily becomes a tool in the hands of ruling classes and colonialists to keep their victims in bondage."

Rayan set out an agenda for the Church in Asia, one that has been mulled over and finally adopted by the most forward-thinking body in the Church today, the Federation of Asian Bishops' Conferences. The Asian bishops said they would reject theological imports and imitations; reappropriate their own theological soil and its promises and possibilities; sow this soil with their own problems, sufferings, and struggles, their own needs, hopes, experiences, and tears; and harvest new humanizing visions that could then create a new reign of justice and peace, now, in this life and on this planet.

As if that task weren't challenging enough, the Asian bishops have come to the gradual realization over the past thirty years that enculturation in Asia demands something more than decolonializing their own theology. The Church in Asia, they said, also had to engage in a dialogue with the Asian people—do some hard listening, especially to the poor, that aimed at a deep, loving, and respectful understanding of their cultures and their religions. This dialogue wouldn't be a substitute for proclamation and evangelization, or a simple strategy for reasons of survival on a continent where Catholics make up less than 2 percent of the population. They pursued this dialogue because they wanted to understand how the Holy Spirit was working even in Buddhists and Hindus.

The Asian bishops, aided by the religious-order priests and their own thinking diocesan priests, seem reconciled to the fact that, however well they get across the Jesus message, they should not expect many conversions, because faith and culture are so intertwined. Hindus in India, for example, cannot convert to Christianity without looking like traitors to their country. I know Asian Jesuits who believe it is enough for them to "proclaim the Gospel—sometimes even with words," and then stand back and let the Holy Spirit breathe where she wills and when she wills.

I can tell you about an Italian Jesuit living in the Muslim world right now who exemplifies what I mean—another Jesuit working on the frontiers. His name is Paolo Dall'Oglio. In 1977, the far-seeing and saintly Jesuit general Pedro Arrupe dispatched him to Lebanon to learn Arabic and Islamic culture—to begin, at age twenty-three, the kind of deep cultural transformation epitomized by the giant missionary to China, Matteo Ricci.

Now, some thirty-seven years later, Dall'Oglio, at age fifty-nine, does not consider himself a giant. But he does think of himself as something of a Jesuit Muslim—"because Jesus loves Muslims, the same Jesus who is alive in me. In a sense, I cannot but be a Muslim—by way of the Spirit and not the letter." He says he is also a syncretist, "culturally *and* theologically—without losing my faithfulness to the mystery of the Church of Jesus Christ."

Dall'Oglio may say he is a Jesuit Muslim, but he looks and talks very much like a twenty-first-century Jesuit, as I quickly learned when I met him a few years ago in a parlor at the Gregorian University in Rome, where he was visiting.[1] When I met him then, he was a tall, animated man on the move with flashing eyes, wearing Nikes, a ski jacket, and a backpack—and coughing through a very full salt-and-pepper beard. "I am sorry," he said, "I have the flu, or something." His English was good—a great deal better, at least, I told him, than my Italian. "Or," he joshed, "your Arabic."

I asked him about his immersion in Islam. "As soon as I arrived in Lebanon in 1977," he said, "I tried to start thinking in Arabic." Among other things, he learned the Heart Prayer in Arabic ("Lord Jesus Christ, be merciful to me, a sinner") and made it as habitual as his own breathing. He came back to Rome for philosophy and theology, but he spent every summer somewhere in the Arab world. And he not only learned what Islam was but also learned to love it, not least from the writings of Catholic Islamic monk Charles de Foucauld (1858–1916) and Catholic Islamic scholar Louis Massignon (1883–1962).

Dall'Oglio produced a doctoral dissertation at Rome's Gregorian University titled "Hope in Islam." He was ordained a priest in the Syriac Catholic Rite and then moved to his first assignment—to Islam, to Syria, where he eventually came upon his future monastery.

Dall'Oglio dug into his backpack to find a picture of Deir Mar Musa, a long shot of a white, fortress-like complex built on top of a cliff. It was first constructed, he said, in the sixth century, frescoed in the eleventh century, and abandoned in the nineteenth century, and then given to him by the Catholic Antiochian bishop of Homs, Hama, and Nebek in 1991. The frescoes in its chapel are priceless.

Deir Mar Musa (it means "Community of Saint Moses the Ethiopian") has an international cast of monks and nuns in their thirties, plus some lay collaborators, including two married couples, and some novices, too. After four years, those who are approved take perpetual vows of poverty, chastity, and obedience, plus promises of contemplation, work, hospitality, and loving Islam. They wear gray woolen habits, cinched with a leather belt. They do not follow any special dietary restrictions but do not eat pork or drink wine when they have Muslim guests.

Shoeless, their heads covered with prayer shawls, kneeling on fine oriental carpets, the community shares an hour of prayer every morning, starting at 7:30, followed by a talk with Dall'Oglio. After breakfast, they work until 2:30 p.m., milking their goats, making cheese, tending their gardens, and constructing a new building for the nuns and female guests. (They have already remodeled a series of ancient caves north of the monastery for the monks and male guests.) After lunch, they take a siesta when they can, they study, and they go on the Internet, creating a virtual monastery in cyberspace at www.deimarmusa.org. In the evening at seven, they have an hour of silent prayer in their ancient chapel. Then they do their Eucharist.

Says Dall'Oglio, "We practice an Abrahamitic hospitality." In fact, hospitality is the whole point of their existence. They want to bridge the tremendous gap between the followers of Jesus and the followers of Mohammed, and they feel they can do this best by meeting with all who come—for a day or for a week—answering their questions, inviting them to join in their prayers, building on their mountain a people's park with and for their largely Muslim neighbors, and joining in their fasts for peace.

In the beginning, they had problems—with both Muslims and Christians who did not understand what Dall'Oglio was up to. He was approached one day by a group of four middle-aged men who charged him with being a spy. "This," he recalls, "was hard to refute. The more I look okay and sound okay, the more I prove how effective a spy I really am. Finally, I tell them, 'All right. Look in my eyes. If you see something that is not sincere, you have every right to beat me. And I am honor bound to let you do it.'"

They withdrew, conferred together, then reapproached him and looked into his deep brown eyes and saw . . . something good. They did not beat him. "Today," Dall'Oglio says, "they're among my best friends."

They have a library at Mar Musa containing all the classic Christian texts ("we have to sink roots deep into our own tradition") and the Koran and some of the classic commentaries on Islam's sacred book. "Our monks and nuns know the Koran almost as well as many Muslims," says Dall'Oglio.

Dall'Oglio sees his work of reconciliation with Islam extending in the future toward some kind of mediation between all the warring parties in the Middle East. "This is very delicate," he says, "but everyone knows that we cannot continue to use religion as an excuse for violence of all kinds. We have to find a way to break through the infernal circle of fear that we feel, all of us." Where to put the focus? Dall'Oglio says it is clear that the people in every religion have to dig deep into their own roots to find the rationales for dealing with everyone in justice and peace. He has found those roots in both the Old and New Testaments. He has found them in the Koran. People who don't go to their roots but follow only the letter of whatever sacred text, he says, are the real troublemakers in this world. "Follow them, and we are doomed."

It remains to be seen whether and how Dall'Oglio can convince mainstream Muslims to repudiate the fundamentalists in their midst. But he says he has to try. It seems like an exciting and crucially important effort. At the end of a long piece in the *New York Times Sunday Magazine* on March 23, 2003, Paul Berman underlined the need. He wrote, "The terrorists speak insanely of deep things. The antiterrorists had better speak sanely of equally deep things. Presidents will not do this. Presidents will dispatch armies, or decline to dispatch armies, for better and for worse. But who will speak of the sacred and the secular, of the physical world and the spiritual world?" Berman went on to say, "President George W. Bush . . . is not the man for that. Philosophers and religious leaders will have to do this on their own. Are they doing so? Armies are in motion, but are the philosophers and religious leaders, the liberal thinkers, likewise in motion?"

I think we can say, "Yes, they are," by pointing to the work of Paolo Dall'Oglio and other Jesuits (and others like American theologian Leonard Swidler) now engaged in interreligious dialogue with Muslims in various parts of the world. This "dialogue" is more than mere talk; it is also working with "the others" to make a better world.

In late July 2013, Dall'Oglio traveled to Ar-Raqqa, a city in north-central Syria on the banks of the Euphrates, to see if he could broker a peace between warring factions in Syria. Shortly after he arrived in Ar-Raqqa, he was kidnapped by Al Qaeda factions and, after some days of conflicting media reports, was finally declared dead. A Western diplomat who'd spoken with Dall'Oglio shortly before he'd crossed from Turkey into Syria in August said Dall'Oglio was fully aware of the risks he was courting and of the deteriorating conditions inside rebel-held areas in Syria. "But he seemed convinced he would be fine and that he had to try to assist in brokering a deal between Kurdish insurgents and the jihadists."

He endorsed the uprising against Assad from the start, dubbing it a "democratic jihad." On the destruction wreaked on the country's landmarks by the war, Dall'Oglio said, "We have the old maps and plans; and we will rebuild and restore it once the regime falls. The most important thing is that the dictator leaves; the rest is easy."

On October 7, 2013, a news bulletin out of Beirut reported that Dall'Oglio was alive and in good condition, apparently well treated by his kidnappers. I have no doubt that he charmed those who were threatening to kill him. It was part of his Jesuit DNA.

While Dall'Oglio was in serious dialogue with Muslims, his brother Jesuit Aloysius Pieris was covering another dialogical frontier—with Buddhists. After finishing his four years of theology in Naples, despite the fact that he'd had no aspirations to live the life of a scholar, Pieris returned to his native Sri Lanka for doctoral studies in Buddhist philosophy at the University of Sri Lanka's Vidyodaya campus, the first priest (in fact, the first Christian) ever to win a doctorate there in Buddhist philosophy. In 1974, after two years of discernment and prayer and consultation with his superiors, he founded his Tulana Research Centre "as a kind of laboratory where people could feel at home and deepen themselves in their own orientation." He has continued to deepen his own knowledge about the sources of Buddhism. Working with its primary original texts in Pali and other Asian languages, Pieris has gone on to publish a number of learned commentaries on Buddhism, and his Buddhist library at Tulana is now a place where Buddhist scholars come to read, reflect, and confer with him.

In preparation for my visit to Tulana in 2001, I knew I had to do some serious homework. I had to read Pieris's *An Asian Theology of Liberation*, a work first published in German in 1988 that was addressed mainly to Catholics; it laid out a program of solidarity with Asia's great religions and with Asia's poor that will take at least a century to come to maturity. Christian monks may lead the way, Pieris wrote. They are the ones now learning "the language of gnosis spoken by Asia's non-Christian monastics and also the language of agape, the only one that the Asian poor can really understand." In other words, for Pieris, the future of the Church in Asia will revolve around basic human communities, with Christian *and* non-Christian membership, "where mysticism and militancy meet and merge: mysticism based on voluntary poverty and militancy pitched against forced poverty."

For Pieris, liberation theology in Asia was more a process than a theology, "a primacy of praxis over theory . . . the radical involvement with the poor and the oppressed. We know Jesus the *truth* by following Jesus the *way*." Pieris wrote that Asian theology cannot become "mere God talk, for in our cultures God talk in itself is sheer nonsense. As evidenced by the Buddha's refusal to talk of nirvana, all words have silence as their source and destiny. God talk is made relative to God experience. The word game about nature and person or the mathematics of one and three have only generated centuries of verbosity. It is wordlessness that gives every word its meaning."

So I knew that when I arranged to spend a week with Pieris at his Tulana Research Centre in a literal jungle outside the Sri Lankan capital city of Colombo, I was getting into some deep theological waters. I even quaked a little when I scanned a leaked copy of a privately circulated paper on Christ that Pieris had delivered to a group of Jesuit theologians in India in August 1999. In it, I found him attacking the doctrine elaborated by the Council of Chalcedon in 451 (which had decreed that in Jesus Christ there is one Divine Person but two natures, one human and one divine). In my seminary days, I'd pondered that proposition a good deal, but I could never really understand it. There were times during my Ignatian contemplations when I'd "watched" Jesus acting as if he didn't have any idea of his special "divine status." There were other times when he did. At his arrest on the night of his Passion, he stayed the hands of those who wanted to help him resist: "Did you not know that if I asked my Father he would send me twelve legions of angels?" But a few hours later, when he was dying on the Cross, he said, "My God, my God, why have you forsaken me?"

I was now delighted to find Pieris saying that the dogma hacked out at Chalcedon was "irrelevant and peripheral to anyone who was thinking at all deeply about the uniqueness of the person and the mission of Jesus."

What *is* relevant, then? According to Pieris, what's important for a Christian in the twenty-first century is not "a *belief* in truths revealed by

God and accurately formulated by the Church but *action* in fidelity to a faithful God who had made a promise of salvation." When I was studying Thomism in a Jesuit house of studies about a thousand years ago, we used a formula to define what we were doing—*fides quaerens intellectum* (faith seeking understanding). Now I found Pieris scrapping that formula on the grounds that we cannot understand a good many things that have been "revealed" and shouldn't break our heads trying.

Pieris suggested a better course: we should see Jesus in the poor and downtrodden of this earth—because whatever we did for the least of God's children on this earth, we did for Jesus. And then maybe we will know more. The heart comes first, then understanding. Pieris quoted 1 John 4:8: "Whoever does not love the neighbor does not know God." And he suggested that understanding is generated by "the encounter with the One who is our Love and our Salvation." He proposed a new formula to help label what it is that Christians ought to be engaged in: *fides sperans salutem* (faith hoping for liberation), a formula that he picked up from Vatican II's constitution on the Church: "Mary stands out among the poor and the humble of the Lord who confidently await and receive salvation from him."

Pieris explained: Mary, the model of the Church, "stands out"—that is, "appears quite conspicuous"—among the "poor and the humble" who hope for and, therefore, receive salvation. The Church that is conspicuously present among "the poor and the humble" in a Marian fashion, hoping for salvation and receiving it, exercises a faith that unfolds itself as a theology of liberation (or salvation). And since God *is* salvation/liberation (as the name *Jesus* literally means), to "hope for salvation" is to hope for that Love that God *is* in Godself and that God *speaks* as God's Word. Pieris wrote, "This is the beginning and the end of an authentic Christology." He added:

> Unfortunately many theologians who criticize the seminal Christologies of Asians do so from within the Chalcedonian frame of mind. One must certainly agree with what Chalcedon was *trying* to say within its own particular paradigm—namely, that the divine and the human allow neither fusion nor fission in the way they constitute Jesus as one personal unity. By acknowledging this truth, we duly express our orthodoxy as well as our solidarity with the faith of the Church. But *how* exactly the two natures remain distinct while being united is a question that appears soteriologically inconsequential and

defies human explanation and therefore cannot be invoked as a criterion of orthodoxy.

I was intrigued by that phrase "soteriologically inconsequential." The *soter* root comes from the Greek word for *savior*. I guessed at the meaning of the whole phrase: It doesn't make any difference if people understand *how* Jesus could have been both human and divine. What matters is that Jesus has given them a plan of action—to be all they can be. That is salvation. What a relief to find a theologian who wasn't trying to mystify the people in the pews. I had to meet this man, because he exemplified some of the salutary variety of thought going on in the Catholic world, epitomizing the kind of freedom that we can expect Catholic theologians to enjoy under Pope Francis.

I took an Emirates airline flight out of Singapore at midnight, a planeload of mainly short, dark-skinned people heading to Colombo, as I was, plus a few dozen Muslims going on to Dubai. Three hours later, coming out of customs with my three bags on a kind of shopping cart, I was met by a little man named Uri, smiling and holding up my name on a cardboard sign. We took off on a dark, twisting ride through what seemed like a densely populated jungle zone. No streetlights, no street signs. "You must have been here many times," I said to Uri after the umpteenth turn in the dark. "Only once," he replied. But I did not fear, because his boss, the owner of the taxi service, was the cousin of my host, Aloy Pieris. I knew I was in good hands.

It was now close to four in the morning, but I found Pieris waiting up for me. He came out to the driveway when we arrived, a diminutive, slightly graying man with a caffe latte complexion, wearing a colorful shirt and a red sarong and sandals. He shook my hand warmly, and then led me to my room. After many twists and turns and steps through the fairly elaborate complex that has gone by name of the Tulana Research Centre for more than twenty-five years, we ended up in the center's only guest room: tiled floor, two cots, one desk, one lamp, one bathroom with a sink, a toilet, and shower. "You may want to undo this netting," said Pieris, "for the mosquitoes." Then, after I pleaded exhaustion and turned down his suggestion for a little talk and a drink, he left me alone in my room.

I was warm and sticky, and I undid the mosquito netting around my bed but quickly tied it up again, because I couldn't see myself ever getting to sleep inside that suffocating cocoon. After unpacking a bit, and brushing my teeth with the tap water and taking my vitamins, I showered and cooled off. I learned later that the normal mode of bathing, often done communally here, is to gather around a small square pool of well water out of doors, dip a pail into it, and pour the water over one's head. So my private shower, even though a cold shower, was a luxury here. I also learned that it was not okay to drink the tap water. In the morning, Pieris gave me an old Johnny Walker bottle, full of the treated well water used here for drinking, to take to my room.

I lay down on my cot at 4:30 a.m. and woke to the songs of the jungle—mourning doves, a koel bird (something like our blue jay), and a rooster crowing in the distance. I showered again, donned a light pair of shorts, a T-shirt, and sandals and went down to a 10 a.m. breakfast of bread, jam, coffee, and a small banana while Pieris joined me for a cup of tea. We dined at a large, circular table in an airy common room dominated by some stunning art. One of the pieces was a bas-relief of Jesus washing the feet of his disciples; it was done by a Buddhist monk, Sadu Janarabaya, who is now studying Catholic theology in Milan, and it may be one of the few portraits of Jesus ever done by a Buddhist monk. Pieris got this artist a scholarship in Italy, not to convert him to Catholicism but to help him be a better Buddhist. "I have never converted a Buddhist to Christianity," he says. "The good Buddhist doesn't need conversion. He is honest, he is generous, he is not caught up in greed or in power games."

We studied this piece by Janarabaya for a time. Then we moved over to another bas-relief, done by another Buddhist, Kingsley Gunatillake. It was called "Jesus Lost in the Temple."

Pieris said, "I let these artists read our Scripture stories, then I leave it up to them to interpret what they read. Doing it this way helps me understand how the Christ event comes across to them and to the others I encounter here in Sri Lanka. For me, it is a form of interreligious dialogue. I think art speaks better than words."

"Jesus Lost in the Temple" looked like it was done in a kind of native sandstone and had a text in Sinhalese going down the left side. It said that Jesus—who was a chubby, almost cherubic figure here in the lower foreground—was "listening and questioning" the elders, whose figures and faces dominated the bas-relief. But their faces were not Semitic faces. I could descry Buddha and Krishna, Lao-tzu, Confucius, Moses,

Socrates, Plato, and Aristotle. Two women were here in this picture to remind those who behold it that women are not to be blocked out of the Jesus community. Pieris quoted Saint Paul's description of the early Church: "neither male nor female, neither slave nor free."

I could see the mother of Jesus in the lower-left foreground reaching out to restrain Jesus, but he was fending her off with his left hand, while gesturing to the elders above him with his right. Pieris explained, "Mary is trying to control the Word of God, but Jesus won't let her do that. He must be about his Father's business. God's business, not the Church's business." Pieris draws a lesson here: "The Church, like Mary here, is to support, not control."

Pieris was one of the most important Catholic theologians in Asia, but almost since the day of his ordination in Naples just before Christmas in 1963, he had been ignoring efforts by Rome to control him and his theological explorations in Asia. These were the early, still-heady days of post–Vatican II Catholicism, when the Church's most original theologians were working on the mandate given in more than one council document that the Gospel message was meant for all humanity and that theologians had a duty to pass that message on in ways that all people could understand.

In a letter to Asian bishops in 1972, Pope Paul VI endorsed this new approach in these words: "The Church must make herself in her fullest expression native to your countries, your cultures, your races. . . . Let the Church draw nourishment from the genuine values of the venerable Asian religions and cultures."

A liberal pope (as Paul VI was—most of the time, anyway) could say this, but the words had never seemed to ring true in the ears of the old colonial, latinizing bureaucrats who were still running the Vatican machinery. One of the investigators in the Congregation for the Doctrine of the Faith (the CDF), the Church's ministry of truth, got after Pieris some decades before for an essay he'd written on liberation theology. Fortunately for Pieris, his Jesuit superior in Sri Lanka challenged the competence of the CDF to even understand what Pieris was saying in English, and, after another exchange of letters, the CDF sent the provincial a note stating there was nothing "intrinsically against orthodoxy" in Pieris's writings but that the CDF thought he was "confused."

Pieris is a citizen of Sri Lanka, known as Ceylon when it became a British tea colony in 1818, after successive dominations by the Dutch and the Portuguese that dated back to the seventeenth century, when Pieris's forebears became Catholic converts. Pieris is thankful they did; otherwise, he would never have received the education he did in the Jesuit order, which he joined at age nineteen at an international house of studies in India. He did his theology in Naples—close to the action at Vatican II during the early 1960s, when he and his classmates often entertained some of the council's leading theologians, including Karl Rahner. Pieris remembers his last encounter with Rahner and Rahner's exact words: "Vatican II is not an end but a beginning. You have to spell out its implications for your people in the context of their life situations."

For the past forty years, Pieris has been trying to do exactly that. At one time he'd had no inclination to live the life of a scholar. "I was a poet and a musician," he recalled. "I wanted to write plays. I wanted to dance. And I wanted to work with the rural youth." At the time, in the late 1960s and early 1970s, revolution was in the air, and Pieris studied with the rambunctious young people in Sri Lanka's cradle of revolution, the university campus, watching them grow from the unthinking tools of others into adult actors in their own futures. Then the Jesuit general, Pedro Arrupe, snatched him up to teach Buddhism at the Jesuits' Gregorian University in Rome and, during the Roman summers, at another Jesuit training ground in Manila, the East Asian Pastoral Institute.

When Pieris returned to Sri Lanka, he felt called to cross-fertilize the socialist concerns of these rural students (and others in Sri Lanka) with their own authentic Buddhist roots. In 1974, he founded his Tulana Research Centre. The word *tulana* comes from the Sanskrit root *tul*, which has a variety of meanings: elevate, weigh, compare, lean toward more important things. In its infancy, though, Tulana seemed anything but important.

"We started with a hundred rupees," recalled Sister Frances de Silva, who had served as Pieris's bookkeeper and general factotum for twenty-five years. A few months after the center's opening, Pieris got a letter from Jean Leclerq, a French Benedictine monk who applauded what Pieris was doing. Enclosed was a check for the equivalent of 240 U.S. dollars, a fortune in Sri Lanka, where a dollar could then buy enough groceries for a week.

Since those humble beginnings, Pieris pursued his pioneering work with one major agendum: to understand Buddhists, not convert them, but rather work with them in what he called "our common struggle for liberation." While Pieris could understand some Jesuits in other places in the world who remain Jesuit priests and also assume the mantle of Buddhist monks, particularly as Zen Buddhists, that route was not for him. "Our people would not understand this double identity," he said, "and therefore I don't claim it."

Instead, Pieris continued to deepen his own knowledge about the sources of Buddhism. Working with its major original texts in Sinhalese, Pieris went on to publish a number of learned commentaries on Buddhism, and his Buddhist library at Tulana had become something of an informal and formal gathering place for a wide variety of people: "People can just drop in, without an appointment. They are free to stay here. We don't have many rooms for them. They generally sleep in our big communal hall and bathe in our communal well, and they eat whatever we have to offer. If they can bring a little rice of their own, or a little coconut, all the better." Life, therefore, was simple and, by Western standards, exceedingly poor. Pieris had an aged houseboy who cooked for him, mostly vegetable curries, but he had no gas or electric stove. On my first morning at the center, I found the houseboy boiling water over an open wood fire.

They had occasional seminars at the center, mostly dialogues between Buddhists and Christians, during which they played off one another's strengths and insights. Pieris said, "In understanding Buddha, we become better Christians. And in understanding Jesus, they become better Buddhists." An all-day seminar begins in the morning with conferences about some particular verses of the Buddhist or Christian scriptures. In the afternoon, they read some contemporary literature dealing with the same subject. In the evening, after dinner, they put on their own dramas or watch a film. "We Sri Lankans love theater," said Pieris, "and dancing, too." Late at night, confreres make their way, one by one, to Pieris's office for a chat; often it is a chat that deals with each person's own individual struggles for liberation, often enough from their own fears.

One day in the early 1990s, Buddhists came to Tulana for a conference that began with a Mass celebrated by Pieris. Later in the day, the pope's nuncio in Colombo, an Italian named Nicola Rotunno, arrived at the center to snoop around. He had heard that Buddhists would be attending, and he wanted to check things out, possibly to see whether

Pieris was caught up in syncretism, a bad word in the Vatican, which means mixing religions, quite ignoring the whole history of religion, a story of creative borrowings, from one religion to another and back again. "Oh, I'm late," he said to Pieris.

"You're not late," said Pieris. "You weren't invited."

"I'm worried about you," gushed the nuncio. "We are colleagues. You don't know how much I care."

Pieris nodded skeptically.

The nuncio said he had to ask. "Did any of these Buddhists attend Mass here today?"

"They did."

"The whole Mass?"

"Yes."

"But we have the Mass of the catechumens and the Mass of the faithful. As you know, the catechumens must leave at the Sanctus."

Pieris scoffed. "These Buddhists are not studying to become Catholics. Therefore, they are not catechumens."

The nuncio protested Pieris's attitude. Pieris wasn't cooperating. He reminded him, "I am the representative of the pope!"

Pieris snapped, "To the government, not to me." Pieris was right. But the distinction is often lost, especially in other countries like the United States. The U.S. bishops have always paid exaggerated deference to the pope's chief legate in Washington; as a matter of fact, the nuncio represents the Holy See to the U.S. government, not the U.S. bishops.

A few years later, after Monsignor Rotunno was transferred out of Sri Lanka, Pieris discovered that Rotunno had made an inquiry about Pieris at his old Jesuit house of theology in Naples. Nothing came of it. Or at least Rome filed no charges against Pieris after Rotunno's complaint.

"What would they charge me with?" said Pieris. "I do not call myself a Buddhist. I am critically loyal to the Church. I have a deep faith in Jesus Christ." And so, because he is so certain and so secure in that faith, Pieris hasn't worried about inquiries from Rome. "We have a great advantage here in Asia, because we work in languages that the men in the Holy Office do not understand."

From an old point of view, the point of view of Cardinal Ratzinger's heresy hunters, the situation in Sri Lanka could only get worse. Pieris has a new generation of young, lay theologians working with him; they are writing in their native Sinhalese. He mentioned one of them, a young man named Shirley Wijesysingha, who has a passion for biblical studies. He got one degree in Scripture from the Biblical Institute in Rome and a PhD at the Catholic University of Leuven. Now in Colombo, Wijesysingha leads a mass movement of people studying the Bible, and his graduates are laypeople who can (and do) preach homilies at Sunday Mass and then also plunge into various sorts of social action. When he writes, Wijesysingha will write in Sinhalese, a language that will be rather impervious to inquiries by the Holy Office (if there is still a Ratzinger-style Holy Office).

Pieris does not just oversee those biblical studies; for years, he has also financed and operated a school for the hearing impaired who could not otherwise find an education in Colombo, still a Third World country existing in a Third World economy. I visited the school one sunny morning in early April 2001 and found that the children had nothing but adoring looks for Father Aloy.

In addition to running this school, with a solid assist from an order of nuns, and supervising a coterie of students and putting on his conferences, Pieris continues to write more books and many more learned articles. During my stay, I found that he rose early and worked far into the night, sometimes in searching conversations with scholars who are writing their theses on Pieris. As of 2001, some two dozen doctoral dissertations had focused on Pieris and on the doings at his Tulana Research Centre.

At the time of my 2001 visit, Pieris's most recent book was a slim, self-published paperback based on private talks he'd given to predominantly Jesuit audiences in 1997 and 1998. As of my visit, *The Christhood of Jesus and the Discipleship of Mary: An Asian Perspective* had brought down no official reprimand from Rome. A surprise, perhaps, for in this book Pieris took up some of the very issues that led to the excommunication in 1998 of his fellow Sri Lankan theologian, the Oblate Tissa Balasuriya, an edict that was later revoked by Pope John Paul II after a worldwide outcry in defense of Balasuriya.

In *The Christhood of Jesus*, Pieris went straight to the heart of the Ratzinger agenda with a gentle attack on the very notion of dogmatic definitions themselves, pieces of legalism, he said, that owe more to Roman law than to the loving words of Jesus and his followers in the early years of Christianity. "Faith," Pieris wrote, "began to be judged, and the deviants condemned, entirely on the basis of one's adherence to the formula of faith" as defined by Church authorities. Result: a set of faith propositions that parallel a legal code, which seem to call for an efficient monitoring system to maintain doctrinal purity, a system that, it turns out, is run by "a powerful clerical class armed with massive punitive powers."

The Church, said Pieris, should have known better from its own history: "The history of the Christological dogmas . . . is not an edifying story of an innocuous development of a teaching; it is a sad story of serious misunderstandings, punctuated by political intrigues and physical violence." He cited the Council of Chalcedon, which condemned the Patriarch of Alexandria in 451. Pieris told me that exactly fifteen centuries later, in 1951, Pope Pius XII revoked the condemnation with an encyclical that admitted confusion over some words in the original edict. Formulas, said Pieris, often do more harm than good, especially if those formulas are asserted as "coming from divine revelation."

In fact, says Pieris, all the Church's formulas are culturally conditioned. As human constructs, they are relative, time-bound, and culturally limited expressions of faith that cannot be used as absolute norms for measuring orthodoxy. But it is precisely on this ground, relativism, that Cardinal Ratzinger's doctrinal police have condemned Asian theologians, who tend to agree with Pieris that dogmas are not divinely revealed at all but guiding statements that serve the believing community as practical aids "to foster and fructify our faith and hope in God who is love."

For Pieris, Vatican II still lives. He keeps pondering its significance for our times, and he keeps writing about it. His latest? *Providential Timeliness of Vatican II: A Long-Overdue Halt to a Scandalous Millennium.* In an e-mail to me, he says this book "is a new way of proving that Vatican II was not a mistake." In September 2013, he e-mailed me to report that he has another personal account of himself heading to press. He calls it *The Genesis of an Asian Theology of Liberation: An Autobiographical Essay on the Art of Theologizing in Asia.*

Liberation theology still lives in the worldwide Church, too, because concern for social justice has become part of the job description for Catholic leaders everywhere. Many dioceses throughout the world have active commissions for peace and justice, run mostly by laymen and laywomen. And students of the twenty-first century's ongoing revolutions have noted that advocates of other liberations have adopted the rhetoric—and some of the arguments—of the liberation theologians of Latin America. They have come up with a more effective formula for those who wanted to be Christ-bearers in the modern world. They got their orders straight out of Matthew 25, where Jesus told the disciples they would be not be admitted to paradise for knowing the right passwords (i.e., abstract truths) but on the strength of their giving food, drink, clothing, and shelter to the poor.

The Belgian Jesuit Jacques Dupuis was a confrere of Sam Rayan, the Indian Jesuit known for his work on enculturation. Dupuis had come as a missionary to India at the age of twenty-four and, by reason of his lifelong attempts at understanding of how the Spirit works, even in Hindus and Buddhists, he became, some forty years later, a key player in the debate about world religions triggered in 2001 by Cardinal Ratzinger's *Dominus Iesus.* This is why I need to profile him here.[2] A Jesuit "on the edge," Dupuis is one shining example of the many Jesuits always going for the *magis*.

He was born in 1923 into a pious, middle-class Catholic family, and his parents enrolled him in a Jesuit elementary school—in the first grade. "In a sense," Dupuis said, "I entered the Jesuits at the age of five." He passed six formative years in that Jesuit grammar school (where he started to learn English) and then spent six more years in a Jesuit secondary school, where he found "four memorable Jesuit teachers." No one was surprised when he followed in their footsteps by entering the Jesuits, along with four of his classmates, at the age of seventeen.

He got the education that was standard in those preconciliar days for all the Jesuits in the world: two years novitiate, two years juniorate (classical studies), three years of philosophy, and then three years of regency—with a slight twist. When his classmates went off to teach in Jesuit high schools in Belgium, he volunteered for the missions in India.

It was in India, at Saint Xavier's College, Calcutta (now called Kolkata), that Dupuis made his first acquaintance with young men who, though not Catholic, impressed him with their goodness and with a kind of attractive piety they had learned from their (mostly) Hindu mothers and Hindu fathers. To Dupuis, it seemed clear that God had revealed himself in and through their Hindu faith. And so now Dupuis began to think harder about the variety of religions in the world. It was now much more obvious to him than ever: these religions weren't bogus. So, then, what were they? Well, he wouldn't presume to say what God had in mind when these religions took shape. "I don't know," Dupuis once told me. "And I don't think Ratzinger knows either." (As Karl Rahner would famously say, "God is and always will be incomprehensible mystery.")

History itself, for Dupuis, was something of a mystery, too. But it was also a *locus theologicus* for him, a jumping-off place for further theological reflection that could promote more realistic (and more peace-making) dialogue between Christians and everyone else. In any event, Dupuis had no other choice than to start thinking new thoughts about the providence of God—in a world where the majority of its people have never heard the name of Jesus. Was the major part of humankind, then, to be denied the "salvation" that comes only through Jesus? He didn't think so. This was Dupuis's first exposure to what he has called "the concrete experience [that] opens one's eyes to reality."

Dupuis's concrete experience in India forced him to examine "the interaction between text and context." He did his theological studies in India, was ordained in India, and was assigned to teach theology in India. In all, he lived for thirty-six years in India, even taking his vacations in India, exploring the country alone on a motorcycle. "I never dreamed I would ever leave India or even ask to go anywhere else," he told me. "I thought I'd live in India, work in India, and die in India."

Then, one day in 1984, Father General Peter Hans Kolvenbach told Dupuis he was being transferred to Rome to teach "other religions" at the Gregorian, something that the general believed Dupuis was uniquely qualified to do. Some Indian Jesuits were glad to see him go. A high-ranking Italian Jesuit told me, "Dupuis was too conservative for them." (It was a fact I confirmed in my own three-week visit to India in 2012, hobnobbing mainly with Jesuits. Older hands told me Dupuis was ordered out of India because he had been such a disruptive force among India's Vatican II theologians.)

Ironic: Dupuis was too conservative in India, surrounded as he was by pioneering, sometimes even radical, theologians like Jesuit Samuel

Rayan. Hard for him, then, to go along with some of the strong stuff Rayan was writing. For example, on the religion of the Jews in Jesus's time, Rayan had this to say:

> Jesus came to decolonize the religion and the theology of the people, which had been occupied by royal, priestly, and wealthy settlers from the time of Solomon. Religion became priest-ridden and expensive, legalistic and burdensome. It had its outcastes and untouchables. It also had its ways of fleecing the poor. Jesus marginalized the temple and all priestly pretensions. The temple is destined to disappear. Worship shall be in spirit and truth. Mercy, not sacrifice. People, not Sabbath.[3]

The Vatican had chosen to ignore Rayan. He was working in the relative obscurity of his native India. Who was listening to him?

However, Dupuis was now in Rome, close to the Gregorian University's official overseers at the Vatican, who watched him for the next fourteen years. There he taught, wrote, and did his research on world religions, in the process catching himself up more and more on the spirit of Vatican II. Two Vatican offices, the Pontifical Council for Interreligious Dialogue and the Congregation for the Evangelization of Peoples, liked Dupuis's approach so much that they recruited him to work on position papers to guide those working with people of other religions. Cardinal Decourtray of Lyons, a member of the Council for Interreligious Dialogue, said that if Dupuis did not exist, the Church would have to invent him.

In the fall of 1997, Dupuis published *Toward a Christian Theology of Religious Pluralism*, a work named one of the year's best by the Catholic Theological Society of America. According to a review in the *Tablet*, the book signaled "a profound theological shift in the Christian understanding of other religions." Dupuis had addressed a central question: How can Christians profess and proclaim faith in Jesus Christ as the one redeemer of all humankind and at the same time recognize the Spirit at work in the world's religions and cultures? Dupuis was not merely asking whether salvation can occur for members of other traditions; he was asking how in God's providence these traditions "mediate salvation" to their members.

Others thought his work important: the book triggered more than a hundred reviews in six languages, as well as articles in learned journals and chapters in books dedicated in whole or in part to a critical evalua-tion of Dupuis's views. And then an all-important critic—Cardinal Jo-seph Ratzinger—came forward to ask Dupuis a few questions. To do that, he might have invited Dupuis over for a friendly cappuccino. In-stead, he wrote to Jesuit General Kolvenbach and told him Dupuis had to stop teaching and instead concentrate on responding to the charge that he was teaching that one religion was as good as another.

Dupuis wasn't saying one religion was as good as another. He had, however, been trying to find in the magisterial documents of his own Church a more open way of evaluating other faith traditions. He had said he was "aiming at a change of mind—and of heart—in my own constituency"—which made him ipso facto dangerous in the mind of the Church's no-change party. But in this, Dupuis had genuinely thought he was following a mandate from the pope himself, John Paul II, who had told the professors at the Gregorian University on Decem-ber 15, 1979, that they should "endeavor to be creative, without allow-ing yourselves to be too easily satisfied with what has proved useful in the past." The pope told the professors they should "have the courage to explore new ways, though with prudence."

That's exactly what Dupuis thought he was doing when he was teaching and doing his research. He was trying to find the good and the true and the beautiful in every religion—which, so many thinking Cath-olics believed, was the only way to bring the peoples of the world (so varied in their beliefs) together.

And yet Dupuis was now under fire. I was surprised to find out that the man who had delated Dupuis to the Holy Office was a Jesuit in Dupuis's own community at the Gregorian University. I have the man's name, but his name is not important, and neither is he. When I asked Dupuis the man's area of expertise, Dupuis growled, "Any damn thing." And it was another Jesuit, an editor of the Italian Jesuits' bimonthly *Civiltà Cattolica*, who wrote that the theology of religious pluralism proposed in Dupuis's book was "problematic and provocative." That review didn't much help Dupuis with the Holy Office, where yet a third Jesuit, a German, was working the Dupuis case.

On December 25, 1998, Dupuis responded to the congregation's first set of questions—even the questions were labeled *sub secreto*— with a two-hundred-page reply. He waited more than six months for the CDF verdict on that reply. Another letter arrived from Cardinal Ratzinger, who was not satisfied with Dupuis's answers; he appended a text of eleven pages containing a doctrinal judgment on Dupuis's book, with a new set of questions to be answered in three months—again in complete secrecy. Dupuis complied, and on November 1, 1999, he sent in his answers—sixty more pages. After that, silence from the CDF. Dupuis stewed and puzzled over papal statements that might give him a clue about his own fate.

On September 4, 2000, Dupuis had his first and only meeting with Cardinal Ratzinger in the cardinal's office on the third floor of the Palazzo Sant'Ufficio. Father General Kolvenbach was with him, along with his advocate, Gerald O'Collins, a kind of defense lawyer. O'Collins had been on the faculty at the Gregorian for thirty years and dean for six of them, and was an advocate for Dupuis because "he was a friend." They cleared up some misunderstandings. Ratzinger's aides had accused Dupuis of writing things he had never written, and Ratzinger apologized for the sloppy staff work.

"What really bothered Ratzinger," Dupuis later told me, "were the questions I raised that no one, not even he, could answer." In what sense did Christ already represent "the fullness of revelation," as the Church had long claimed? And did the Church possess that fullness? Anyone who had studied Church history knew the answer to the second question: the Church has always been somewhat short of the mark. In answer to the first question, Dupuis knew that Jesus made a good beginning with his life, death, and resurrection. But what about the endtimes? Won't Christ complete his revelation then, when we will see him "face to face" and no longer "dimly"? "Asking questions like these," Dupuis told me, "is what finally got me into trouble."

After that meeting in Ratzinger's office, it took the Holy Office six months to endorse a final compromise with Dupuis. Finally, on February 26, 2001, the Holy Office issued a "notification" regarding Dupuis that was surprisingly mild. It reported that Dupuis had acknowledged "ambiguities and difficulties" that might lead readers of his work to some wrong conclusions. But Ratzinger demanded no changes in Dupuis's book—only that the Holy Office's critique of Dupuis's book be included in subsequent editions.

Within hours, Father Kolvenbach issued a press release that put a benign spin on the story. He said the notification "recognized" Dupuis's book "for the seriousness of its methodological research, the richness of the scientific documentation, and the originality of its exploration." Kolvenbach also said, "On this solidly established dogmatic basis, we hope that Father Jacques Dupuis can continue his pioneer research."

Dupuis was waiting for the Holy Office to make up its mind when I first met him through the Australian Jesuit Gerald O'Collins. I became a friend of Dupuis. O'Collins said Dupuis took a liking to me because, as O'Collins put it, I was "a jolly fellow" and Dupuis was going through a profound depression. I think O'Collins meant that I knew how to listen to Dupuis's stories, draw him out, laugh at his sardonic humor, and not betray him with premature stories in *Newsweek*. I started calling him "Jim," as O'Collins did. Soon I found myself having supper with the two of them almost every Friday night, either in the refectory at the Gregorian or at the Abruzzi, a restaurant around the corner from the Greg.

Only then could I come even close to breaking through Dupuis's everyday persona, which, to most of the faculty and students at the Gregorian University where he was living, was "gruff and grum." Most of the Jesuits on the faculty kept their distance—which is probably the way he liked it. He was a serious theologian, given to heavy reading and thinking and writing—mostly in English—and he was not at all interested in small talk that would take him away from his work.

"In the community here at the Gregorian University," one senior professor told me, "Dupuis is considered something of a curmudgeon. Nice enough, mind you, but he doesn't talk about the weather or Italian football, and he doesn't gossip. He doesn't even give you a nod in the hallway." In a sense, then, I was closer to him than many in his own community.

Dupuis didn't seem to have any hobbies or favorite foods or favorite movies. His eyes only brightened when I asked him good questions about his favorite thing: theology. I also found that whenever Dupuis talked about his "trouble," he said the word with a kind of lilt in his voice. If it was trouble, even trouble that gave him an ulcer, I thought it was also a kind of happy trouble, for it put Dupuis into the ranks of those (admittedly few) pioneering theologians (many of them in Asia) who were helping give Catholic theology what little vitality it had at that time. During Vatican II, there had been a lot more exciting theologians like Dupuis around the city. The Church had never been more alive.

Thirty-five-odd years later, the only theological opinions that merited public attention were those of John Paul II and Benedict XVI.

Like any other Jesuit, Dupuis lived simply. He occupied a single small room on an upper floor of the Gregorian University that served as his bedroom and his office. It was the cell of a man vowed to poverty, but I couldn't help feeling that Dupuis was rich, too. He had the morning sun streaming in on him through a window that looked out on the garden of the Colonna Palace, he was surrounded by hundreds and hundreds of books, and he had a big, oversized desk and a computer perched at its side. What more could a scholar want?

A little more space? Perhaps. At Christmas 2000 I had sent Dupuis a large poinsettia to brighten up his room, where he lay recuperating from surgery on his ulcers. "How'd you like the plant?" I asked. "I took it to the infirmary," he said, without remembering to say thanks. "I had no place for it in my room."

We discussed the Sri Lankan Jesuit theologian Aloysius Pieris. Dupuis frowned when I asked him to comment on what I thought was a brilliant piece Pieris had written on Jesus. But he liked Pieris's writing on liberation theology, and he seemed to be on the same page with him. "The primacy of orthopraxy—doing right, a word often paired with the word *orthodoxy*, thinking right—seems to be plain gospel truth," Dupuis wrote in a 1999 piece for *Louvain Studies* called "'The Truth Will Make You Free': The Theology of Religious Pluralism Revisited." He went on: "In John's Gospel Jesus says, 'He who does what is true comes to the light.' Discipleship leads to the knowledge of Jesus. . . . Only then can theology become truly relevant to the human condition." Or, as the bishops attending the Asian Synod affirmed in 1998 (I am offering a paraphrase crafted by Dupuis), "The discovery of the person of Jesus is more important than teaching doctrines about him and must in any case come first in a context where experience is paramount in religious endeavor."

Dupuis only lived another three years after the close of the Holy Office trial, his health broken by his ordeal and his disposition no more winning than before. He was no longer teaching. But he was now much better known and more esteemed for surviving Ratzinger's attacks on his theology. He had more invitations than ever to speak all over the world.

At first, I had a hard time explaining to myself that Dupuis's most severe critics were Jesuits. What I finally decided was this: that twenty-first-century Jesuits are no longer in lockstep—if indeed they ever were. They are the advance guard of a Church that is growing up in a new kind of freedom, founded on the person of Jesus, God made flesh, who chose to enter human history and start his pilgrim people on a march through that history.

In the middle of the birth-control debate, I'd realized some up-to-then hidden corollaries of that idea: that we who are members of Christ continue to grow through time and, as extensions of the living Christ, continue to deepen understandings of our mission but not necessarily at the same rate and not always with the same clarity in New Zealand as in New York. Hence, in a Church that is an extension in time of the Christ who came to make men and women free, we realize that we can differ from one another—even from our so-called leaders—and still be good Catholics. We began to understand that there were graduations of truth and that our positions on specific moral questions could and would differ—even change over time.[4] Otherwise, we would be lost in fideism: reason could never prevail, only the fiat of a pope acting like an ayatollah who would brook no opinion other than his own.

By a happy miracle, we do not now have a pope acting like an ayatollah. In his July 2013 interview with the Jesuit editors, Pope Francis said:

> The dogmatic and moral teachings of the Church are not all equivalent. The Church's pastoral ministry cannot be obsessed with the transmission of a disjointed multitude of doctrines to be imposed insistently. Proclamation in a missionary style focuses on the essentials, on the necessary things: this is also what fascinates and attracts more, what makes the heart burn, as it did for the disciples at Emmaus. We have to find a new balance; otherwise even the moral edifice of the Church is likely to fall like a house of cards, losing the freshness and fragrance of the Gospel. The proposal of the Gospel must be more simple, profound, radiant. It is from this proposition that the moral consequences then flow.
>
> The Church is the people of God on the journey through history, with joys and sorrows. Thinking with the Church, therefore, is my way of being a part of this people. And all the faithful, considered as a whole, are infallible in matters of belief, and the people display this

infallibilitas in credendo, this infallibility in believing, through a supernatural sense of the faith of all the people walking together. This is what I understand today as the "thinking with the Church" of which Saint Ignatius speaks. When the dialogue among the people and the bishops and the pope goes down this road and is genuine, then it is assisted by the Holy Spirit. So this thinking with the Church does not concern theologians only.

Compare this to the words of Pope Pius XII's encyclical *Humani Generis*, promulgated on December 12, 1950:

This deposit of faith our Divine Redeemer has given for authentic interpretation not to each of the faithful, not even to theologians, but only to the teaching authority of the Church.

This is as good a piece of evidence as any of how, as the world changes, popes change, too. Since Pius XII, an aristocrat through and through, was vaunting the exclusive right of the Church's magisterium to give "an authentic interpretation" of the faith sixty-four years ago, most of the people in the Third World had turned away their colonial overseers and taken on the adult responsibilities of governing themselves, while the Fathers of Vatican II were in the throes of delivering a whole new definition of the Church as the entire people of God. History had embalmed many of Pius XII's certainties.

Pope Francis is, as are most of us, a man of his age, a new age in which the people have a legitimate voice that must be heard. He doesn't think his Church ought to be run by some kind of intellectual elite: other thinking Catholics ought to have a say as well. In the *America/Civiltà* interview, he said that we must be very careful not to think that this people power in the light of Vatican II (he even dared to call it a kind of infallibility) is a form of populism—whatever that means to Pope Francis ("populism" is an abstraction). In this context, I think he meant that the people should not feel they have sovereign power in the Church, nor should any pope. Christ's pilgrim people should be on a journey together. At any rate, here is what he said:

No; it is the experience . . . of the Church as the people of God, pastors and people together. The Church is the totality of God's people. I see the sanctity of God's people, this daily sanctity. There is a "holy middle class," which we can all be part of . . . holiness in the patience of the people of God: a woman who is raising children, a man who works to bring home the bread, the sick, the elderly priests who have so many wounds but have a smile on their faces because they served the Lord, the sisters who work hard and live a hidden sanctity.

He called this steadiness in the faith "the common sanctity." He might well have called it "the common sense of the common people."

He went on in the *America/Civilt à* interview to say,

> I often associate sanctity with patience: not only patience as taking charge of the events and circumstances of life but also as a constancy in going forward, day by day. This was the sanctity of my parents: my dad, my mom, my grandmother Rosa who loved me so much. In my breviary I have the last will of my grandmother Rosa, and I read it often. For me it is like a prayer. She is a saint who has suffered so much, also spiritually, and yet always went forward with courage. This Church . . . is the home of all, not a small chapel that can hold only a small group of selected people. We must not reduce the bosom of the universal Church to a nest protecting our mediocrity.

The pope who comes across in the *America/Civiltà* interview is obviously a man of the people. His father was an engineer and his mother a housewife. By his own account, he was a movie buff as a boy and now a soccer fan. He was (and is) much like the vast majority of us, and he makes sure we know it with small, but important, symbolic gestures, like trading in the papal Mercedes for a Ford (and then, later, a Renault with two hundred thousand miles on it). In such modest ways, he has already taken a step toward eliminating the ancient, toxic class system in the Church, the ecclesiastical class that protects us from heresy and sin with a series of "little rules" that have no relation to the way most people live.

8

LIBERATION THEOLOGY

Soon after Jorge Bergoglio's election, far-left Catholic liberals dug up his record on liberation theology during his six-year term as provincial of the Argentine Jesuits and, later, archbishop of Buenos Aires. They claimed that Father Provincial Bergoglio had not come to the defense of two of his social-action Jesuits when the military that had taken over Argentina had them arrested for subversion. Bergoglio's defenders, including one of the arrested Jesuits now living in retirement in Germany (the other one has passed on), said Bergoglio had done what he prudently could, helped free the two men, and had them deported to safety.

Bergoglio's critics scoffed, charging that he had never completely joined in with all the other Latin American Jesuit provincials in their support of liberation theology. They backed their opinion with the testimony of a former head of the British Province, Michael Campbell-Johnston. In 1977, Campbell-Johnston had visited all the Jesuit social-action centers in Latin America. His purpose: to encourage the Jesuits in those centers and their collaborators to stay in solidarity with others in the movement known as liberation theology; they were committed to the fight for bread and justice for the poor, already working on strategies to overturn the arrangements between business interests and government officials that were keeping the poor poor. They told Campbell-Johnston they were concerned about the Jesuits in Argentina, who were strangely silent about efforts by the military junta's leaders to "disappear" their political opponents. Campbell-Johnston also had good reason to be worried. He had spent years as a Jesuit missionary in El Salvador, where he saw the U.S.-backed military dictatorship in action, and would later reel in horror with the rest of the world when military goons assassinated Archbishop Oscar Romero while celebrating Mass, and he was just as shocked by the execution of six Jesuits at the Jesuit's Central American University in El Salvador in 1989.

So, let's cut back to Father Campbell-Johnston, visiting Argentina at the end of his 1977 trip, asking Bergoglio, the Jesuit provincial, why he had not spoken up about the estimated six thousand political opponents of the junta in Argentina who had been imprisoned and tortured, and about another twenty thousand people who had been "disappeared." They spoke at length but "could come to no agreement," as Campbell-Johnson reported in the *Tablet* in April 2013. He went on to say,

> On returning to Rome I received a copy of a letter addressed to the pope and signed by more than four hundred Argentinian mothers and grandmothers who had "lost" children or other relatives and were begging the Vatican to exert some pressure on the military junta. I took it into the secretariat of state but never received any acknowledgement.

No reply from the Vatican's secretary of state? That raised even more questions. How complaisant was the Vatican itself and its nuncio in Argentina, Pio Laghi, with the murderous actions of the junta? And if Laghi and the Vatican knew what was going on, how much pressure did Laghi bring to bear on the young Jesuit provincial to keep silent? I needed to know more, so I e-mailed Campbell-Johnston and asked him to elaborate on his meeting with Father Bergoglio. I asked, "What did you want Father Bergoglio to do, and why didn't he want to do it? What did you say, and what did he say, and what did you say?"

Campbell-Johnston didn't care to say. He wrote me, "I can't remember any more of a conversation that took place some thirty-five years ago." To myself, I wondered why this good father couldn't remember a crucial and historic conversation, made more historic by the fact that this Father Bergoglio had just been elected pope. Unless Campbell-Johnson was suffering from dementia (and he wasn't), he should have remembered. It is obvious to me that he just didn't want to join in with Pope Francis's liberal critics—whether out of deference to the man who had become pope, or because the Jesuit general had asked him to cool his criticism, I was not sure. (My suspicious self leans toward the theory that Bergoglio was listening too hard to Pio Laghi, the papal nuncio in Buenos Aires from April 1974 to December 1980, who supported the junta. Future scholars will study Laghi's reports to Rome during this period. They may well find Bergoglio's Vatican report card filled with As, not only during Laghi's term in Argentina but also during the years that followed—until Bergoglio was tapped by the next papal nuncio to become an auxiliary bishop of Buenos Aires.)[1]

So I let go of Campbell-Johnston and sought answers elsewhere to my questions: What did Father Bergoglio fail to do, and why did he fail to do it?

I got a quicker answer than I expected from Paul Vallely, the British journalist whose April 2013 book, *Pope Francis: Untying the Knots*, I discussed in chapter 3. In this book, Vallely reported that after the horrifying episode in which Bergoglio's two priests had been abducted by the junta, when he later became a bishop in Buenos Aires and then archbishop, he got a new, less deskbound perspective on the struggle between the affluent members of Argentinian society (who'd backed the junta) and the country's downtrodden underclass. Vallely said that Bergoglio had simply undergone a change of heart and that the change happened during the time he came to know the poor in the slums of Buenos Aires.

Vallely quoted Guillermo Marcó, Archbishop Bergoglio's aide for eight years, who said that his boss "must have talked to half of the poor people in the city's villas." Marcó said that, during his fifteen years as "bishop of the slums," Bergoglio began to see how the economic system oppressed so many in Argentina. During the country's 2001 economic crisis, which forced Argentina to default on its $94 billion debt to foreign banks, Bergoglio had developed an understanding that what the poor needed was not charity but justice. And he even went on in 2007 to tell his Latin American bishops that the "unjust distribution of goods" creates "a situation of social sin that cries out to heaven and limits the possibilities of a fuller life for so many of our brothers." He said that people were poor because of "unjust economic structures"—a shorthand expression that might take hundreds of pages to explain. It refers to the current exploitive labor situation (to use a very concrete example) in which a company like Nike sets up shoe-making facilities in Third World countries that pay workers less than a dollar an hour and then turns around to sell the shoes in the United States for more than a hundred dollars a pair.

In retrospect, Bergoglio came to see the value of what the liberation theologians were attempting to do—push for reforms of practices in the business world that were keeping the poor poor. Sound like Karl Marx? Yes. But so what? In this, who could say Marx had it wrong? Bergoglio began to pay homage to the sacrifices of those who had paid with their lives for "espousing Marxism" when all they were doing was organizing unions of workers demanding a living wage. In 1999, just a year after he became archbishop, on the twenty-fifth anniversary of the murder of Carlos Mugica, the first social-action priest martyred in the Buenos Aires slums, Bergoglio gave instructions that the remains of the priest should be disinterred and honored.

Throughout the slum parishes, Bergoglio and his priests supported the *cartoneros*, who make a living sorting through the city's garbage to find and sell recyclable materials. "Bergoglio helped them to form a union and to turn this work into something from which they can make a decent living," said the spokesman of the archdiocese, Federico Wals. Vallely declared that this union organizing was "exactly the kind of work [that], two decades earlier, [Bergoglio] had condemned."

Furthermore, as a bishop and then archbishop of Buenos Aires, Bergoglio became an important player at meetings of CELAM, the Latin American Episcopal Conference that tried, after Vatican II, to turn the Church of the rich and the privileged into a Church of the poor. The bishops' populist manifestos at Medillín in 1968, at Puebla in 1979, and at Santo Domingo in 1992 provided the theoretical underpinning for the Latin American Church's turn toward an involvement in matters of concern to society (not simply "the Church"). At CELAM's last general conference in May 2012 at Our Lady of Aparecida in Brazil, Archbishop Bergoglio took the lead. He delivered—and probably wrote most of—CELAM's gigantic analysis of the state of affairs in the entire continent. He left no doubt about the Church's "practical obligation to set things right here on earth."

"What shines through all this change is that Bergoglio is a pragmatist rather than an ideologue," Vallely concluded. "Just before he left for Rome and the conclave, he penned what turned out to be his last Lenten message to the people of Buenos Aires. Morality, he said, 'is not a "never falling down" but an "always getting up again."'"

It seems that in the celebrated July 2013 interview with Pope Francis, *Civiltà*'s editor, Antonio Spadaro, did not ask the pope to give an account of his leadership of the Jesuits during the years of the junta. Father Spadaro backed rather gently into the question by asking him about his years as provincial in Argentina. Francis confessed, "My style of government as a Jesuit at the beginning had many faults. That was a difficult time for the Society: an entire generation of Jesuits had disappeared. Because of this I found myself provincial when I was still very young. I was only thirty-six years old. That was crazy."

Papa Francesco went on to explain himself, but in the vaguest terms:

> I had to deal with difficult situations, and I made my decisions abruptly and by myself. My authoritarian and quick manner of making decisions led me to have serious problems and to be accused of being ultraconservative. I lived a time of great interior crisis when I was [assigned to a Jesuit house of studies] in Córdoba. It was my authoritarian way of making decisions that created problems. Over time I learned many things. The Lord has allowed this growth in knowledge of government through my faults and my sins.

In fact, two Argentinian journalists who had a long interview with Bergoglio just before he became pope say that Bergoglio admitted to "hundreds of errors" when he was a young provincial in Argentina. Bergoglio told the two journalists, Sergio Rubin and Francesca Ambrogetti, that he hadn't beaten himself up over his failures; he'd read a book written by longtime professor at the Gregorian, American Jesuit John Navone, called *The Theology of Failure*, that propounded the refreshing notion that we all fail, but so what?

Rubin and Ambrogetti do not linger over the story of Father Jorge Bergoglio's twenty-two months in Frankfurt, Germany. He was fifty when he went there in March 1986, after having served six years as provincial in Argentina (1973–1979) and then some years as rector of the Jesuits' Colegio Màximo in Buenos Aires. He went to Saint George, a Jesuit house of studies, to pursue a doctorate on Romano Guardini (the Jesuits housed a large collection of Guardiniana there). We do know that after twenty-two months in Frankfurt his provincial, Victor Zorzin, ordered him back to Argentina, his thesis only half finished. Why? No one seems to have asked, and no one will say. What we do know is that after his return, Zorzin assigned Bergoglio to be spiritual father to the scholastics in Córdoba and put him under some severe restrictions. According to Elisabetta Piqué, Rome correspondent for the Argentine daily *La Nacion*, and author of the biography released in November 2013, *Francis: Life and Revolution*, Zorzin did not allow him to make phone calls without permission, and his correspondence was "controlled."

In the Society of Jesus, this kind of severe discipline is rarely warranted unless the man has told his superiors that he has fallen in love, or unless some fellow Jesuit has found out he is having a love affair and "manifests" him to the provincial. Then the provincial moves in, gets the man transferred, and cuts off all communication between the man and his lover. I cannot imagine any other scenario that would call for such moves. Pope Francis has confessed he is "a sinner" and that he has made "hundreds of mistakes." This may not be pious nonsense. He may simply be telling the truth.

In my opinion, it is not a shameful thing for a priest to fall in love. It happens. (How frequently, no one can say.) It happened to Thomas Merton when he was in his fifties. It also happened to Karl Rahner, also in his fifties, during Vatican II. For all the work Rahner was doing as a theologian at the council in 1962, he found time to write 110 love letters to German novelist Luise Rinser—123 in 1963 and 276 in 1964, sometimes three or four letters a day—competing all the while for Rinser's love with another council father, a Benedictine abbot, only identified in Rinser's published correspondence with Rahner as M. A.

Sometimes the priest will leave the active ministry and marry his love. Sometimes (as in the cases of Rahner and Merton) he will renounce his love and go back to his cell and his ministry, wiser for the experience and more compassionate to everyone. If this is what happened to Jorge Bergoglio, it would explain at lot about his "conversion" at Córdoba and his subsequent compassionate ministry among the poor in the slums of Buenos Aires (and his constant preaching about "God's mercy"). I believe that if the world were to find out that Jorge Bergoglio had a love affair in Germany, it would love him even more—for being human. (Thomas Merton once wrote that "to be holy is to be human.")

Pope Francis never seems to get tired of saying that it's okay to be human and, since we humans are such a sinful lot, that it's okay to be a sinner, too. Not to say that falling in love is a sin. Was it Augustine who said *Ama et pecca fortius*—"Love and sin more strongly"? How many

Marilyn Monroes are there out there who can say, "I do sin, but I am not the devil; I am just a small girl in a big world trying to find someone to love"? A lot of them, I suspect, and I imagine that many are now fans of Pope Francis. As Pope Francis keeps preaching joy to the world, he is encouraging us to learn to forgive ourselves.

Months before Pope Francis confessed his sins in the *America/ Civiltà* interview, Tom Reese, now news analyst for the *National Catholic Reporter*, judged that Father Bergoglio did what he could when he was the provincial in Argentina. "In the face of tyranny," Reese concluded,

> there are those who take a prophetic stance and die martyrs. There are those who collaborate with the regime. And there are others who do what they can while keeping their heads low. When admirers tried to claim that John Paul worked in the underground against Nazism, he set them straight and said he was no hero. Those who have not lived under a dictatorship should not be quick to judge those who have, whether the dictatorship was in ancient Rome, Latin America, Africa, Nazi Germany, Communist Eastern Europe, or today's China. We should revere martyrs but not demand every Christian be one.

So, what was so wrong with liberation theology? Why all the tumult? As it turns out now, nothing. Well, nothing more than the prospect that liberation theologians—like Leonardo Boff, Gustavo Gutiérrez, Juan Luís Segundo, and Jon Sobrino, among others—threatened to empower Latin America's meeker citizens, and perhaps even go so far as to send them into revolt against their capitalist exploiters and the politicians they were bribing. From the perspective of the continent's power brokers—and the U.S. Central Intelligence Agency—liberation theology had to go.

But did it? If Jorge Bergoglio once had reservations about liberation theology when he was provincial in Argentina, he's certainly had ample opportunity to educate himself in the three decades that followed. After his conversion, he became a man of the people, more inclined to agree with early liberation theologians like Father Boff and others who insisted that in Latin America the Church *had* indeed been siding with the 1 percent of the population that owned 99 percent of the land and that the Church *had* to pay more attention to the poor—as Dom Hélder

Câmara, the birdlike, ascetic archbishop of Recife, Brazil, had been urging ever since the close of the Second Vatican Council.

Bergoglio had to consider, it is true, that Pope John Paul II did not support liberation theology—or, rather, he was not sure whether he was for it or against it. The pope commissioned one negative letter on liberation theology in 1984, but he had another drafted in 1986 that seemed to cancel the first. He was being chivvied on all sides, with the Latin American bishops pushing from the left and his own nuncios in Latin American capitals pulling from the right, warning him that Marxism was taking over the clergy in Latin America. (When Hélder Câmara heard those charges, he complained, "When I give food to the poor, they call me a saint. When I ask why the poor have no food, they call me a Communist.")

John Paul II should have treated the nuncios' reports about a Marxist clergy with some skepticism, but there is no evidence that he did. He gave every indication that when he looked at priests like Ernesto Cardenal, the priest-poet who had become the minister of culture in the Sandinista government of Nicaragua, he saw images of the Communist commissars he had known in Poland.

It did not help any when the Holy Office got into the discussion. That happened when John Paul II appointed Joseph Ratzinger its prefect. In much of the 1980s, Ratzinger, who'd spent his early teens in Bavaria as a member of the Hitler Youth, went after liberation theologians with a quiet efficiency. On March 11, 1985, his office issued a notification on Leonardo Boff's book, *Church, Charism, and Power*. Boff's work endangered the faith, the congregation said, in its concept of dogma, in its understanding of sacred power, and in its overemphasis on the prophetic role of the Church. In 1992—the year that Bergoglio was made bishop in Buenos Aires, and after his conversion at Córdoba—Ratzinger finally and formally silenced Boff. He was not to publish, teach, or speak publicly until further notice.

I do not know how Bishop Bergoglio received this news. Did he feel some sympathy for Boff? I cannot imagine he would have felt good when he saw the authorities in the Roman Curia and the papal nuncios ganging up on Boff. I think he was then beginning to see that papal nuncios cossetted the rich as a matter of course, and that Ratzinger, the theologian, resented liberation *theology* because it was more about liberation than it was about theology.

Ratzinger's words on that occasion, however, offer a clue as to his motivations. He said that Boff "had still not cleansed his ecclesiology from the elements of dissent and internal class struggle." As Ratzinger would have been making this pronouncement, the newly consecrated Bishop Bergoglio would have just been beginning his ministry to the poor in the *villas* of Buenos Aires. He could not have failed to note Ratzinger's word choice—"class struggle." Could the wording have betrayed the Vatican's real, underlying problem with liberation theology all along? That disciplining Boff was a class thing, something that had very little to do with Catholic dogma at all and much more to do with Boff's threat to the Church's long-standing alliances with the rich and powerful in Latin America?

To hear Cardinal Ratzinger's side of the story, his campaign against Boff was "not just secular politics." He cast the debate in the starkest terms of good versus evil: "The antagonism between a world under the power of the Evil One and the disciples of Christ will never be mitigated," he told one journalist, Vittorio Messori, "but will grow ever more bitter in the course of time." And he had a little sermon for his liberal critics:

> It is time to find again the courage of nonconformism, the capacity to oppose many of the trends of the surrounding culture, renouncing a certain euphoric postconciliar solidarity. Today more than ever the Christian must be aware that he belongs to a minority and that he is in opposition to everything that appears good, obvious, logical to the "spirit of the world," as the New Testament calls it.

Ratzinger couldn't have made any clearer his diametric opposition to Vatican II and *Gaudium et Spes*, the council's signature document. But how could he prove he was right? One touchstone for him: the Cross. In rebelling against their lot in life, he suggested, these new liberationist Christians were putting their hopes in "secular political progress" instead of accepting "the Cross of Christ."

There was something terribly abstract about that judgment, lodged by a man who had spent his whole life behind a desk. He had seen little of the Cross, while the active proponents of liberation theology got to know the Cross on rather intimate terms. Bergoglio knew that thousands of them—many priests and nuns, but a good many laypeople besides—were martyred at the hands of the Latin American military.

And many who were not murdered found their struggles ending in apparent failure. This, too, was part of the Cross—a manifest imitation, many of those who suffered believe, of Christ himself, who didn't want to die but accepted his death at the hands of the Romans and certain Jews for daring to speak his truth to their power.

We may not have to guess much longer about Pope Francis's final verdict on liberation theology. In *Pope Francis: Untying the Knots* Paul Vallely reports that the pope has asked Boff to send him what he has written on ecotheology because, as Francis told Boff, he wants to issue an encyclical on the environment. Make of that what you will, but it seems Pope Francis is in the process of giving us another Vatican take on liberation theology. On September 10, 2013, Religion News Service reported that Francis will meet "in the next few days" with Father Gustavo Gutiérrez, "the Peruvian theologian and scholar who is considered the founder of liberation theology." Another surprise: "The meeting was announced . . . by Archbishop Gerhard Ludwig Mueller, prefect of the Congregation for the Doctrine of the Faith, the Vatican's doctrinal watchdog, during the launch of a book he coauthored with Gutiérrez." The head of the Holy Office collaborating with the father of liberation theology? What other surprises lie ahead?

9

PIONEERS

Here I would like to tell you about the best Jesuits I have known, the pioneers who, in their zeal to advance the Jesus message, did not and do not fear to take risks. They did so in accordance with the theory that if their experiments proved a success, their example would make a difference, for the greater good of the people of God and for the greater good of humankind. In effect, their work anticipated and paved the way for the revolution that has begun with the election of Papa Bergoglio.

If as provincial in Argentina Father Bergoglio had been loath to take risks, now as a pope with Jesuit DNA he is in a position to pioneer a whole new way of being the Church. After his September 19, 2013, interview with the Jesuit editors and his interview with *La Repubblica*'s Eugenio Scalfari a few days later on September 24, there was no mistaking the pope's intent to create a new kind of Church along the lines recommended by the majority fathers of the Second Vatican Council: to let the bishops be bishops, to open the Church to modern culture, and to have a dialogue with other religions and nonbelievers. Scalfari may have misconstrued the pope's words when he reported Francis as saying that "very little was done" to carry on with the updating of the Church launched at Vatican II. (Scalfari did not record his interview, nor did he take notes. He left the Casa Santa Marta and reconstructed the conversation from memory, though he did check his story with the pope before he went to press and, according to the pope's press spokesman, Federico Lombardi, the pope said to go with it.)

Pope Francis surely knew that the council had encouraged a new, more open spirit in the Church. The council made us more real, more human, and more loving. It brought all the world's religions closer together. It helped us realize that the world is a good place—good because God made it—and that he made it because he loves us and loves the world as well.

There was one thing the council did not do. It did not give the people a voice, a vote, or a sense of citizenship in their Church, not even through their bishops. After the council, bishops were still papal lackeys, too willing to say "How high?" when the Curia said "Jump." Francis knew that. He told Scalfari that the members of the Curia ("a leprosy in the Church") had far exceeded their authority. And he had already asked his eight cardinal advisors to give him some advice on "Church governance"—which could only mean that there was something wrong with the way the Church had been governed of late. (And how has it been governed? Under an absolute ruler ruling absolutely.)

I do believe Scalfari got it right when he quoted the pope as saying, "I have the humility and the ambition to want to do something" about that. A reporter or editor does not forget words like *humility* and *ambition* when they come from a pope. I would argue that those were the exact words that came tumbling out of the pope's mouth—*humility* because of his lifelong efforts to be like Jesus, who came not to be served but to serve, and *ambition* because of his habitual commitment to go for the *magis*, the greater glory.

The pope's daring can only embolden other pioneers in and out of the Society of Jesus, can only encourage the order's most imaginative men today to "move to the edge" as boldly as John Paul II and Benedict XVI held them back—through "thirty-five years of terrorism" (as stated in chapter 2). If Papa Bergoglio's Jesuit DNA (mainly his openness to change, *ad majorem Dei gloriam*) keeps coming into play, my guess is that he will urge on the Church's pioneers—Jesuits and everyone else "impelled by the Spirit." Then we will have a happier Church, one that will not set itself against every culture but, rather, strive to be incarnate in every culture, while the Church, in turn, gives the world more hope and more joy. To best illustrate how that will happen, I will profile some Jesuits who have had the smarts to think outside the box and the courage to attempt new things, AMDG.

For me, Marie Joseph Pierre Teilhard de Chardin epitomized the Jesuit on the edge. The Jesuits should give him a special Frontiersman Prize (except that the Jesuits do not often give special prizes) for the number of times he stepped out of the box to do things his way.

Ordained a Jesuit priest in 1911, Teilhard did graduate studies at the National Museum of Natural History in Paris; served as chaplain, medical orderly, and stretcher bearer in the French army during World War I; received his doctorate in science in 1922; became president of the Geological Society of France; and was appointed professor of geology at the Catholic University of Paris. In 1923 he began taking a series of scientific expeditions to China and writing on the coming together of God and matter in the Incarnation. When he wrote a paper that was critical of the Church's teaching on original sin, the general ordered him to stick to writing on science and banished him to China for twenty years. There, he turned to paleontology and was part of the team that discovered Peking Man.

As a scientist, a humanist, and a Jesuit, Teilhard felt compelled to write on the evolution of the species, which was tolerable to his superiors, and on the evolution of the Church, which was not. His major work, *The Phenomenon of Man*, was a mystical mixture of science and religion and did not see publication until after his death in 1955 in New York (where he had been living in enforced exile). Friends published this work and his *Divine Milieu*, both of which detailed a philosophy of the future of the universe. They went on to become bestsellers and later knocked the red socks off many a bishop at Vatican II. That popularity may have prompted Cardinal Ottaviani, in June 1962, seven years after Teilhard's death, to issue a warning from the Holy Office about the theologian. Shortly afterward, on December 3 of that year, I had a conversation about Teilhard with Cardinal Ottaviani. "He wasn't writing theology," the cardinal protested to me. "He was writing poetry."

The writings that so alarmed the Church's chief doctrinal watchdog were only Teilhard living out his Jesuit DNA. Early on, when he was thirty, he'd written:

> If there is one thing that I fear less than anything else, it is, I believe, persecution for my opinions. When it comes to questions of truth

and intellectual independence, there is no holding me. I can envis-
age no finer end than to sacrifice oneself for a conviction. This is
precisely how Christ died. . . . *I believe the Church is still a child.*
Christ, by whom she lives, is immeasurably greater than she imagines. [emphasis in original]

Teilhard's Jesuit training encouraged him to use his imagination.
The exercises made it impossible for him to be anything but outstanding in the service of the Kingdom, to do everything *ad majorem Dei
gloriam*, and, though he would do it under obedience to his superior, he
was encouraged to do it "his way"—that is, in a way best suited to his
particular talents. In his first long retreat, thirty days doing the exercises
of Saint Ignatius, and in his yearly exercise-oriented seven-day retreats,
he had been taught under a rubric called the Rules for the Discernment
of Spirits to figure out for himself how to do things his way. This he
figured out by asking himself whether his inspiration was coming from
"the good spirit or the bad." His discernment, which included an assessment of his own particular predilections, led him into the world of
science.

I met my first pioneer Jesuit on a visit to my hometown of Phoenix in
1953. I was a scholastic at the time, and Father George Dunne was a
priest still in his forties serving at a Jesuit parish in Phoenix, part of the
California Province, after he'd been sent back from St. Louis for his
spirited, public attack on segregation in Saint Louis University's dorms.
The Phoenix Jesuits were having cocktails in the rectory before dinner,
and they'd invited me to sit in and listen to George Dunne's reflections
on his already stormy life in the order. Maybe these Jesuits thought it
good for me—then only five years along in my training and still in the
process of acquiring my Jesuit DNA—to know one of the province's
giants, an exposure that might inspire me to be a better Jesuit.

Nine years before, Dunne had established himself as an early cru-
sader against racism with his article "On the Sin of Segregation," published in *Commonweal* in 1945. "In the field of racial justice," he'd
written, "the American ideal and the Catholic ideal coincide. Our Catholicism only deepens our commitment to justice. As Americans who
are Catholics we have a twofold obligation upon us and, therefore,

a double shame when we fail. When we fail, we fail not only our country. We fail Christ."

Dunne had spent that year in St. Louis, where he'd been assigned to
the Jesuits' Institute of Social Order, one of twenty such research centers around the world aimed at exposing an economic system that was
exploiting the poor and marginalizing men and women of darker skin.
Since Dunne was then living in the Jesuit community at the university,
he could hardly help noticing that the school had separate dorms for
blacks and whites. In a campus publication, Dunne pointed out that his
own Saint Louis Jesuits were still caught up in "social sin"—a relatively
new concept in post–World War II America. No surprise, then, that his
superiors sent Dunne back to his California Province. There he was
assigned to teach political science at Loyola University in Los Angeles,
but, in the spirit of *magis gloriam*, Dunne wanted to do more than
classroom teaching: he wrote and produced a play called *Trial by Fire*,
which was about the bombing death of a black family in a middle-class
white neighborhood in Fontana, a steel town east of Los Angeles. Liberal audiences and critics in Los Angeles, Chicago, and New York made
his play a big hit in 1948.

Dunne may have aspired to take up writing after the example of a
famous uncle, the celebrated American humorist Finley Peter Dunne,
who'd delivered his daily wisdom through the heavy brogue of an Irish
immigrant with uncommon common sense named Mr. Dooley. George
Dunne was too serious a guy to take up such a pretense, but, like Mr.
Dooley, he seemed to go looking for trouble. That same year, 1948,
Dunne turned up in the pages of the *Los Angeles Times* as a champion
of the Hollywood craft unions that had gone on strike. That did not
endear him to the archbishop of Los Angeles, James Francis McIntyre,
a staunch Republican who had spent some years working on Wall Street
before joining the seminary. McIntyre suggested to the Jesuits that
Dunne's presence in Los Angeles was no longer needed. So the priest
left to do a year's "research" at the Jesuit villa at Phelan Park in Santa
Cruz. From there his California provincial sent him to Phoenix, where
he would be unlikely to stir up much trouble. Arizona was a conservative state then. Its Democrats tended to be Southern Democrats, not
much interested in social justice for their laboring-class Hispanics and
blacks. Republican politicians did what the newspaper, the banks, the

mines, and the railroads told them to do: keep taxes low, and pass right-to-work laws that all but killed the labor movement in Arizona.

The exile in the desert didn't exactly mean that Dunne was done. In 1949 he somehow managed to show up at Harvard to engage in a series of highly publicized debates with Paul Blanshard, a first-class anti-Catholic bigot. He turned that Blanshard debate into a book, *Religion and American Democracy*, and continued to publish his articles on social-justice issues in *America* and *Commonweal*.

The California Province had recognized Dunne's excellence early in his career. Back when he was still a scholastic, he'd been sent to study in China, and then, in the mid-1940s, he was off to the University of Chicago to get a doctorate in political science (this was long before the province made a practice of sending its best men to get their PhDs at Harvard and MIT). There he wrote his dissertation on the Jesuit missionary Matteo Ricci and other Jesuit missionaries who'd worked in China during the Ming and Qing dynasties. Dunne's dissertation (and even his publication of that thesis, "Generation of Giants," by the University of Notre Dame Press in 1962) was ahead of its time.

Dunne told a fascinating tale—how Ricci and his Jesuit confreres in China were busy planting the Gospel in a new kind of soil. They petitioned Rome for permission to celebrate Mass in Chinese, and they got that permission but found ways to ignore it (no doubt fearing the criticism of other China missionaries). But they did attempt to adapt the Chinese people's ancestor devotion (not worship) to a Catholic ceremony that would win the hearts of the Chinese people. Franciscan missionaries in the nearby Philippines heard about that and protested to Rome that the Jesuits had accommodated themselves to Chinese superstitions.

Ricci and his contemporaries insisted that the traditional Chinese devotion to their dead was "cultural" and not "religious." They did not have the archeological sources to prove this, but modern historians have shown that the so-called superstitious rites were part of Chinese tradition, holdovers from the primitive ways that a primitive people utilized to handle death. One ceremony called for a grandfather's survivors to place food at his burial place—the idea being that Grandpa would need some sustenance on his journey into the next life. Some of the simple-minded imagined that Grandpa would actually find a way to partake of the fruit and vegetables set before his bier. But no thinking Chinese—

certainly not the Confucian intellectuals the Jesuits knew—actually believed that.

Dunne pointed out that the Jesuits' critics (a Dominican and two Franciscans) based their negative reports to Rome's Holy Office on some conclusions derived from their hurried visits to "unlettered rustics" in three small villages. In their own reports to Rome, the Jesuits claimed the facts (as related by their Dominican critics who'd been dispatched from the Philippines to establish a beachhead for their own brand of Catholicism) were "misinterpreted and misrepresented."

For almost one hundred years, a half dozen popes issued varying decrees condemning Chinese Christians who practiced their "superstitious rites." On July 11, 1742, Benedict XIV issued the bull *Ex Quo Singulari*, which forbade any toleration of the ancestral rites and banned further debate under pain of severe ecclesiastical penalties. It was a move that George Dunne says changed the history of the world. Giving Jesus a Chinese face in China might have made China a Catholic country today.

It took a while, but, as George Dunne observed, "times changed." On December 8, 1939, the Vatican authorized Christians to participate in ceremonies honoring Confucius and also to perform the "ancient manifestations of civil respect before the deceased or their pictures."

In 1990, I was pleased to find George Dunne's memoir, *King's Pawn*, in the bookstalls. To get his take on some of the players in the ups and downs of his life, many of whom were players in mine, I started first on page 83 to read about Dunne's nine years of exile in Phoenix, where Clare Boothe Luce had discovered me writing for the *Republic* and wondering who I was and what I wanted to do with my life. When I told her I wanted to work for *Time* and cover the upcoming Vatican council, she said she thought she could be of some assistance. That led to a tryout with *Time* and, soon, an assignment in Rome, one of the major positive turning points in my checkered life.

And so, from my narrow and certainly selfish perspective, I had nothing but awe for Mrs. Luce. George Dunne didn't share my awe. He'd received several invitations to the Luces' winter home just off the eighteenth fairway in Phoenix's Biltmore Estates. At his first encounter, a golf date with Luce, he'd found her too busy for golf. She told him that President Eisenhower had been admitted to Walter Reed with a severe attack of ileitis, preventing his attendance at an upcoming summit meeting in Paris. That sent Luce into action. She phoned Vice President Dick Nixon and told him that, no matter what others advised, he had to take the president's place in Paris. Then she proceeded to phone a long list of others, including William Knowland, the Republican leader in the U.S. Senate, and Joe Martin, Republican speaker of the House, to make sure they got Nixon to the summit. At Luce's insistence, Dunne went off to play eighteen holes with the younger of her two secretaries, leaving Luce behind "exuding an aura of power as she rallied people in Washington and across the land to save the country—and the world."

Dunne took some relish in telling readers about his last encounter with Clare Luce, a dinner party at the home of Frank Cullen Brophy (whose mother, Ellen Brophy, had founded the Jesuits' Brophy College Preparatory in Phoenix). After dinner, she took charge of the conversation, spent some time putting down President Franklin Roosevelt, and then launched into an anti-Semitic diatribe. Dunne's reaction:

> While inwardly writhing, I listened for some time to her anti-Semitic absurdities. Meanwhile, Frank Brophy, who was wholly innocent of anti-Semitism but like many others not insusceptible to the glamor of famous women, had been nodding in apparent agreement with her every statement. Finally, my reserves of self-control eventually exhausted, I intervened. "Frank," I said, "why do you agree with all of this nonsense? Simply because it comes from Clare Boothe Luce?" The temperature of the room dropped sharply. Mrs. Luce's monologue came to an abrupt end, and it was followed by a sharp exchange between the lady and myself. A few minutes later, she took her leave.

Dunne wrote about his "rather pyrotechnical meeting" with Luce to John Courtney Murray—the Jesuit priest who would soon go on to be so instrumental in crafting *Dignitatis Humanae* at the Second Vatican Council. Murray responded, "You have seen one facet of a multifaceted woman. You have seen the facet which I call—and she is aware of this—*the from-rags-to-bitches side.*"

Dunne's was an honest memoir and, therefore, to me an enjoyable one. Despite his above-mentioned encounter with Luce, it is neither a "tell-all" nor an account of his sins, "which are many." Dunne even goes easy on the sins of others he knew well. For example, he cites the case of Jean Daniélou, the French Jesuit who cut a quite liberal figure at Vatican II but turned markedly to the right and grumpy after he got a red hat. When Daniélou attacked the general superiors of all the major religious orders at a meeting in Rome (under the chairmanship of Pedro Arrupe) for allowing their subjects to appear in public without their soutanes, Dunne wrote him a note:

> Dear Jean,
>
> I have just [heard] your inappropriate remarks over Vatican Radio. Permit me to give you some brotherly advice. Make your own the self-admonition of the Psalmist: "I shall put a gag in my mouth."

Dunne added only this: "Daniélou died a few months after this in somber and tragic circumstances. I greatly regretted his death, but not the message I had sent to him." Dunne did not mention the somber and tragic circumstances—that Daniélou died of a heart attack slumped over a prostitute in her Paris apartment. He was not wearing a soutane.

The province put Dunne on ice for nine years in Phoenix for making trouble in Los Angeles. And by "making trouble," I mean, of course, that he'd fought against injustice wherever he found it and done it with the kind of flair that could only arouse anger in more than one bishop, in more than one college president, in more than one provincial. I was delighted to learn in his memoir that he'd had problems with Zachaeus Maher, the superior general's North American assistant, and no fewer than four California provincials—Joe O'Brien, Carroll O'Sullivan, Pat Donohoe, and John F. X. Connolly. This is sometimes the fate of Jesuits who enjoy doing something different. Getting in trouble, AMDG, with superiors means they must be doing something right. Some of them stay in the Society anyway, and some do not. George Dunne did because he had a higher tolerance than I for ambiguity (and for dumb superiors) and because he had a firmer resolve to swim upstream, paying less attention to what others thought and more, I suspect, to what Jesus thought.

In his memoir, Dunne says his call to the priesthood was "not a love letter but a stern call to take up the Cross and follow Christ." He says he never turned back, satisfied that he had given up all things for God, even though he admits he doesn't know God, only that he exists. God doesn't get a single reference in Dunne's index, but Zach Maher gets thirty-one. And Dunne admits that, though he prayed, he wasn't very good at it. He says that before Timothy Manning went on to become archbishop of Los Angeles and then a cardinal, while still a young auxiliary bishop, he once told a group of priests that "George Dunne has the makings of another Martin Luther."

Dunne says this was a bit of hyperbole. His life, he writes, was not "a record of brilliant achievement but, rather, of many failures." The God who writes straight with crooked lines seemed to be moving him around on a cosmic chessboard (hence the title of his memoir, *King's Pawn*), but providentially and mysteriously from one successful challenge to another in the cause, mainly, of justice and peace. This, of course, was part of Dunne's Jesuit DNA.

He once gave a retreat to the theologians at the Jesuit house of studies at Alma in the Santa Cruz Mountains, and was stunned when he walked into the refectory toward the end of the eight days and was met with a rising applause. He got in trouble for that with the *patres graviores et rotondiores*, even Zachaeus Maher, who wrote to him that the applause "may seem a small thing to you, but it is a straw which shows which way the wind is blowing. Such worldly demonstrations have no place in our communities."

Dunne, you see, ought to have been inspiring the scholastics in that retreat with calls to a higher spirituality. Instead, he was focusing on the ideals of feeding the hungry and clothing the naked and finding decent housing and justice in the workplace for poor blacks.

Though George Dunne never aspired to "higher office," he was given positions of high responsibility. Late in life, he showed everyone how he could handle that responsibility when he ran the Peace Corps training at Georgetown University for more than a dozen years. And from 1969 to 1972 he led an ecumenical consortium at the UN in Geneva, which had been tasked with trying to follow up on a general agreement between Eugene Carson Blake, head of the World Council of Churches, and Pope Paul VI, that all Christians should be working together for the good of humankind and not for the aggrandizement of institutional religion.

When Dunne was sacked as director general of the consortium—which had been organized under the acronym SODEPAX for "Society for Development and Peace"—a fellow worker wrote him a note praising him for his style of management: "You allayed the fears of [the

World Council of Church's] bureaucrats in Geneva and [the Curia's in] Rome who thought that SODEPAX was going to become a power-grabbing machine, which would threaten their own kingdoms. In this connection, Dr. Blake recently and quite seriously dubbed you a saint."

Dunne made light of that assessment. He was sure that Blake's criteria for sanctity "would not pass muster" with Rome. But it does with me. Dunne was always more interested in putting hierarchy aside and getting people to work well together as people—and with humor. One night during an international conference on peace in Baden, Austria, he got all the participants together and took them to a cellar pub. Everyone made their entrance through a slide that propelled them—ecclesiastical dignitaries, government ministers, distinguished international jurists—through a huge barrel onto a floor below. "Their spilling out on the floor to laughter and applause added greatly to the camaraderie of all," he recalled. Dunne recommended adopting the barrel entry "as a ritual to be observed at disarmament conferences, summit meetings, and interchurch theological discussions."

Michael Czerny is another of my Jesuit pioneers—a Canadian who, ordained a priest in 1973, has spent most of his active life guiding others (Jesuits and non-Jesuits) into peace and justice actions at the highest international level. Superior General Kolvenbach tapped him to work at the Jesuit Curia's Social Justice and Ecology Secretariat beginning in 1992. I heard that by 2002 Czerny had helped the provincials of Africa and Madagascar set up the African Jesuit AIDS Network (AJAN) to encourage Jesuits and their coworkers in sub-Saharan Africa to help people with AIDS. As a correspondent in Rome for *Newsweek* and the *Tablet*, in the early autumn of 2002 I had to ask Czerny why the Jesuits were getting into the AIDS business at all. The Jesuits were not medical people, after all; they were primarily missionaries of Christ. [1]

Czerny was a busy guy, but he agreed to tell me why one Saturday morning that September, on the sun-dappled roof of the Jesuit headquarters overlooking Saint Peter's Square. He'd just returned from ten days in Johannesburg with a team of twenty-two Jesuits and seven laymen, covering a UN summit meeting on sustainable development, trying to understand how the world's governments proposed to save the world from itself.

"It was a complicated affair," Czerny said, "with action going on simultaneously in four different arenas. It took all of our combined energies to gather the facts—I'm not even sure how well we did that—and then, to try to figure out how they all added up."

Czerny (pronounced *chair-knee*) raised his eyebrows and wagged his shaggy, bearded head, as if to say that summarizing Johannesburg was an impossible task but, as a modern Jesuit who knows how important it is for his mission to give due attention to the press, he would attempt it anyway. When he was finished with me, he'd go to his computer and write up his last dispatch, which would soon be flashed around the world to an e-mail list of eight thousand who'd signed up to get his daily dispatches out of Africa.

Czerny, born in 1946 into a family that escaped to Canada from Czechoslovakia after World War II, said that the United States has only one vote in the UN General Assembly. But it has a weighted vote in the World Trade Organization, which is the eight-thousand-pound gorilla in these Earth Summits that eats whatever it wants to eat. Earlier preparatory meetings in March at Monterrey, Mexico, and then in June at Bali, set the summit agenda. Its rallying cry was "sustainable development," which required translation: "People need to find ways of making their living without running the environment into the ground."

The first Earth Summit, in Rio de Janeiro in 1992, produced much awareness but little of substance. It was supposed to be about a range of environmental issues, but it ended with a mighty conclusion that the world needed to cut back on the profligate burning of fossil fuels. It was something that few had the willingness to do—certainly not the oil companies, which have a $10 trillion investment in the current energy system, nor the people they serve with cheap fuel, nor their governments. China and India did nothing to cut back on carbon emissions, and arguments about the real dangers of global warming go on and on.[2]

But rather than throw up their hands in despair, environmentalists turned to projects that were more doable. They noted that more than a billion people have no access to clean water, while 2.4 billion people defecate in their backyards or in the street. Past efforts to deal with these problems focused on building large centralized infrastructures that are very expensive: big dams, big reservoirs, big aqueducts, and centralized waste-treatment plants. So, say the experts, we need small projects at the local level—for example, energy-producing windmills and solar panels.

"That's the currently popular idea," said Czerny. "It's true as far as it goes. In fact, the Church is the world's biggest agency pushing sustainable development. Christians, priests, and sisters working in the developing countries make a contribution worth billions, even if it goes unaccounted.

"But opting for sustainable development isn't enough. It gets the First World off the global hook. It's an excuse for not solving the biggest issues, like overfishing the world's oceans and closing up the ozone hole. Yes, the people of the Earth need little solutions. They need big solutions, too."

I said, "So Johannesburg was a failure?"

"We can't let it be a failure," he said. "The poor can't afford a failure. We have to mine what was honest and true in Johannesburg and move ahead from there—on behalf of the poor. Eighty percent of the world's people are poor. They scrape out a living on 13 percent of the world's income."

At the summit, the nongovernmental organizations (NGOs) were assigned their own compound in Nasrec, home to a sports complex some thirty kilometers from the summit's plenary sessions (which were held in a wealthy suburb of Johannesburg). The NGO Global Forum was full of booths. The Jesuit Order, as an NGO, had its booth, too, with a banner that said "Finding God in All Things." This is one of the Society's mantras, and it should provide even right-wing critics with the religious rationale for the Jesuits' appearance at all at an international conference on economic development. The Jesuits believe that making a more just world is one of their main reasons for being—not simply because they are responsible citizens of the planet but also because they believe they are working, as their motto says, *ad majorem Dei gloriam*. This is what makes Czerny more than the sort of priest whom Cardinal Ratzinger once charged with being "a mere social worker."

"Wandering around Nasrec," said Czerny, "was like surfing the Web: the same unlimited variety of ideas, options, urgencies, languages, and faces." He found the variety impressive but also felt "a sense of fragmentation, even disorientation."

He said that an analysis of what happened at the summit—"it was like a four-ring circus"—has just begun. "We learned a lot. But what do the facts mean? When we are able to add things up, then we have to say what needs to be done. Eventually, the people of the world will decide. Public opinion will make a difference." What did Czerny, who at the time had been directing his order's social-justice secretariat for ten years, learn at the summit? "We are living in a monopolar world," he said. "We know that the only real changes that occur in the world come about with democracy. Messy as it is, democracy is the only thing that works and keeps working. But democracy was bypassed in Johannesburg. Those few who wrote the UN's Political Declaration and the Plan of Action did so in secret. None of us, no members of the press, none of the nongovernmental organizations, could attend meetings of the inner circle, much less have any influence on the plan," written, in effect, by the world's business conglomerates.

So what did the Jesuits think they could do about that situation?

Czerny said, "We get the facts, we get them out to the world at large, we rely on public opinion to force a change."

"Isn't that a bit quixotic?" I asked.

"Prophetic," he said. He was using the word in its Old Testament sense: speaking out, crying alarm. The order's promotion of justice was a prophetic strategy that would lead the Jesuits into social and political arenas that would incur the wrath of the rich and the powerful—and, in certain countries, of the military goons they employed. No one could forget Superior General Arrupe's charge to the 223 assembled members of the Jesuits' thirty-second General Congregation in 1974:

> Jesuits are never content with the status quo, the known, the tried, the already existing. We are constantly driven to rediscover, redefine, and reach out for the magis. For us, frontiers and boundaries are not obstacles or ends but new challenges to be faced, new opportunities to be welcomed. Indeed, ours is a holy boldness, a certain apostolic aggressivity, typical of our way of proceeding.

"Some of us," he affirmed, "will find martyrdom." The delegates spent a good deal of prayer and discussion over Arrupe's charge. They finally endorsed the order's new direction in Decree 4 of the thirty-second General Congregation. Among them was a young provincial from Argentina who, forty years later, would be elected pope (and take the symbolic name Francis) at one of the most crucial moments in the history of the Church.

Pope Francis, the first Jesuit pope, made it clear to the cardinals gathered in the Sistine Chapel even before his election that Arrupe's forty-year-old challenge was still very much with him—so much so that the words fell from his lips spontaneously without any seeming calculation at all: that he felt the Church itself needed to get out of itself and back out "to the edge" where the saving, liberating message of Christ was most needed.

Since Arrupe's manifesto of 1974, Father Bergoglio (and later Archbishop Bergoglio) could not help noting how members of his order had followed the superior general's lead (and in some cases, like George Dunne's crusade in the 1940s against racism in the United States, had even anticipated that lead). The liberation theology in his own Latin America (which puzzled Jorge Bergoglio when he was a young provincial in Argentina) was one example of Jesuits going boldly where no one had gone before.

So, in fact, was the order's commitment in 2002 to put a big part of its energy into the fight against AIDS in Africa—which the order's leadership in Rome made sure that every Jesuit around the world knew about, including Archbishop Bergoglio of Buenos Aires.

I asked Czerny why Jesuits were so involved in matters that are not per se priestly. He laughed. He knew that I knew that Father General Arrupe had put justice and peace at the heart of the Jesuits' mission. He also knew that I knew that a few hundred Jesuits were involved in a number of social-action projects under the banner of the International Jesuit Network for Development. There, Jesuits were in action seeking debt cancellation for nations trapped in poverty, pushing policies to break the debt cycle, and promoting sustainable development throughout the Third World.

I told Czerny that some still don't understand why Jesuits are involved at all in social-action projects that are not priestly. "Sure," said Czerny with a smile. "If a Jesuit teaches chemistry (which is not a priestly activity) in one of our high schools, no one questions that, because Jesuits have been teaching chemistry for five hundred years. But working in the field of human rights? That's different. People have to get used to seeing a Jesuit wearing jeans digging a ditch alongside a group of African women who are barefoot."

Czerny said he realized that mainly laymen and laywomen have to get involved in social action. That's a legacy from Vatican II, whose crowning document urged the people of God to roll up their sleeves and keep on with the work that Jesus began, the work of redemption: "Thy kingdom come, thy will be done *on earth* . . ." And many people were contributing to that. The Jesuit Refugee Service, for example, employs several thousand men and women around the world. But only eighty-three of those who work for the JRS are Jesuits. Still, said Czerny, Jesuits may have "the radical freedom" to take a lead in certain areas, like Nairobi, a freedom that many laypeople do not have.

I cite Nairobi because that's where Czerny was going on his next assignment—to head the African Jesuit AIDS Network. Somberly, he talked about the rationale for this new effort: to found a mission to help AIDS sufferers in Africa.

"Those suffering with HIV/AIDS," Czerny told me, "need and deserve the same attention that our biblical tradition requires for the orphans, widows, and strangers in our midst—that is, a response that conveys God's preferential love for them." He said he wanted to involve Jesuits and others in every African country to help develop "responses appropriate to the local circumstances" and build the national working groups into an effective African network "with its own voice," one that will reach out to share information, expertise, and other resources with the whole Church in Africa.

Czerny's voice deepened. "We have to be very close to those who suffer and those who care for them. AIDS hits at the core of a person's existence in a way that no other problem does, and at every level—physical, personal, spiritual, sexual, familial, social, psychological, economic. It's all about life—and death."

Czerny went on to spend eight years in Africa running the African Jesuit AIDS Network, coordinating its struggle against the pandemic, pretty much ignoring the overpublicized flap about condoms. He recruited a few Jesuits and laypeople to work at the small AJAN headquarters in Kangemi, a very poor settlement on the outskirts of Nairobi. A first step would be to go out to the ten Jesuit provinces or regions in Africa to learn how Jesuits could deal with people afflicted with AIDS and their families—and still keep up with all their other apostolic activities. The Jesuits had to teach them to teach their people how not to get HIV and then, if they came down with the infection, what kind of pastoral counseling and home-based care they could give them and what kind of medications they could arrange for them. They taught some families how to start their own businesses (to generate income for themselves). They brought in medical and nutritional support.

During Czerny's years in Africa, he worked to support the wide and diverse range of initiatives by Jesuits and their coworkers in AIDS ministry, to develop best practices, and to encourage the development of new programs. When he left in early 2010 for another assignment in Rome (at the Pontifical Council for Justice and Peace), he left AJAN House in the care of a team headed by a Jesuit priest from the Central African Republic, Paterne Mombé.

From there, Mombé reports today on the AJAN website that, because of recent medical advances, AIDS is no longer considered an emergency and appears to be sliding down the agenda of international priorities. "But we are only too aware that the pandemic remains a threat to millions of people, families, and communities across sub-Saharan Africa, and we are determined to continue doing our utmost to be with those who are affected, to make sure they have all they need to live life to the full, and to prevent the further spread of the pandemic."

Bill Cain is a New York Province Jesuit with the Jesuit DNA who has found another credible way of preaching the Gospel. He does it (as Jesus did) by enlightening people's minds and enkindling their hearts with stories. Cain has found he can do that best by bringing his stories to a stage before a small audience—or, when he can, by producing his stories for millions on network television. He could do that as a Jesuit, because Jesuits have a long history of working in theater, dating back to 1551. For three centuries, Jesuit colleges and universities were renowned for their theatrical productions. They were usually pious productions, promoting religious and moral virtues for the students and audiences. Now Cain puts his own stamp on that tradition by writing plays that are anything but pious productions because, though audiences have changed since the sixteenth century, they still have need for art that is virtuous—plays that speak the truth and challenge us to goodness.

As a student at Boston College, Cain gravitated to the theater. It was during one college production that took place in the cancer ward of a hospital that Cain discovered his calling: "In the face of this terrible disease, in the face of leukemia, our performance made people human. Something happened." He felt the presence of God. "I knew then that I needed to do this for a lifetime."

Even after he joined the Jesuits, he never left the theater, and the theater never left him. During theology in Cambridge, Massachusetts, he founded the Boston Shakespeare Company and ended up serving as its artistic director for seven seasons. Cain then moved to the South Bronx to teach in a middle school and to continue to teach himself more about the special craft of writing plays. In 1989 he wrote a play about the school where he was teaching and the violence he saw in the neighborhood. *Stand-Up Tragedy* premiered in Los Angeles at the Mark Taper Forum, where it had a charmed run. The play went on to win awards in Hollywood and, in 1990, appeared on Broadway. Film and television producers came looking for Cain, and he spent a dozen years writing for network TV.

In 1997 Cain wrote and produced a TV series for ABC called *Nothing Sacred*. It was about an inner-city parish in New York featuring some very human priests confronting one crisis after another, sometimes even their own personal crises as priests.

Nothing Sacred won awards, too. In the late 1990s, it won a Writers Guild of America Award and a Humanitas Prize, along with a Peabody Award. The Peabody citation read in part:

> *Nothing Sacred* provided an honest portrayal of the complexity of faith in the modern era. In its all-too-brief run on network television, the program was fiercely unafraid to interweave into parish life such contemporary issues as abortion, HIV, class struggles, and racism.

Television dramas about Catholic priests confronting contemporary issues offended Bill Donohue, U.S. Catholicism's pit bull and moral watchdog. "A priest who is struggling with his homosexuality?" asked Donohue. "We don't have gay priests, and, if we do, we don't put them on television." He launched a boycott of the series, even before he had seen a single show. ABC let it run for twenty episodes before it finally succumbed to pressure from Donohue's Catholic League for Religious and Civil Rights.

Even so, doing *Nothing Sacred* made Cain feel that he had produced the kind of art that "speaks the truth and challenges us to goodness." Some of the show's episodes spoke some truth (and made people think) about the institution called the priesthood. This was five years before the Church's sex scandal first broke in Boston before spreading to the whole nation and the world, bringing on a shame that made even the most loyal Catholics start asking why the Church still insisted on celibacy, a rule set a thousand years ago that was obviously being observed now in anguish (or in the breach) by so many otherwise good men. It's not that celibacy tends to produce rapists. But mandatory celibacy makes some priests feel they are so special that their first-class status allows them to tamper with children with impunity.

Cain went on to write more daring plays because he believed that "theater is a place where nothing is forbidden and ultimate truth is on our side." In 2009 he wrote and produced *Nine Circles*, a one-act play about the Iraq War, which was performed in cities across California, Massachusetts, Arizona, and Colorado. It won the Harold and Mimi Steinberg/American Theatre Critics Association Award for best script premiered professionally outside New York City.

Cain's source for *Nine Circles* was the case of Private Steven Dale Green, formerly of the 101st Airborne Division, who was convicted in 2009 of raping and killing a fourteen-year-old Iraqi girl, murdering her family, and later setting them on fire. Green, who said he was following orders from the other soldiers also involved in the act, is now serving five consecutive life sentences for his crimes. Cain told interviewer Robert Israel why he wrote *Nine Circles*: "I had read a story about a soldier who tried not to be a killer. Indeed, he had become baptized during his basic training so he wouldn't have to kill. I am a Jesuit priest who is supposed to find the presence of God everywhere and to celebrate it." In creating a fictional work for the stage based on this horrific story, he found that presence by constructing tense scenes meant to emulate the nine circles of hell from Dante's *Divine Comedy*. During the course of the play, the audience learns of Private Reeves, the character based on Green, and the atrocities he has committed, his subsequent punishment, and his execution by lethal injection. The turning point comes when the actor playing Reeves stands naked onstage, engaged in a ritual act of ablution that calls to mind an earlier scene in which he'd discussed baptism with a priest.

The actor stands before a makeshift sink, rinsing his torso with a sponge. Audiences gasp as the actor struggles to rid himself of his dark demons. Before the final curtain, the actor stands center stage under an ever-brightening light and delivers a seven-minute monologue. His gnarled words sputter forth to reveal a slowly dying mind.

In a note on the *Nine Circles* script, Cain writes, "As the intensity of the light grew, the moment became a transfiguration. It isn't an antiwar play—that's a kind of warfare on its own. It's a play that wants to make war unimaginable. And—at least in the silence that follows the blackout at the end—it is my experience that it succeeds. For a moment. How does one say 'no' to war? It's not in the language we use. I am asking audiences to look at themselves, to ask how, individually and as a nation, we can seek an answer to this question."

In 2011, Cain saw his play *Equivocation* open at the Oregon Shakespeare Festival. Audiences there were sure they were watching an allegory about Abu Ghraib and weapons of mass destruction, even though the play was set in Shakespeare's England. In the play, Cain imagines that Shakespeare's troupe at the Globe Theater in England has been commissioned by King James I to write the government's version of the Gunpowder Plot. (The Gunpowder Plot, an unsuccessful attempt to blow up the House of Lords in 1605, remains a mystery to this day—though the government convicted a Jesuit, Henry Garnet, and had him drawn and quartered for planning it.)

Shakespeare (whom Cain calls "Shagspeare," or "Shag" for short) and his theater company have a problem: They do not believe the government's version, so how can they get the show together and still tell the truth? Does Shakespeare lose his head for telling the real story, or does he lose his soul for writing propaganda?

On one level, this is a story about actors putting on a play, but, on another level, it is about the messiness of democracy. Cain claims that in 1605 Shakespeare's troupe was the world's only functioning democracy, and even this one wasn't functioning all that well. One critic said *Equivocation* is *A Man for All Seasons* put through a Stoppard blender.

Cain's play *How to Write a New Book for the Bible* made its debut at the Berkeley Repertory Theatre in October 2011 and has played all over the country since then. It owes its success to its timelessness. Cain says, "It's about the innate revelation that exists in every family." It's a comedy with a serious theme about a man named Bill who moves in with his mother when she becomes too frail to care for herself, a tale that celebrates a mother's love and a son's devotion. Cain has a thesis: Every hundred years every family ought to add a new book to the Bible, to look back on their experience, to recognize the darkness and claim the luminous. "Every family," he says, "creates a sacred story out of love. The Bible is not a rulebook. The Bible is the story of a family. And if there was the revelation of the divine in Abraham and Sarah, there's the revelation of the family in everyone's parents and everyone's children."

Cain now lives in a Jesuit community on 14th Street in Lower Manhattan. His fellow priests scatter all over the New York area in a variety of ministries. Cain's ministry, the theater, takes him farther afield, as he follows his plays coast-to-coast and workshops many of his plays at the Ojai Playwrights Conference, an arts enclave sixty-five miles north of Los Angeles.

Cain is a witty, honest interview, as evidenced by some exchanges I found on the Internet. Madeleine Oldham of the Berkeley Repertory Theatre asked Cain some questions about *How to Write a New Book for the Bible*, and their discussion bears repetition in full.

Madeleine Oldham: Why write this particular play?

Bill Cain: The play focuses on three people: my father, my mother, and my brother. These are exquisite human beings, and I wanted to ritualize in some way the wonder of their lives as a way of celebrating them. I think the history of both religion and drama is the sins of the parents are visited on the children—as told by the children. And whether that's Adam and Eve have ruined our lives or James Tyrone and Mary Tyrone [*Long Day's Journey into Night*] have ruined the lives of their children. This is not my experience. My experience is the opposite of the general tradition; I have a huge sense of the blessing of my parents' lives being passed to the next generation, and I wanted to make a ritual of that passage of life visible. Most of drama really is pointing the finger backwards. And comedy is where we get to celebrate. There's a drama in generosity as well. I don't think the only drama is in the scarring or the losses. I think there's great drama in self-sacrifice and kindness and the cost of kindness. And that's a ritual I would like people to enter. And exit less afraid and more joyous.

Madeleine Oldham: What do you hope people will walk away with when they see this play?

Bill Cain: I hope they walk away with a great sense of joy, walk away carrying less fear about how life ends. My parents both gave off light as they died, and they found a way to make their deaths a summation of the goodness they had received and given for their whole lives. The play is very funny. And I think the reason for that is my parents understood that death does not negate life but it's one of the things in life. I hope the play works as a celebration of all of the darkness and light and not just some of it.

Madeleine Oldham: How does being a priest affect your playwriting and vice versa?

Bill Cain: I'm a Jesuit priest, and the Jesuits weren't founded to live in a cloister or a monastery. We're supposed to go into the world, find the presence of God there, and celebrate it. I'd say that was a pretty good description of what all of us in theater do as well. Theater is always proclaiming "attention must be paid" to what is neglected and holy. Willy Loman. Antigone. Blanche. In this play—Mary. The jobs of writer and priest—as "Bill" says in the play—are closely related. In both, you point and say, "Look. Look there. That person you haven't noticed—he, she matters."

Madeleine Oldham: Do you write in other formats? What attracts you to writing for the stage?

Bill Cain: I wrote for television for many years and loved doing that. *Nothing Sacred* for ABC TV was one of the great experiences of my life. We didn't last long—one season—but, while we lasted, we created a national community, and it was an extraordinary experience. I don't find much difference between stage and television. I love them both for the same reasons—gathering a community around a story (with any luck, with some laughter) always widening the circle of inclusion. I love theater for its intimacy and television for its vast reach.

Madeleine Oldham: Does the process of creating a play look the same for you each time? If not, how was this one different from others?

Bill Cain: All are time-consuming, wracking, lonely, and . . . why do I do this?

Madeleine Oldham: What's next in your writing world after this play?

Bill Cain: Finishing an overdue film script about Greg Boyle—a Jesuit who works brilliantly with gang members in Los Angeles. He talks about the basic quality of love being "no-matter-what-ness." I love that.

Madeleine Oldham: What haven't you done yet that you'd like to?

Bill Cain: I'd like to try pole-vaulting at least once. Skydiving at most once. I'd like to live in Florence for a while and soak up some Dante, Canterbury and soak up some Chaucer, Dublin and read the second half of *Finnegans Wake*. Someday I'd like to really clean my room. I'd like to, for once, fold my laundry as soon as it comes out of the dryer. I'd like to do a one-man show—or maybe I'd just like to be the kind of person who could do a one-man show. There is a great deal of writing I would like to memorize—James Agee's poem "Dedication" and Teilhard's *Hymn of the Universe*. I'd like to go back to studying karate. That feels like unfinished business. I'd like to go back to teaching middle school in the Bronx—nothing was ever better than that. I'd like to write a play a year for the next ten years. Or a really good play every two years. Or a great play—once. I'd like to write a new book for the Bible.

Writer Tim Treanor of DC Theatre Scene asked Cain questions about art, faith, and moral responsibility. In reply to some of the questions, Cain was modest enough and humble enough to say, "I don't know."

Tim Treanor: You faced outspoken hostility from the Catholic League and some other sources for your work on *Nothing Sacred*.

Did your battles on behalf of that show inform some of the moral questions you raise in *Equivocation*?

Bill Cain: Not consciously. It would be nice to think we were "fiercely unafraid." Personally, I was scared to death every single day. Though we laughed a lot, I think we all were. We were just trying to tell the story as we knew it.

Tim Treanor: Have you experienced tension between the need for artistic integrity and the authority of the Church in your own work? If so, how have you resolved the tension?

Bill Cain: (a) Yes. (b) Who says you resolve the basic tensions of your life? Those tensions—among others—are the generating engines of your creativity.

Tim Treanor: Who are the great truth-tellers now among our artists?

Bill Cain: I don't know. I know that when I was teaching in the South Bronx, kids were able to speak devastating truths regularly and powerfully. Whether their voices will make it into print and media, I don't know. Who are the truth-tellers now working? In many varying ways I have been touched recently by the Dardenne brothers' films, Athol Fugard, *Restrepo*, Mark Rylance, Richard Bean, the National Theatre of Scotland's *Black Watch*, Taylor Branch, David Garrow, *The Wire*, *Friday Night Lights*, Paul Taylor [Dance] Company, the food at Homegirl Café, James Agee, and, always, Anne Frank.

Tim Treanor: Have you found your commitment to the religious life to be more helpful or more challenging to your work as an artist?

Bill Cain: Art and religion? I always feel that I am at the threshold of both. I hope to make it across the starting line some day.

Tim Treanor: Is there anything else you'd like us to know?

Bill Cain: I'm trying to do my best. Apologies for the failures, the shortfalls, the omissions. I always think that the next one will be better, and, who knows, maybe it will be.

10

NOT JUST ABOUT STRAY DOGS

Now here's another pioneering Jesuit—John Baumann, a handsome guy, now seventy-five years young, who founded something called the Pacific Institute for Community Organizing, or PICO, way back in 1972. If Pope Francis (who keeps talking about himself as a pope of the poor) knew what Baumann has been doing for the past forty years, he would hug him. He hasn't exactly been ministering to the poor. He has been empowering the poor—and doing it so quietly that few have noticed what he's been doing. He is a leader who leads by hanging back and letting others take charge.

So I am not going to start this story by telling you all about John Baumann. I want to tell you about a woman he has empowered named Gloria Cooper. Through her story, you must understand that there are hundreds of other Gloria Coopers in the PICO firmament who have similar stories to tell, all because of John Baumann. You will understand what makes a revolutionary like Baumann a revolutionary without needing me to keep talking about him. You just need to know about his people. This is the way Baumann wants it. He doesn't need the glory. The people like Gloria Cooper don't need the glory either. You, my readers, need to learn about Gloria Cooper so you can take a look at Jesuit DNA from a different angle—which is all wrapped up in the two Latin words, *magis gloriam*. For John Baumann and the people of PICO, "greater glory" means that while once they didn't think they could do very much, now they can do almost anything they want to do.

I first saw Gloria Cooper in action on May 1, 2004, speaking to a crowd of more than two hundred in a ballroom at the Washington Court Hotel on Capitol Hill. Copper skin, flashing eyes, great teeth, and a dress that I cannot describe now except to say that I remember it was as pretty as she was, and maybe yellow. I wasn't paying much attention to what she wore. I was paying more attention to what she said and the way she said it.

"We got to tell people," she shouted, "that they, too, shall overcome, because we are all speaking the same word at the same time. We are saying our children are in pain. We are saying our elderly have no health care. We are saying our young people who have gone to college and done the right thing cannot afford to buy a house." Her voice kept rising, like that of a preacher from the Bible Belt. Some of the more than two hundred people in that ballroom must have been from the Bible Belt, too, because they kept chiming in with shouts of "Amen!"

This was not a revival meeting. For three days, some 150 leaders and staff from the national PICO network had been trying to figure out how they could make an impact on Washington. But they quickly figured out that when it came to getting a hearing in Washington, "Washington" didn't really exist. "Washington" was an abstraction, or, if they wanted to think concretely, "Washington" was thousands of faceless bureaucrats. They decided what was more real to them: the existence of their own representatives in Congress, people they elected back home to give them a voice in a town where even million-man (or million-women) marches had become as common as crab cakes.

Their own representatives. Yes, Gloria Cooper was telling the crowd their own representatives were the key. We did live in a representative democracy. If the crowd really believed that, then they knew their representatives had the power, but they couldn't use it to stand up for them until those representatives understood what they wanted them to stand up for. And they wouldn't understand that unless and until their own people spoke up. This was the point Gloria Cooper was trying to make, waving a microphone in her left hand like a baton—a mike she hardly needed, given the power of her voice, rising and falling and drawing the crowd closer to the palm of her hand.

"We got to create an echo chamber," she cried.

"Amen!" came the response.

"So it's important you understand."

"Amen, Sister."

"So we go back to California, we go back to New York, we go back to Louisiana, and we create that echo chamber."

"Amen. Yeah. Amen."

"And we make them hear the stories, and we make them feel the pain. They won't know unless we tell them about it."

"Yes! Amen!"

"We are challenging you to go back and tell your people. Let them know there is hope."

"Amen! Amen!"

"Let them know there is hope."

"Yeah! Amen! Amen!"

"So we don't go home and sit down and do nothing. We say, 'We have a solution.' We say, 'We have a solution.' We say, 'We have a solution.' And we make them hear us."

The crowd broke into song. It sounded like a spiritual.

> I've got the victory, praise the Lord!
> I've got the victory, praise the Lord!
> I once was bound in sin and misery.
> I've got the victory, praise the Lord!

Later, after the crowd had hugged their goodbyes and headed back to their hometowns, Gloria Cooper told me who she was and where she had come from.

I said, "Are you a preacher's daughter?"

She laughed. "Yes! My daddy, A. D. Cooper, is still a preacher. He was eighty on December 3, and he's been a preacher for forty-one years in San Diego."

"Now, how did I know that?" I asked. She grinned, understanding that I was paying her a compliment, and she plunged right in to tell me her story. She knew that was why I grabbed her away from her well-wishers. One of them said he thought "Gloria is very excited about all of this." A longtime PICO organizer challenged that. "How do you know," he asked, "*when* Gloria's excited?" As far as he knew, since he hardly ever saw Gloria Cooper when she wasn't on PICO business, this woman was always excited.

Gloria Cooper seemed to epitomize what I was beginning to see as the secret of PICO's success. This was a woman who had risen from her very humble beginnings to the presidency of the PICO network in San Diego and a seat on its national board.

"I was born in Shreveport, Louisiana," she said. "Shreveport was segregated at the time. When I was three years old, I knew the difference between black faucets and white faucets. I knew they had two ordering and pickup windows at the Dairy Queen, one for whites and another one for blacks. I knew I belonged at one and didn't belong at the other." She remembered the white folks in Louisiana who didn't count her as a human being, or her six brothers and two sisters. She recalled the time one of her brothers was ordered into a bayou filled with alligators to dive for a white man's false teeth. (He refused and was beaten.)

When the family moved to work a farm near Amarillo, Texas, she found white folks had the same "go fetch" expectations. One day, the lady of the manor ordered the young Gloria Cooper to come into the house. "'Chap'—she called everybody 'Chap'—'you come in and help me clean my toilets!'"

Cooper was only five years old at the time. She stomped her little foot and said, "No!"

Cooper smiled at the recollection. "'Zoura—her name was Missouri, but everybody called her 'Zoura—broke three or four switches on me, but I wouldn't do it. My momma told me I shoulda helped 'Zoura, but I told her, 'As long as I'm alive, I'm not gonna clean no white man's toilet.' And I never did."

Her five-year-old gumption never faded. In 1954, when Cooper was ten, she and her family moved to San Diego, where her father had found work as a tile-setter. (Sure, he soon became a preacher, but in his little black church in those days, the ministers at the Antioch Church of God in Christ earned their bread, like Saint Paul did, with their hands, six days a week, preaching for free on Sundays.) At first, some of the family lived with her dad's aunt. Others camped out with her aunt's friends until the Coopers could get on their feet financially.

But Cooper and her brothers all went to school and made something of themselves, well instructed by their dad, who always told them, "Yesterday ended last night. Live today, and trust for tomorrow." And they were also taught well by their mom, Ozell, who became a preschool teacher after the kids were old enough to not need her at home. Both of her parents are still living, and Cooper says that they intend to live on for many years to come because they have good genes. Her grand-father, A. D.'s father, died last year at the age of 103.

Cooper attended San Diego city schools, but she didn't go to college because she wanted to get married and have kids of her own. She had two—a son, Tony, and a daughter, Felicia—and then, eventually, she took in a niece, Talesh, and Felicia's playmate, Andrea, whose parents didn't seem to want her. So she raised a boy and three girls.

"They never gave me any trouble. No drugs. No gangs. It took a lotta prayer, I think. And hard work. I kept those children so busy that at night all they could do was go to sleep. Tony was in the Optimist Club band; the girls were all cheerleaders. I was a cheerleader mom. We all cleaned the house together on Friday nights so we could do all these other things on Saturday. And then we'd go to church every Sunday." After graduating from San Diego State University, Felicia became a district counselor for the San Diego Unified School District, and An-drea became an analyst at the University of California–San Diego. Ta-lesh is now in the U.S. Army; she made E-5 in less than two years. Her fourth, Tony, originally dropped out of college after finding a good job. He'd said, "When I get ready to go back to college, Mom, I'll tell you." And Cooper had replied, firmly, "Fine, and when you get ready to go back to college, you'll pay for it." She was only telling Tony what her dad had taught her: "You always got to pay your own way." Years later, when Tony decided he was ready for college, he paid his own way, taking out $40,000 in loans. (He's still making payments.)

Finally, in her forties, Cooper was ready for college, too. Busy and time-strapped as she was—divorced after fifteen years of marriage, head of a household, and working full time for the local telephone company as an engineer—she enrolled at National University and got her degree after six years of night school, yet somehow still finding the time to start working for the PICO chapter in San Diego, called SDOP, the San Diego Organizing Project.

Along with SDOP's other members, Gloria Cooper started helping to change the face of San Diego. She did it as a volunteer, not a paid staffer. PICO leaders are always volunteers, never paid staffers. Cooper explained her reasons: "As a volunteer," she said, "nobody can fire me. I can speak my mind. I can let others know when there's an inequity. I can let others know people are hurting. I can let others know there's a drug house next door."

Soon, Cooper was speaking out at meetings of the local school board, helping to spearhead SDOP's proposed Six-to-Six program, designed to give inner-city kids a place to go from six in the morning (when, frequently, both parents were off to work, already at work, or coming home from work) until six at night.

Administrators for the city of San Diego had a lot of sympathy for the Six-to-Six idea. They knew what the problem was and knew how it impinged on the health of San Diego (and their own self-interest). Statistics informed them that most inner-city crime occurred between 2 p.m. and 4 p.m. That was when latchkey kids were on the loose. SDOP's suggested solution made nothing but sense to the City of San Diego: get the kids off the street after school.

Cooper remembers, "We wanted to put our kids in after-school classes. And the city council agreed. They gave the program one and a half million dollars. But we were only half-finished with our plan. We also needed the cooperation of the San Diego Unified School District, and its board members were balking. In private meetings with us, they said the school district couldn't afford after-school classes. They wanted to know, couldn't they just provide babysitting? We said, 'No, we want a credentialed teacher there, not just a babysitter. We need an academic learning center that can help the children get up to grade level.'"

Even though she knew the school board couldn't match the City of San Diego's $1.5 million, Cooper led a delegation of 250 parents to the next board meeting. There, she stood up and said, "You're telling me you can afford to fund *water polo* north of I-8, but you can do nothing about the twenty worst schools in the city that are south of I-8? Well, we'll pray for you. And two weeks from now, we'll be back."

Then Cooper and her crowd got up and walked out of the meeting while reporters from the print press took notes and TV news cameras ground away. Two weeks later, as Cooper had promised, the same crowd, even larger now, marched to the school-board meeting carrying candles in their hands, ready to hold a vigil if the board again said no.

Cooper laughs at the recollection. "We were all primed and ready for a candlelight demonstration, but we didn't sit down real good before the chairman said, 'Gloria, you can have it.' The school board gave us what we wanted, gave us everything we needed."

How did they do it?

Gloria Cooper says, "It was how PICO taught us."

The Pacific Institute for Community Organization started out with a name that was deliberately nondescriptive. If the people in East Oakland, California, the marginal neighborhood where the organizers would begin their work, wanted to come up with their own name rather than the name of some national organization, well, that would be up to them. And they did choose their own name. At their first convention in 1975, the PICO people in Oakland called themselves the Oakland Community Organization. Today the OCO is part of PICO and its programs on statewide and national issues.

But if you'd asked the OCO back in 1972 what they were selling, they would have looked at you with a blank stare. They weren't selling anything. They were just trying to survive over here on the seamy, wrong side of San Francisco Bay and make as good a life as they could under the circumstances for their kids.

This is just the way PICO's early organizers wanted things to take shape. They were in Oakland to build an organization of, by, and for the people. Only one way to do that: encourage the poor to speak for themselves and do for themselves.

Imagine this scenario: A group goes down to City Hall to present a petition for, oh, say, the demolition of a long-abandoned home across the street from the elementary school in their neighborhood and now the site of a good many observable drug transactions, night and day. Who can make the most credible case before the mayor and the city council? An outside organizer? A respected senior lawyer who lives in the neighborhood? Or a young couple with three children in the school? The organizer might make the most telling case. The lawyer might be very eloquent. The young couple will speak with passion, because they're speaking about the safety of their own kids. Odds are the mayor and the city council will understand where this young couple is coming from, listen to their plea, and act on it. Odds are the reporter who is there covering for the morning paper will include the young couple's entreaty in his council story. Odds are the reporter from Channel 2 will not fail to tell his cameraman, "Roll on these guys!"

That, at least, was the theory when PICO got going in 1972 in Oakland. John Baumann and his fellow organizer, a Jesuit classmate named

Jerry Helfrich, now deceased, thought, "No one wants to hear *us*. Let the people speak for themselves."

Over the course of its forty-year history, the theory worked. PICO's two Jesuit founders stayed in the background while the organization looked, on the surface, like nothing more than a group of poor and lower-middle-class people, at first in Oakland and then, as time went on, in fifty other inner cities across the nation, each group using one of the only tools they had—their sheer numbers—to make America's political and economic institutions live up to their democratic promise.

'Twas said that PICO's founders trained with Saul Alinky in Chicago, which branded PICO's early identity. It is true that PICO was an Alinsky-type organization producing smart leaders who knew how to get what they wanted using the machinery of democracy—freedom of speech and assembly, free speech, and free press. Alinsky was an anti-establishment liberal and a social critic, not a Communist (as some claimed) but dangerous, because he really believed in American-style democracy—and nothing else. He had no highfalutin', abstract theories, no utopian ideals. "I just hate to see little people kicked around," he said in his book called *Reveille for Radicals*, which he published in 1946 to explain his sassy, anti-establishment methods to the college kids of the time, who made Alinsky one of their heroes.

As it turned out, Oakland soon learned that PICO was much more than your typical Alinsky-type organization. When PICO started to make a splash in Oakland, reporters discovered that PICO's prime movers were indeed Alinsky acolytes, but they were also far more than that. An early story about PICO in the *Oakland Tribune* carried the ominous headline "Who's Rocking the Boat in Oakland?" The article said two young men—they looked like they might be graduate students from Berkeley—had been going around East Oakland knocking on doors and asking people how they felt about their city.

According to the *Tribune*, the two young men were priests, though they were hardly identifiable as priests because they were always dressed in Levi's. Even more intriguing: they were Jesuits working "for the greater glory of God."

So, was PICO a Catholic thing? Professedly not. Baumann and Helfrich didn't even whisper religion. They knew how to get action going in Oakland's neighborhoods by encouraging the people—not the Church—to take charge.

Alinsky would have been impressed with PICO's successes at organizing through the years. He would have been absolutely delighted on
May 2, 2000, when three thousand delegates from a dozen local PICO
affiliates in California marched on Sacramento to expand health care
for the working poor. They didn't get everything they asked for, not
immediately, but they won enough support in the California legislature
to demonstrate their power to reshape public policy in the nation's most
populous state. They demonstrated their power to deal with one of the
most knotty social issues in America (as no other action group anywhere
in the United States had yet been able to do). For PICO, committed as
it was to doing things for the poor, there couldn't be any more important issue. Reforming America's three-tiered health-care system would
make all the difference for families at the lowest rung of the economic
ladder—the very people Saul David Alinsky hated to see kicked around.

In 1967, PICO got its jump-start from Pedro Arrupe, the Jesuit
general in Rome, who had just been elected the year before, not long
after the close of Vatican II. On November 1, 1967, Arrupe addressed a
letter to American Jesuits that urged them into the battle against "racial
injustice and grinding poverty."

Arrupe pointed out the disconnect between America's ideals, as embodied in the Declaration of Independence, and America's execution of
those ideals. He wrote, "The dignity of human personality, the unity of
the human race, and the equality of all men are of the very essence of
the Christian Gospel, which proclaims our common purpose, our common redemption, and our common destiny."

His own American Jesuits, more than seven thousand strong, the
supposedly elite order in the Church, didn't seem to understand that
"the dignity of human personality, the unity of the human race, and the
equality of all men are of the essence of the Christian Gospel." Since
the Civil War, some Jesuits had distinguished themselves in their work
with various minority groups, but they'd been doing very little for the
black people in America. As those educated in their twenty-eight Jesuit
colleges and universities had advanced economically, educationally, politically, and socially, Arrupe said, "the Society of Jesus tended to become identified more and more with the middle-class, white segment of
the population."

Arrupe said it was "humbling to recall that, before the Civil War,
some American Jesuit houses owned Negro slaves and humbling to

remember that, until recently, a number of Jesuit institutions did not admit qualified Negroes."

He asked the American Jesuits to examine their consciences and ask "why so little effort in the past has been expended on work for and with the Negro." He suggested the Society's training did not eradicate the acceptance of certain stereotypes and prejudices acquired in youth, the insulation of far too many Jesuits from the actual living conditions of the poor (and of most Negroes), and an unconscious conformity to the discriminatory thought and action patterns of the surrounding white community.

True, he conceded, the U.S. Jesuits talked a good game, "becoming more aware of their Christian obligations." But the Society hadn't committed enough manpower and resources to the fight against the problems of race and poverty or used this potential "vigorously and courageously in the service of Christ's poor." And so Arrupe suggested ten concrete actions. Among them, he wanted to see Jesuits on the faculties of Negro colleges and inner-city high schools, and he wanted to see Jesuit high schools and colleges recruit qualified Negroes for faculty and staff positions. Even more concretely, he recommended separate Jesuit residences in a poor Negro section of one or more of the major cities in each province. "Those who would live in such a house would be prepared to lead lives of poverty accommodated to their neighborhood in order to make the humble and poor Christ present among those whom they serve and among whom they live." And those assigned to what he called "the Interracial Apostolate" should get intensive training in the particular problems of the inner city so they could "meet with understanding the spiritual and material needs of the poor." He recognized that this new realignment of manpower and resources might carry with it some costs, but he didn't see any other way "to meet the crying needs of our brothers in Christ who languish in degradation and inhuman poverty."

John Baumann remembers being thrilled by the general's challenge, not only because it was his own general speaking but also because he had a special admiration for Arrupe himself, already a legend before he'd been elected general in 1966.

Arrupe had been a missionary in Hiroshima when the A-bomb had struck on August 6, 1945, killing half the city's population and setting the whole city ablaze. Having received medical training before the

Spanish Jesuits had sent him to Japan, Arrupe treated hundreds of the men, women, and children who survived the atomic blast, doing surgery without anesthesia, cutting human flesh with household scissors, wondering as he worked why so many victims were suffering from this peculiar sunburn that, after a few days, only worsened, suppurated, and ultimately penetrated to the bone.

If Arrupe had a particularly good feel for the kind of postwar world in which everything had changed by the atomic bomb (as Albert Einstein had said) except our way of thinking about it, it was no wonder. He wrote, "There are millions of men and women in the world, people with names and faces, who are suffering from poverty and hunger, from the unjust distribution of wealth and resources and from the consequences of racial, social, and political discrimination."

No surprise that Arrupe was soon telling his troops they should become "men for others" and that their faith should aim first at "doing justice."

And by 2005, despite its colorless, almost meaningless name, PICO had become a network of more than a million mostly poor and middle-class families working in more than 150 U.S. towns and cities.

It was a process that put them in contention with the comfortable, who were used to diverting a disproportionate measure of public monies to their own sleek neighborhoods, and with businessmen who had become rich by levying high rents for substandard housing or charging the poor 200 percent interest on short-term loans.

PICO members sometimes speak like prophets of the Old Testament—crying out for the common good in communities where they find much evidence of the common greed. Most of the time, they seem more devoted to democracy than they do to the deity, but this is only because, in public, at least, in a land of many faiths, they have found in the language of American freedom, as codified in the Declaration of Independence and the Constitution, sufficient reasons to pursue what God has always seemed to want for humankind: liberation.

PICO's members are linked to four faith traditions: (1) the social Christianity of the historic black Churches, (2) the social Gospel and Christian-realist perspectives in liberal and moderate Protestantism, (3) the strongly evangelical but socially responsible orientation of the Church of God in Christ, and (4) the intellectual resources, working-class commitments, and Hispanic cultural ties of Roman Catholicism. It

has those links because, historically, these are the faith traditions that
have gravitated to the leadership of PICO's founder and president, John
Baumann. I say "gravitated to the leadership" because Baumann (who
may be one of the most laid-back social reformers in America) doesn't
go out looking for congregations to affiliate with PICO. They come to
PICO mainly because they admire what it's doing—(1) for the better-
ment of various cities around the country and (2) for the people who get
involved.

This second goal—for the people's own personal growth—may be
more important than the first. Sociologists who like to put pretentious
names on what most of us take for granted as part of our cultural give-
and-take call this growth *human capital*. The term is useful because it
makes us think more deeply about what goes on in PICO. When people
in the organization—like Gloria Cooper—grow, they become assets to
their communities, assets that redound to the good of those who are the
beneficiaries of those assets. When the kids that Gloria Cooper and her
allies helped keep off the streets in San Diego's Six-to-Six program did
not get caught up in the city's crime and drug scene but instead went on
to earn their college degrees and get hired to the kind of jobs their
parents had never dreamed of, they became part of the human capital
of San Diego—in the sense that they produced goods and services for
San Diego and made their community richer. Like *venture capital*, this
human capital grew. The Gloria Coopers of San Diego made invest-
ments in others, often enough in their own children, who, they hoped,
would grow up and take their productive places in the community of
San Diego. And the funny thing about this kind of human capital? It
was something like love—the more they gave it away, the more they
had left.

In the late 1960s, John Baumann was finishing off his last years of
study for the Jesuit priesthood—"doing theology" is what they called
it—at Alma College in the redwood-covered foothills of Los Gatos,
California. He was steeping himself in the Church's intellectual tradition by studying the Fathers and Doctors of the Church and wondering
where his provincial would send him after ordination. Many of his classmates would go on to pursue higher degrees and become college professors or prep-school teachers. Some would zip off to the missions in
Africa or Asia. Some few would become parish priests or prison chap-
lains. Very few would launch out into absolutely unique ministries. One

of Baumann's contemporaries, Nick Weber, became a professional clown. Another, Bill Cain, became a Hollywood producer, as we saw in the previous chapter.

Baumann said, "I knew right then and there I didn't want to go teach at one of our high schools—which is probably where my provincial would have sent me. I wanted to go where the action was." But where to go? Where could he learn "faith doing justice"?

At the time, Saul Alinsky was the flavor of the month in *Time* and *Newsweek*. P. David Finks, a priest who worked with Alinsky in Rochester, New York, said that though Alinsky was an atheist, he was like one of the great mystics—and a devout troublemaker. Alinsky carried a business card that read, "Have Trouble, Will Travel." He was a romantic loner like Rick, the Humphrey Bogart character in *Casablanca*, a pushover for a real dame or someone in trouble. He loved a fight, preferably toe-to-toe with university presidents, corporation executives, big-city mayors, or arrogant Church leaders. He once called James Francis McIntyre, cardinal archbishop of Los Angeles, "an un-Christian, prehistoric muttonhead," though presumably not to his face. Another time, when he got off a plane at an airport in the Deep South and saw a delegation of twenty Ku Klux Klanners in white sheets waiting, or so he assumed, to do him some harm, he walked up to one of them and shouted "Boo!"

So when John Baumann and Jerry Helfrich found out that Alinsky had set up a training center in Chicago, they told their provincial they wanted to go work with Alinsky and learn how to change the world. The provincial said, "Alinsky? He's a Communist. No. You will not be going to Chicago."

They did some calling around and found that Alinsky had a long, creative association with the Catholic Church in Chicago. Way back in the 1940s, Bishop Bernard J. Shiel had introduced Alinsky to Marshall Field, the Chicago blueblood billionaire, who got Alinsky started in his efforts to help the people know their own power—once they learned to get along with one another. The Poles, Mexicans, Negroes, Lithuanians, Hungarians, and Germans in Chicago all hated one another, and they all hated the Irish, because the Irish were the power structure. Alinsky got all these people pulling together, once he convinced them they had the power of numbers. "Power," he told them, "goes to two poles—to those who've got money and those who've got people."

Baumann and Helfrich kept providing their provincial with news bulletins from Alinsky's battlefields in Chicago. Finally, the provincial relented and sent them to a summer assignment in Chicago—not to study at Alinsky's Industrial Areas Foundation but rather at an Alinsky-inspired spin-off, the Urban Training Institute. This was a multifaith endeavor under the direction of Jim Martin, an Episcopal priest who enkindled in his students (including a dozen other Jesuits from around the United States) a fire for social reform in a city badly in need of it. Chicago was a bastion of wealth and privilege—for those who already had wealth and privilege. For too many of the rest of the city's citizens, it was a hellhole.

They learned that firsthand when Father Martin sent them on a weekend adventure, dressed like bums, to explore some of Chicago's chanciest neighborhoods on foot. Their mission: to survive from Friday night to Monday morning with no more than $5 in their pockets. Bonding with other bums, they not only survived but also learned compassion—on both the giving and the receiving end. Jerry Helfrich recalled:

> I made my way on foot through the neighborhood and ended up in the black neighborhood. So, apparently, did John Baumann, 'cause some of the black gang leaders came up to me and said, "Something funny going on. There's another white guy in the neighborhood, too." They were compassionate. They figured we were both "in trouble," and one of them gave me two dollars to get something to eat and to catch a bus out of their neighborhood. Then they watched me eat and watched me walk out of their neighborhood, glad to see me go, because "If we get hurt in our neighborhood, no one cares. If you get hurt in our neighborhood, the cops will be on us."
>
> In the white part of skid row, I got no sympathy and a lot of hostility. I was obviously bringing down the neighborhood. Heard this from shopkeepers and older, retired men who spent their days playing cards. They kept demanding that I go find a job. By contrast, the black people were sympathetic. They thought I was in trouble, so they wanted to help. The white people thought I was in trouble, so they wanted to hurt me. That's where I first learned to love the black people. I went back to the black community.

For the rest of the summer, they went on to learn community organizing in Chicago, as a young man named Barack Obama would do decades later. (You may remember that, during the presidential campaign of 2008, when the Republican vice-presidential candidate, Governor Sarah Palin of Alaska, pointed out Obama was only a community organizer, some wag replied, "Jesus was a community organizer. Pontius Pilate was a governor.")

After that summer in Chicago, Baumann and Helfrich returned to California for their second year of theology, where, Baumann recalls, "my studies came alive for me. Theology was no longer an abstraction; it became concrete and personal. My faith had been transformed, and theology gave me a way to think about my summer experience. Faith entailed being more active in the struggle for justice." He confessed:

> I now had a better understanding of why I'm called to serve; theology is about the real world; it interacts with people. It's about putting Gospel values into action. I began to understand better the Ignatian spirituality that had been an integral part of my life through prayer and retreats to "finding God in all things." God is present in our world and active in our lives. If we believe that God is among us, how can we allow divisions based on ethnicity, religion, or background to create animosity, injustice, or violence? I better understood the meaning of becoming a contemplative in action. I began to see that it means allowing God to flow into my relationship with people. It is about the core values of the Gospel—justice, integrity, love, hope, healing, compassion, service. It is about Faith that does Justice. It is about a life of service to others to work for justice and the common good that stems from the dignity, unity, and equality of all people; every aspect of social life must be related to faith in order for it to attain its fullest meaning.

After Baumann and Helfrich were ordained, the California provincial, caught up in the spirit of Father Arrupe's insistence that "Jesuits are never content with the status quo, the known, the tried, the already existing," sent the two priests to San Francisco's strange and mysterious East Bay to try their hands at community organizing.

In their beginnings in Oakland, they found an immediate home in a Catholic parish. This might have identified them and their work as a strictly Catholic thing but for the fact that Baumann and Helfrich didn't put their energies into preaching the Gospel and celebrating Mass. They started knocking on doors, asking people what troubled them, for they had zeroed in on one of the worst neighborhoods in one of California's most problem-ridden cities, statistically at the top of many charts when it came to unemployment, school dropouts, and drug use. Oakland was a city in pain.

Getting people to open up about their lot in life represented a radical new departure in the Catholic Church. For centuries, Catholic clergy had been urging their people (people like the downtrodden folks in Oakland) to be content with their lot in this sorry little world—salvation would come in the next life. Now, because they had adopted a new theology that emerged in the early 1960s, Baumann and Helfrich had a new, more worldly (but more meaningful) message to convey. It sprang from their own deep faith following of Jesus, who said that he had come that we might have life and have it more abundantly. But since the young priests' message was aimed at everyone in town, they chose to not couch that message in Jesus-speak. Instead, they simply said they wanted to help make Oakland a better place.

Making Oakland "better"? What did that mean? The two had some high-level, deep-think answers, but they didn't use them. They could have said they were trying "to bring more justice to Oakland." They could have said they were part of the time-honored spirit in America, where significant elements of the population that had long suffered injustices of all kinds, most notably African Americans, Hispanics, and poor whites, were thirsting for justice and equal opportunity. They could have talked about the sweep of history, the passing of power from elites to the people that had been going on throughout the world for more than two centuries in one form or another, sometimes through revolution (as in the American experiment launched in 1776 or in the French Revolution of 1793), and sometimes by a peaceful process in which people long subjugated by their foreign masters began to assume responsibility for themselves (as in the decolonializing of Africa and Asia during the 1960s).

They didn't talk about all that. Rather, they asked the people in a little downtrodden Oakland neighborhood what they needed. They knocked on dozens of doors and talked to people "one to one," and they found an overwhelming majority of mothers telling them what they needed most: to get the stray dogs out of their neighborhood. The dogs—some of them rabid—were biting their kids and making them sick. "Well," the two Jesuits said, "you can do something about that. You can organize."

Organize? Baumann and Helfrich tried to explain: Acting alone, people had very little power. A public official could ignore a single citizen phoning City Hall. Acting together, people might have a great deal of power. A public official would have a harder time ignoring a dozen phone callers. Or a hundred marching on City Hall. And so, on the advice of Baumann and Helfrich, the people of Saint Elizabeth's parish did some research about animal-control policies in Oakland. They hailed a passing patrol car and asked the officer, "Who can do something about the stray-dog problem here?"

They found out that Luther Giddings, the man in charge at the Alameda County's animal control, couldn't do much. He only had four men and two trucks to cover the entire county. So two hundred men, women, and children from the neighborhood marched into a meeting of the county board of supervisors, with a TV news crew behind them, demanding the supervisors give Mr. Giddings the budget he needed to do his job. When the supervisors said yes (what else could they do, given the sudden presence of two hundred angry citizens and a television news crew?), Mr. Giddings had what he needed to do a better job. Needless to say, he made sure the Saint Elizabeth's neighborhood got the same attention as some of the hillside communities in the county—no, even more attention, because, for some odd reason, upscale Piedmont didn't have many stray dogs on the street.

So how do two highly trained Jesuit priests justify spending their time—their whole lives, actually—helping a poor neighborhood in San Francisco's East Bay do things like get rid of stray dogs?

Baumann and Helfrich were up to a great deal more than that. They were bringing the Jesus message to a piece of the world in words that people could understand. It was not pious claptrap. It was the core of the Jesus message, his mission statement: "I have come that you may have life and have it more abundantly." Baumann and Helfrich were trying to bring life to this community by helping its people understand the power they have when they organize. And soon the people enlivened themselves. They started to become all they could be, which is another name for salvation. For Baumann and Helfrich, that was enough. They didn't talk to the people about God or religion because they didn't have to. Baumann says, "We saw religion here as a part of the why of our work but not the how."

A dozen years later, PICO realized it needed to set a new course. Its issue-oriented neighborhood model did not give their PICO chapters any staying power. Once PICO volunteers resolved an issue, they were gone. What PICO needed was more of a solid, permanent base. So they looked around for people who had a stake in making local political leaders accountable. They found them, mostly, in inner-city Catholic parishes, Baptist congregations, and synagogues. The people who worshipped there already had the sense of sharing that comes with any healthy community. They already had the religious language that gave their worldly causes an otherworldly passion. Soon, PICO began to reach out to the pastors and rabbis and imams in inner-city Oakland anxious to translate their faith and the faith of their congregations into action. Their people had the power of their faith. They were steeped in ideals that they had learned from their holy books—powerful, inspiring ideas like human dignity, the common good, love of neighbor, and concern for the least among us. PICO helped them learn how to build on that power to address the root causes of the problems they faced in their daily lives.

PICO was not based on one faith but many. From every faith and no faith. PICO people came in all shapes and sizes—white, black, brown, yellow. You saw the faces of those who had been inspired by PICO to stand up for the equality and dignity supposedly guaranteed to them under the U.S. Constitution marching on the California capitol in Sacramento. You saw men, women, even children, laughing together and feeling good about themselves because they had a sense that they were becoming all they could be, everything that America's founding fathers imagined when they had designed a nation conceived in liberty and dedicated to the proposition that all men (and women) are created equal.

For most of U.S. history, it would have been impossible for Alinsky-style revolutionaries to work with Catholics and Episcopalians and Baptists and Presbyterians and Jews, all collaborating together. Not, that is, until the Second Vatican Ecumenical Council, which reversed more than four hundred years of bitterness between Catholics and members of other religions, who the Church said could never achieve salvation because they didn't have "the one, true faith." It was a bitterness that had divided the American people from the very beginning. For most of U.S. history, Catholics and Protestants were enemies. Officially, at least, they couldn't even engage in joint civic ventures to create more civility and a more just society. Catholics were told they couldn't even enter a Protestant church. If you went to a friend's wedding in the First Baptist Church up the street, you were ipso facto excommunicated.

Now many PICO chapter meetings began with prayer. In October 2013, Baumann told a meeting at Boston College's School of Theology and Ministry:

> Faith places our human efforts on behalf of justice within a larger spiritual context. Opening prayers and reflections at community meetings serve to remind us that our efforts are ultimately in service to God and a response to God's abundant love for us. Working in a faith context brings a sense of humility to our work often not found in secular politics. It can also bring a capacity for perseverance and hope and a protection from cynicism and despair. Faith challenges us to keep our eyes on the horizon and to locate our work in a moral vision. Opening prayers and reflections at community meetings serve to remind us that our efforts are ultimately in service to God and a response to God's abundant love for us. Working in a faith context brings a sense of humility to our work often not found in secular politics. It can also bring a capacity for perseverance and hope and a protection from cynicism and despair. Faith challenges us to keep our eyes on the horizon and to locate our work in a moral vision.

In 2004, at age sixty-nine, Jerry Helfrich passed into the light, but John Baumann, looking far younger than his chronological age would suggest, continues to preside over PICO in his deceptively low-key manner. Today PICO is made up of more than a thousand member institutions (including congregations from more than thirty-seven different faith traditions) representing 1.2 million families in 250 cities and 18 states.

Several years ago Baumann was asked to see how he could translate the PICO idea to another culture in other lands very unlike the United States. And so he ended up working with Cardinal Óscar Andrés Rodríguez Maradiaga—archbishop of Tegucigalpa, Honduras—and all the Catholic bishops of Central America. Those bishops now have a contract with PICO. Their hope: that PICO will show their people how to make democracy work in Honduras, El Salvador, Nicaragua, Costa Rica, and the Canal Zone. (Maybe someday those bishops can find someone who can show them how to make democracy work in their Church.)

Taking PICO to Central America could be a dangerous move. As the history of the past few decades there has shown, people who enjoy almost absolute power in many of these countries have ordered the deaths of men and women trying to teach democracy.

In the last few years, Baumann and his lieutenants have also made PICO into a national lobby—with its volunteer leaders making periodic assaults on various governmental agencies to promote profamily policies in education, housing, health care, neighborhood safety, and immigration. Clergy from the PICO National Network cross partisan divides to fight for needed resources for working families, make neighborhoods safer, increase access to health care, and create housing opportunities in cities and towns across America. The PICO people tell members of Congress and their top aides, "We represent a lot of churches, a thousand religious congregations, schools and neighborhood institutions, and one million families working in 150 cities and towns, and we all vote."

Baumann summed things up in his October 2013 talk at Boston College: "Our most important contribution as PICO is to support the development of people's spiritual gifts, social talents, and personal growth. At the very heart of our mission is the process of helping people help themselves." Most of those people are citizens of our inner cities, many of them living below the poverty line.

John Baumann found one way to help them do better. And be better.

11

STILL JESUITS

I need to add to my honor roll of pioneer Jesuits a number of men who left the Society but have continued to work in the real world (as they say) for the greater good of the people of God. Their stories help illustrate my thesis: that there is a special something about the Jesuits that drives them to keep risking more in their efforts "to christify the universe." The expression comes from Pierre Teilhard de Chardin—his reformulation, maybe, of what we pray for in the Our Father: "thy kingdom come."

Edmund G. "Jerry" Brown Jr., current governor of California, spent almost four years in the Society of Jesus at the Novitiate of Los Gatos, then left and went on to the University of California–Berkeley for his undergraduate degree and then to Yale for his law degrees, while his father, Edmund G. "Pat" Brown Sr., was serving two very productive terms as governor of California.

When Jerry entered politics in 1969 (as a candidate for the Los Angeles Community College District board of trustees), his name recognition alone won him an easy victory over 123 other candidates. Name recognition did not hurt him when he ran for (and won) the office of secretary of state the very next year and then, in 1974, the governor's seat. As soon as he was sworn in, still living in the spirit of his vow of poverty, he forsook the newly constructed governor's mansion in Sacramento for a small apartment near the capitol and traded in his predecessor Ronald Reagan's chauffeur-driven limo for a Plymouth Satellite. (Sound familiar?)

He was careful with the people's money, too. He racked up a $5 billion surplus in his first term, and in 1977 he sponsored the "first-ever tax incentive for rooftop solar," among many other environmental initiatives. He appointed more women and minorities to office than had any previous California governor (and in 1978 he named the first openly gay judge in the country). He sought the Democratic nominations for president of the United States in 1976 and 1980, and he was the Democratic candidate for the U.S. Senate in California in 1982, but was unsuccessful in all three attempts at higher office.

After his Senate defeat, Brown took a time-out. He jetted to Asia. He visited Mother Teresa in Calcutta, ministering to the sick in one of her hospices. To a reporter there he explained, "Politics is a power struggle to get to the top of the heap. Calcutta and Mother Teresa are about working with those who are at the bottom of the heap." Nevertheless, he saw those at the bottom of the heap as no different from himself, and their needs as important as his. "Serving them," he said, "is attaining as great a state of being as you can."

The next year, he studied Buddhism in Japan. When he returned to the United States, he told a reporter he could now take a critical distance on some of his more comfortable assumptions: "Since politics is based on illusions, zazen [sitting in prayer] definitely provides new insights for a politician."

In an interview with *Rolling Stone*, his then-girlfriend, pop singer Linda Ronstadt, referred to him as "Governor Moonbeam," and many were still calling him Moonbeam when he dropped by the *New York Times* in 1981 for a Q & A with the editors on the thirteenth floor. For the better part of an hour, he amused the editors with his sardonic humor and stunned them with his encyclopedic knowledge of U.S. politics. After he departed, managing editor Abe Rosenthal said to his colleagues, "Well, he's no California flake."

In 1992 he made another spirited campaign to secure the Democratic Party's nomination for president of the United States, even winning some primary races against Bill Clinton. In 1999, he pulled back from his highest ambitions in order to do the best he could do in a somewhat lower office. He ran for and won election for mayor of Oakland and was reelected for a second term—a popular white guy in a black city. He followed his Oakland gig with four years in Sacramento as the state's attorney general, and then he ran for governor again, beating his Republican opponent, Meg Whitman, the former eBay CEO with a net worth of $1.6 billion. She tried to buy the election, spending $177 million on her campaign. Brown spent $36 million. Final score at the polls: Brown 53.1 percent, Whitman 41.7.

At age seventy-five, Jerry Brown is still going strong, despite battling prostate cancer, which he says is "under control." He is happily married to Anne Gust, a Stanford grad and Bay Area lawyer twenty years his junior, who spent years as an executive at Gap before joining her husband's staff as a special aide, first when he ran for attorney general and then in his return to the governorship after nearly thirty years.

He says he is still a Jesuit at heart and still follows the Jesuit motto *age quod agis*—literally, "do what are you doing." For him, this means devotion to his job. He works hard and can go seven days a week—for the greater good of the people of California. In 2012 he drove a ballot measure to victory that put billions into the state treasury. When added to a host of cuts he was able to make in the state budget, he ended a decade of deficit spending with a solid surplus. The bulk of the new money goes to California's elementary schools and into its triple-tiered system of higher education, to start paying California educators what they are worth. He could look upon that, too, as doing something for the greater good of the people of California.

Robert Mills Holstein lasted in the order for eight years, and then left some five years short of ordination for law school and a career as a personal-injury lawyer. But he never really left the Jesuits. He walked out of a visit with Father General Kolvenbach in 1998 with an extra spring in his step because the general had just told him, "Mr. Holstein, you are still a Jesuit." Bob loved that because he hated the term *ex-Jesuit*. The Jesuit homilist at his funeral Mass in January 2003 told a standing-room-only crowd that Holstein "just considered himself a Jesuit who was a little ahead of his time."

Holstein died a little ahead of his time, too. He was only sixty-one when he underwent cardioversion, a fifteen-minute electrical procedure, not surgery, that pushes a wire up through the groin and jump-starts the heart to bring the beat to a normal rhythm. As the wire was withdrawn, the doctor did not notice that an artery had been severed— and left Holstein to die in the arms of his wife.

Loretta Holstein was herself a former Dominican nun who ran the Holstein law firm and attended to the couple's five grown children while her husband pursued various causes in California and in a world he was determined to change. Robert spent years organizing annual November demonstrations at the gate of the U.S. Army post at Fort Benning, Georgia, part of a national campaign to close down the Army's School of the Americas, which was training Latin American cops and military men how to kill the U.S. missionaries who were there to help the meek get bread and justice.

In 1997 Holstein spent two months in the U.S. federal prison at Lompoc, California, for crossing a line at the Fort Benning gate in 1995, his second offense for civil disobedience, the first having occurred during another demonstration at Fort Benning. The demonstrators only succeeded in getting the U.S. Department of Defense (which was once more honestly called the Department of War) to change the school's name to the Western Hemisphere Institute for Security Cooperation— mostly referred to as WHINSEC, another one of the Army's confusing but amusing acronyms.

After Holstein's prison term, he went right on fighting the U.S. Army, organizing ever-increasing numbers of mostly young people attending some twenty-eight Jesuit universities and forty-seven high schools in the United States to make the annual trip to Fort Benning. He also poured much of his time and considerable earnings into causes aimed at helping the poor.

Holstein served on and contributed to many boards—among them John Baumann's Pacific Institute for Community Organizing (PICO). He helped fund an inner-city Catholic school in Oakland and Verbum Dei High School in South Central Los Angeles, an experimental program for minority students who work a day each week for Los Angeles firms that each, in turn, donate $25,000 a year back to the school. He and Loretta set up an endowed chair in religious studies at the University of California–Riverside, and they were major contributors to the Jesuit School of Theology in Berkeley.

Holstein was a player in the California Democratic Party, a fundraiser for Democrats who wanted to make a difference in the lives of the poor. He was instrumental in the 2002 passage of a global-warming initiative in the California legislature and gave backing to a bill designed to provide health care and education benefits to the poor. On January 9, 2003, not long after Holstein's tragic death, State Senator John Burton adjourned the legislature in Holstein's memory.

Robert Holstein was a rollicking good, and often profane, storyteller who loved duck hunting and steelhead fishing. He had a cabin near Fort Jones in the High Sierras that he readily offered to his friends, including Jerry Brown, the late House speaker Tip O'Neill, and San Francisco mayor Willie Brown.

In 1955 the California Province sent Michael Saso, a classmate of mine, to its China mission, partly because he was driven by *magis gloriam* and partly because he was a gifted linguist. (He now speaks two Chinese dialects and some Tibetan.) After ordination in the Philippines, superiors sent him to Yale to get an MA in Chinese studies and then to London University's School of Oriental and African Studies, where he received a PhD. He did his doctoral dissertation there on Taoism and Chinese popular "folk" religion, and on Taoism and Tibetan tantric Buddhism as paths leading to apophatic, or wordless, prayer.

Mike is now a promoter of and true believer in wordless prayer. "In apophatic prayer," he explains, "you don't talk a lot; you listen." Eastern and Western Christianity split in 1054 over this issue. Saso says, "They had political and theological differences, too, that don't make much sense to moderns, but then neither does the notion that anyone would want to destroy the unity of the Church over the right way to pray."

But they did. The Patriarch of Constantinople (and his followers) believed prayer was a heart thing. The Patriarch of Rome (the pope) said prayer ought to be more of a mind thing. And so East and West went their separate ways. Soon afterward (counting in Church time, in the thirteenth century, that is), intellectuals from the great medieval universities like Bologna and Paris rediscovered texts of Aristotle, thanks to scholars from both Judaism and Islam who had unearthed them from dusty shelves of the great Library of Alexandria. Thomas Aquinas, a Dominican friar from southern Italy who was teaching at the University of Paris, produced a masterwork that summed up much of all that Christians believed, the *Summa Theologica*. (Among other things, the *Summa* proved the existence of God five times over.)

Once the popes understood what prestige their Church derived from such a towering intellect as Thomas's, they gave him and his disciples their special blessing. Their scholastic theology became a standard throughout the Western Church, even to a point in the nineteenth century that the Roman Church decreed that everyone studying for the priesthood had to become steeped in it. Catholicism became a very heady exercise indeed. But it was always a danger when it contributed more to a man's pride in himself than his humility before God. (The Second Vatican Ecumenical Council tried to restore some of "the heart thing" to Catholicism, and it looks like Pope Francis is trying to do that, too.)

Mike was studying in Kyoto, Japan, when he met Nariko Akimoto and, after leaving the Jesuits, married her (with permission from Rome). They moved to Honolulu, where he became a professor at the University of Hawaii. Nariko later left him in Hawaii (they got an annulment) to raise their two daughters (now in their twenties, living in Los Angeles). Like Matteo Ricci, Mike Saso has become as Chinese as the Chinese, and a Zen Buddhist monk besides, even as he was welcomed back into active priestly ministry by the bishop of San Jose. He has been busy, still going for the *magis*, as a world-renowned expert in Asian spirituality and author of eighteen books, including *Mystic, Shaman, Oracle, Priest* (published by the University of Hawaii Press in 2012). In that book, he writes:

> I am firmly convinced that using the Jewish Kabala *Zohar*, the Kashmir Saivite woman poet Lalla, and the Islamic Sufi *Conference of the Birds* vastly enhances the ability of the Christian, priest, minister, and laity alike to do contemplative prayer and engage in peaceful dialogue. These, along with Buddhist Zen and Daoist "centering" meditation, are spiritual practices, not "faith" or "dogma" statements. They are indispensable tools for interreligious dialogue. Through these encounters, prayer experience—freed of dogmatic dispute— becomes a powerful tool for inner sanctity and world peace. Such encounters are extremely important today in our war-torn twenty-first century.

Mike Saso spent a dozen years studying matriarchal tribes living on the south shore of Lake Luguhu in the Tibetan Himalayas (where he owns a small house and has been adopted by a Tibetan family). With funds that he has begged, he has helped build five colleges in Tibet.

From 1990 to 2004, he ran a program for U.S. college students (and others) in Beijing, educating students in Chinese language and culture. He provided intensive Chinese language instruction in the morning and in the afternoon seminars on Chinese culture (history, literature, philosophy, religion, journalism, economics, and ethnology) and took the students on four trips each year to places of cultural and religious significance in China. Whew!

Eugene Bianchi, another of my Jesuit classmates, left the Society as a young priest at Santa Clara after he had fallen in love with one of his beautiful students, a former nun. The marriage didn't work out, and he tried again and again, until he found his soul mate, Peggy Hermann. For more on his search, see his frank memoir, *Taking a Long Road Home* (2010). After getting his doctorate at Columbia in 1966, he became a lifelong professor of theology at Emory University—and something of a skeptic about the Jesus of history. In 1992 he edited an anthology with Rosemary Radford Ruether, *A Democratic Catholic Church: The Reconstruction of Roman Catholicism*, a work that offered ideas, a bit ahead of their time, on democratizing the Church. In 2002, in collaboration with political scientist Peter McDonough, Bianchi wrote *Passionate Uncertainty*, a noted and somewhat negative book about the future of the Jesuits in America. In his last years at Emory before retirement in Athens (Georgia, not Greece), he became an authority on creative aging. He is founder of the Emeritus College at Emory and he keeps publishing new stuff on aging, plus some darn good poetry, on his general website.[1] Still going for the *magis*.

David Myers was an Oregon Province Jesuit for fifty-two years and has been a missionary to the Yaqui Indian community near Phoenix for the last forty. He runs his mission to the Yaquis out of their dirt-floor chapel in the poor community of Guadalupe, Arizona (unincorporated until Myers urged the people to become a city in 1974), and he continues to win admiration from the legal community for practically giving away his legal expertise for free to Arizona's most downtrodden. He has received awards from the State Bar of Arizona, the Maricopa County Bar Association, the Thomas More Society (a Catholic lawyers' guild), and the Sandra Day O'Connor College of Law Alumni Association at Arizona State University.

Myers pooh-poohs the praise he receives for his work with the Yaquis. "My mission," he says, "is to convert the rich to Christianity. My own people, who are white, rich, and well educated, are the ones who need help, not the Yaquis. The Yaquis are the ones who give good examples, and they suffer from the abuse of my people: suffer on the job, suffer in the schools, suffer in public opinion. They are a downtrodden people living in a slum only because the rich have violently pushed them there."

Members of Guadalupe's Yaqui Indian community love Padre David because he serves them as a compassionate priest who speaks to them in plain English and in their own Spanish, and because when they are in trouble he takes their side in court. He charges his clients a sliding fee based on their own earnings. If a laborer is making $9 an hour, for instance, his fee for the laborer is $9 an hour. He usually says, "My hour for your hour." But then he says he feels ashamed "because my client is supporting a wife and five kids, and I am not." He also says, "If I don't have enough to live on, I don't get mad at my client; I get mad at his employer who underpays him."

Myers gets no salary from the Catholic Church. He has never passed a collection basket and will not accept stipends for weddings and funerals. He says he does not believe in "a professional clergy." He does earn a small salary from the Maricopa County Community College District for teaching an ethics course to generally oversubscribed classes at South Mountain Community College—where they'd never before offered a course in ethics.

Curiously, none of his ministry changed when Phoenix's Bishop Thomas Olmsted forced the Jesuit provincial in Oregon to dismiss Myers from the Society in 2009 and also ordered him out of Arizona. Myers says the bishop has no power to send him away. He remains at Guadalupe, still serving the Yaquis, who ignore a sign posted by the bishop at the door of their church telling them Father Myers is "not authorized to participate in the sacraments" in Phoenix. They know nothing of the bishop's beef with Myers and still revere him, flocking to his Masses, baptisms, and funerals. In effect, the people of Guadalupe are telling the bishop, "This isn't your church. It is ours." (They are right. The Yaquis have legal title to Our Lady of Guadalupe Church.)

Myers doesn't know what he is doing that bothers Bishop Olmsted. He has not been presented with any charges and has yet to meet Olmsted face-to-face. But then, many of the 147 priests in the Diocese of Phoenix can say the same thing. When they call the bishop, they are shunted off to one of Olmsted's aides.

Not many Jesuits would be comfortable living as Dave Myers does, under an official cloud, near his church in a Phoenix slum. When you ask him how he is doing, he smiles and says he is confident he's doing the Lord's work. "That's all I need to know," he says, encouraged by a recent note from Frank Case, an Oregon Province Jesuit who once held a top position at the order's headquarters in Rome: "You are doing what any Christian, any Catholic, any Jesuit, should be doing, working with the poor. You are the quintessential Jesuit."

Myers says he isn't quite sure what *quintessential* means—which is his way of making light of Case's compliment. For the record, *quintessential* has come to mean the most perfect example of its type—the most perfect embodiment of something. The word comes from ancient Greek philosophers who spent a good deal of time speculating about the nature of the world around them and, from what they could tell by their primitive science, decided that the universe was composed of four essences: earth, air, fire, and water. That wasn't good enough for another Greek philosopher named Pythagoras, who posited a mysterious, invisible, unnamable fifth essence out there that "rises above" the other four. Quintessence. The fact is, among American Jesuits David Myers has taken Pedro Arrupe's "faith doing justice" beyond even a fifth level.

John Dear, the Maryland Province Jesuit who left the order on December 20, 2013, is another kind of quintessential Jesuit. During his thirty-two years in the Society of Jesus, Dear followed the lead of Jesuit Daniel Berrigan in his peace witness, and in some ways he has out-Berriganed Berrigan. In the 1970s, when Berrigan was being arrested and clapped into federal prisons for protesting U.S. military actions in Southeast Asia, he found few cheerleaders among his fellow American Jesuits. But now, several decades of ruinous overseas military adventures in Afghanistan, Pakistan, and Iraq, as well as the buildup of the U.S. war machine that has bled the nation's resources—in other words, history itself—has vindicated Berrigan. Now ninety-two and ailing, Berrigan has finally earned a hero status among many of his fellow Jesuits.

The strange thing about the Dear case is this: that the Jesuits who have watched Dear in action, emulating Berrigan and then some, have given Dear so little support. He figures that, based on private correspondence with his fellow Jesuits, no more than a hundred (out of more than two thousand U.S. Jesuits) seem to make the connection between Jesus's witness for peace and his own witness. He has been arrested more than seventy-five times, spent more than a year of his life in jail, and written two books that make a case for nonviolence in general, and an end to our nation's commitment to nuclear arms in particular.

In an hour-long telephone conversation on January 10, 2014, Dear told me that a whole succession of Maryland provincials have urged him to leave the order because of his work for peace. In 1987, one Maryland provincial proclaimed, "Jesuits are not pacifists, not nonviolent, and do not work for peace." He then stood up and kicked Dear hard in the shin and said, "Let me see you be nonviolent now!" Dear showed him what Jesus would do—by not retaliating. You might say he turned the other shin.

James Shea, Dear's most recent provincial, found a somewhat less violent way of dealing with Dear. In 2010, Shea put him under a form of house arrest for a time, and told him, "Nothing you have done over the last ten years has had anything to do with the Society of Jesus." According to Dear, Shea explained that the Maryland Province was closing all of its projects that serve the poor, and it would henceforth concentrate its dwindling manpower on the province's universities and high schools. Dear told me the Jesuits at Loyola University in Baltimore hold an annual Mass at which, after Communion, they bring their nearly one hundred ROTC cadets into the sanctuary to profess an oath to defend the Constitution of the United States against all enemies, foreign and domestic. "I told my provincial that I consider this a blasphemy, a mockery of Jesus and the Eucharist, but he said he had no problem with it." I have asked two Maryland Province Jesuit friends if it is true that the province has cut back on its social-action projects. Their responses were careful and equivocal. Neither James Shea nor his communications chief have returned my phone calls asking for confirmation that the Maryland Province now considers Pedro Arrupe's "faith doing justice" a dead letter. I do know this—the Maryland Province lists no social-action projects on its website. The California Province lists five.

I wanted to ask James Shea what outside forces compelled him to deal so harshly with Dear. I do know that he moved Shea out of New Mexico at the request of Santa Fe's Archbishop Michael Sheehan, who was troubled when Dear was leading peace demonstrations at the Los Alamos National Lab. Dear says Sheehan is led by a combination of U.S. dollars and U.S. politics. "Sheehan raises a lot of money out of Los Alamos," he says, and is only one of a majority of American bishops who, for at least three decades, "have been recruited by the Republican Party." Which is why, Dear says, "dozens of bishops all across the country have banned me."

In any event, after Shea put Dear on the shelf in Baltimore for five months, Dear asked for a leave of absence so he could return to New Mexico and discern what the Holy Spirit wanted him to do with the rest of his life. (At age fifty-five, when the U.S. Jesuit's median age is sixty-five, Dear is still a youngster.) During his discernment, his Jesuit DNA compelled him to ask himself, "Is it for the greater glory of God to let my light be buried by my superiors or for the greater glory of God to let my light shine?"

Framed that way, his course was clear. He told his provincial he had decided to leave the Jesuits. Dear told me, "I left because for three decades they have made my life miserable—all because of my peace work. It's tragic, and sad, and I finally couldn't take it anymore. The story of the shin kick was just one of a hundred stories I could tell about the way I've been treated over the years." For some time, he had been bolstered by the belief that a majority of the Jesuits around the world sided with him—including Jesuit General Peter Hans Kolvenbach, who gave him a formal apology in 1995 for the way he was being treated by his own province for challenging the U.S. war machine. Until his interview with me on January 10, 2014, Dear told me he hasn't spoken publicly about his chief anguish—the withdrawal of support for his peace actions on the part of his fellow U.S. Jesuits. Like the Old Testament prophets, Dear should expect brickbats, not bouquets, for speaking plainly. On the tenth anniversary of 9/11, he wrote in his weekly column in the *National Catholic Reporter* that we celebrate the Pentagon's warmaking efforts—and continue to live in fear: "We were attacked, so we bombed Afghanistan, Iraq and Pakistan, killed hundreds of thousands of people, tortured thousands more, rebuilt our nuclear installations, threw out our basic liberties and spied on millions. In our so-called war on terrorism, we became the biggest global terrorists, threatening the planet with drones, bombs, and a spanking-new nuclear weapons arsenal."

But now, suddenly, and to the shock of many,[2] Dear is an ex-Jesuit. "I've devoted my life to the cause of peace," Dear told me, "because I was a member of the Society of Jesus. I thought the point was to follow Jesus, who was nonviolent, blessed the peacemakers and commanded us to love our enemies." He raised his voice here on the word "Jesus" to make sure I understood the heart of his commitment. "My inspiration comes from Jesus," he told me, "not from St. Ignatius of Loyola."

I include Dear in this chapter because he has been reaching for the *magis* through his years in the Society—and now he's decided to keep doing so outside the order. Ironic, that he is leaving the order's official ranks because of his Jesuit DNA. But it makes perfect sense to me and to many of my ex-Jesuit friends who have contributed to the greater good of the people of God in more significant ways out of the order than they could have done inside it. We are a dangerous bunch because of our Jesuit DNA; it helps us act with more freedom (and speak out with more freedom) than many of our fellow Jesuits, still so tied to institutional concerns. (They have all these schools to run, you see.) Now Dear is one of us, willing to pay the price for his following of Jesus in the twenty-first century. It is a part, he admits, of his Jesuit DNA—and part of what Dear seems determined to do, whether in the order or outside.

He has one regret: that, without faculties from a bishop, he cannot celebrate Mass any longer. Pained by that prospect, Dear has sent a letter to the pope, explaining why he left the Society, asking that, even if he cannot get faculties from a U.S. bishop, he be allowed to celebrate Mass as part of his peace ministry. I hope Pope Francis will hear his plea. He has known how misguided an authoritarian Jesuit superior can be. He was one, once.

For now, Dear will be joining the staff of Pace e Bene, a small international group that works to promote Gospel nonviolence, and he is helping another group called Campaign Nonviolence, which is promoting demonstrations in every U.S. congressional district before the elections this fall to protest war, poverty, and environmental destruction, beginning with a national gathering September 21 in Washington, D.C. He thinks this campaign is for God's greater glory, too.

12

THE MAN IN THE WHITE SUIT

At Vatican I, on July 18, 1870, some six hundred bishops fled Rome rather than vote *placet* on Pius IX's decree *Pastor Aeternus*, which declared him infallible. Exactly 593 bishops stayed on to give this slightly mad pope the vote he thought he needed to shore up his temporal power over the advancing forces of the Risorgimento. Strictly speaking, only one pope after him, Pius XII, ever made such a solemn irreformable definition (when he declared in 1950 that the Blessed Virgin Mary had been "assumed," body and soul, into heaven). But it was a decree that has bedeviled the popes and the Church ever since, for it gave leave to most of Pio Nono's successors to endow themselves with a kind of creeping infallibility, assuring us that whatever they said about anything came directly from God—including their absolute authority. This guaranteed us a great collection of certainties to guide us through life's ups and downs. Our Protestant and Jewish friends could make no such claims, so we went through life feeling quite pleased with ourselves, sure that if we just listened to the pope we would go to heaven—after a short stay in Purgatory, of course, to have our sins burned away. That's how we felt, at any rate, through the reigns of Pius X, Pius XI, and Pius XII. Maybe that's why we bought into this absurd idea so completely. It made us feel privileged—even cocky.

Then Angelo Giuseppe Roncalli came waltzing into the papacy. Not only did he not exercise his infallibility as Pope John XXIII, he never even came close to suggesting that anything he had to say was infallible. (His secretary, Loris Capovilla, told me his boss used to joke about it.

The pope would say, "Looks like rain today," and Capovilla, playing the straight man, would say, "Are you sure about that?" and John would say with a laugh, "Well, I'm not infallible, you know.")

Until Pope John called his Second Vatican Council, the popes before him, leaning on *Pastor Aeternus*, pretty much avoided the word *change*. But then, over the course of four years in the early 1960s, Pope John's parliament reversed a good many things in the Church that hadn't changed for centuries. The more publicized moves of Vatican II—like putting the Latin Mass in the vernacular, exonerating the Jews of deicide, and declaring that everyone (of whatever faith or no faith) could get to heaven—made thinking Catholics almost euphoric. It also discombobulated many who had enjoyed living in a Church that never changed.

In 1963 Pope John appointed a commission of experts to see if the Church could do anything to lessen the pain of many couples trying to follow the teachings of Pius XI and Pius XII that said birth control was "a grave sin." When, after four years of secret meetings, that commission told John's successor, Paul VI, how the Church could assure the people of God that responsible parenthood was no sin, Paul VI had to reject their recommendations (in his 1968 encyclical *Humanae Vitae*) because he was stuck with the pronouncements of Pius XI and Pius XII. ("Stuck," his advisors claimed, because the moral judgments of the two Piuses were "irreformable." And anyway, what were they to do with all those people they'd already condemned to hell for using birth control?)

For the next thirty-two years, Paul VI's successors remained just as stuck—stuck on the birth control thing, and also stuck in their view of the world, divided between the Church that prayed and the world that sinned.

Then came our first Jesuit pope. Not only was he unafraid of change, but his Jesuit training also prompted him to launch a series of big and little changes that astounded the world. Mostly by symbolic gestures (rather than by decrees), he came down from his throne to tell the world he was not God. He refused to move into the Apostolic Palace, he traded in his big black Mercedes limousine for a Ford (which he drove himself), and he insisted members of the papal court not call him "Your Holiness" or "Holy Father." He told his Vatican Press Office to refer to him as "the bishop of Rome," not "the pope," a move that implied he was no greater than all the world's other bishops.

In 1983 Jean-Marie Roger Tillard, a French Dominican, came out with *The Bishop of Rome*, which delineated the difference between an imperial papacy and a servant pope. His impeccable historic scholarship was largely ignored until recently, when this Jesuit took over and signaled that he understood Tillard's lesson, taking the name Francis, making himself accountable and available to the press, and putting the Church into reform mode. "I think like a Jesuit," Francis told members of the press—which means that he is constantly driven to rediscover, redefine, and reach out for better ways of doing things. More natural for him to look for change than to stay the same with "a certain apostolic aggressivity," in the words of Jesuit General Pedro Arrupe, "a holy boldness." Even the word *holy* was subject to a reformulation. Judging from the way the new pope ran through each day—giving interviews to nonbelievers, stopping to talk and joke in the hallways with fellow residents at Casa Santa Marta, phoning a lesbian mom to express his sympathy over her problems—it seemed that he was living out Thomas Merton's definition: "to be holy is to be human."

It was this quality, this ease in his own skin, that most endeared him to the world's press, with a modesty and sense of humor reminiscent of Pope John XXIII but rarely seen in John Paul II, the hard-nosed media star, or in Benedict XVI, the remote doctrinal enforcer who had an answer to every question. To Benedict/Ratzinger, homosexuality was an abstraction, something so certainly "disordered" that he would deny ordination to any man who was gay. To gay priests, Francis could only say, "Who am I to judge?" And later, by way of explanation, "When God looks at a gay person, does he endorse the existence of this person with love or reject and condemn this person? Here we enter into the mystery of the human being."

For Benedict, there was no mystery; for him, homosexuality was an abstraction: penises are made to go into vaginas, and male sperm is made to fertilize female eggs. That is the way God made us—another way of saying that same-sex sex is "against the natural law." Francis could come right and say this (he undoubtedly believes in the natural law), but he doesn't—which maddens many gay Catholics; if he's not going to condemn same-sex sex, they say, then why doesn't he give it his blessing? If he doesn't, well, then, he must not be as liberal as his climbing down from the throne implies, so we can expect he will be as backward as his predecessors on much more important issues, like giving full citizenship in the Church to women.

Francis has chosen a different, more human way of dealing with homosexuality. He goes beyond definitions. He prefers to talk with gays, really listen to them, ask them why they stay in the Church or how they pray. How utterly human! His humanity, I submit, is why the editors of *Time* magazine made Francis their Man of the Year for 2013. Deserting the Chair of Peter (a throne), he could better emulate Jesus in that poignant scene with the woman taken in adultery, about to be stoned by a hypocritical mob. "I won't condemn you," Jesus told her, and then he turned to the mob and advised "the man without sin" in that mob to throw the first stone. Yes, Jesus also told the woman to go and sin no more; if Francis does not say as much to every gay man he encounters in his daily rounds (for many a gay cleric works in the Vatican these days), it must be that he isn't too sure the man *is* sinning. We sin, says Thomas Aquinas, because we are caught up in passion or habit (a condition that lessens our freedom) or in a compulsion we do not understand.

Francis can understand that; he's a self-confessed sinner himself, a man who says he is likely to miss the mark again—which makes him like every other man on the planet. As a reporter, I would like to know what fifty-one-year-old Father Jorge Bergoglio was doing in Germany that got him called home only halfway through his doctoral work there and put under strict discipline. No phone calls and controlled correspondence implies that Francis (at least in the eyes of his superiors) had sinned and was still tempted to sin "with another." I'd prefer to think he had simply fallen in love with, maybe, a beautiful German novelist, as the Jesuit Karl Rahner had during Vatican II. I would hardly consider falling in love a sin, but rather a special grace not given to every man and hardly ever to a Jesuit. But not even a reporter has a right to ask such an intimate question, and even if I did, neither Francis nor his Jesuit superiors would be obliged to answer it.

No wonder Francis can laugh at himself: he, a sinner, who is also now a pope. God must surely have a sense of humor—to make him the 266th successor of Peter, the Fisherman, all decked out in a white suit, setting out to light a fire in the heart of the world! Pope Francis can take some consolation in recalling that the first pope, Peter, was a sinner, too, on the eve of his Lord's Crucifixion.

That Francis can even imagine himself lighting a fire in the heart of the world tells us more about his Jesuit DNA, a spirit of optimism that tells him he can always do more. This is not simple bravado. Francis is in a perfect position, for example, to bury the Church's thousand-year-old blunder, the nonbiblical understanding of papal primacy itself so insisted on by the popes of the second millennium that it has split the Church between East and West to this very day. Who better to reverse that history than the pope himself, the man recognized by the most conservative members of his flock as holiness itself?

I do not think it is out of place for me to call up a political paradigm, for the East-West split in the Church was, in the beginning, far more a matter of politics than of theology. I dare to say Francis has something like the power of Richard Nixon, whose possession of the most solid anti-Communist credentials allowed him to befriend Communist leaders in China during the 1970s without being deemed a traitor at home—a move, by the way, that helped give Chinese society its own special brand of prosperity that resembles nothing so much as the fruit of capitalism. I like to think the election of Francis is a gift of the Holy Spirit herself: since he still possesses absolute power in a very real juridical sense, he (and only he) can demonarchize, demythologize, and (something now in process) decentralize the papacy. This would be his way (and a most sensational way) of undertaking the immense task he announced at the very beginning of his papacy—rebuilding a Church that was in almost total disgrace and disarray.

It was the Church's arrogance and denial that put the Church into this disgrace and disarray. Were our priests having an evil way with children? No, said many of the Church's leaders (including two popes). Not wanting to hear the now-undeniable facts, they said, "Perish the thought. Priests are holy by definition." In fact, many priests were tampering with children while many of their chaste colleagues knew what was going on but did and said nothing to stop them. Worse, out of loyalty to the clerical caste, they covered up the perfidy of the priests among them. Clerics were a special breed, you see. Their celibacy itself was supposed to prove they were not like other men and, therefore, could do anything they wanted, with impunity.

Analysts said this attitude (which they call *clericalism*) was the principal cause of the priest-sex scandal, an attitude best described by the Boston police officer who caught a drunken priest driving the wrong way on a one-way street and wrote in his report, "The monsignor thought the one-way sign did not apply to him."

The way to make this attitude a part of past history is to figure out ways of making churchmen accountable, not by securing their promises to do better in the future, but by setting up a system that demands accountability-or-else from the Church's priests and high priests. The bishops who for too long have emulated the nonaccountability of the pope himself by holding themselves immune from all impertinent inquiry should know that this kind of arrogance will automatically make them ex-bishops.

Faithful Catholics do have the right to ask questions and to demand the Church set up the same kind of machinery common in every democracy: accountability from their leaders, who promise it by the very act of standing for election. In the Church today, bishops and priests are not held accountable to the people as mayors and governors are, and therefore they are not accountable at all. The only practical way we can get accountable bishops—and, by extension, equally accountable priests—is to elect them, and if they abuse our children or misuse the dollars we put in the collection baskets, we unelect them.

Vatican II taught us to expect as much by redefining the Church as the people of God. It gave us a new view of ourselves when it urged us to wake up and grow up as Christians, with an ongoing mandate from the God who took flesh and dwelt among us to bring light and salience to a world that was already redeemed and didn't know it.

Pope Francis keeps repeating this message. We should care more about Jesus than the Church, and it is this refocus that has, paradoxically, given many who left the Church an impetus to come back. Furthermore, we take a fancy to Francis's Jesus, who does not want us to obsess over our sins but to give ourselves a break. We're all sinners, but so what? That shouldn't stop us from serving God and one another by making a better world.

On November 24, 2013, Pope Francis released a forty-eight-thousand-word "exhortation" called "The Joy of the Gospel" that was long enough and detailed enough (though not quite formal enough) to be an encyclical. In keeping with the tone he'd struck from the beginning of

THE MAN IN THE WHITE SUIT

his papacy, he was talking about the changes needed to make his Church—indeed, the whole world—a more joyful place. With infectious exuberance, he said he had a dream: to enlist "all the members of the People of God as missionary disciples" who would "transform everything—the Church's customs, ways of doing things, times and schedules, language and structures—to make a better world."

It was a pep talk, and more. He offered the Church a road map of sorts for navigating the complexities of the modern world, using the words of Jesus as a compass for what he called "a new phase of evangelization, one marked by enthusiasm and vitality."

In his exhortation, Francis repeated the word *change* nineteen times and used the word *evangelization* (or a variant of it) even more—exactly 208 times. *Evangelism* is a difficult "churchy" word that can only puzzle non-Christians, and so, recognizing that, Francis made sure to tell everyone what it meant:

> An authentic faith . . . always involves a deep desire to change the world, to transmit values, to leave this earth somehow better than we found it. We love this magnificent planet on which God has put us, and we love the human family that dwells here, with all its tragedies and struggles, its hopes and aspirations, its strengths and weaknesses. The earth is our common home, and all of us are brothers and sisters. . . . All Christians, their pastors included, are called to show concern for the building of a better world.

Pope Francis described the things that are getting in the way of making a better world. He issued a fourfold *no* to (1) an economy of exclusion, (2) the idolatry of money, (3) a financial system that rules rather than serves, and (4) an inequality that spawns violence. His twentieth-century papal predecessors had taken exception to these trends before. Francis cited them possibly to demonstrate he was not so different from them, although, in fact, the tone of his leadership could hardly be more different. They kept saying no to the world, and Pope Francis keeps saying yes—except to the world of capitalism, and even there he didn't call for its overthrow, explaining that the world has experts better qualified than he to come up with some reforms to make the capitalist system more benign. Still, he couldn't help observing there is something wrong with a system that keeps one billion souls perpetually hungry. "Can we continue to stand by when food is thrown away while people are starving?"

Rush Limbaugh, the most popular commentator on the far right end of the radio dial in the United States, rushed to the defense of capitalism. He told his fourteen million listeners, "The pope here has now gone beyond Catholicism here, and this is pure political. Somebody has either written this for him or gotten to him. This is just pure Marxism coming out of the mouth of the pope."

Limbaugh was only giving voice to a popular and simplistic notion (in the United States, anyway) that "we shouldn't mix politics and religion." For decades, even the most conservative U.S. Catholic bishops have been telling their people they *should* be mixing politics and religion. Religion alone, religion that has no resonance in the real world, may comfort me. But if it does not challenge me to help thee, then it is not the religion given us by Jesus, who is reported to have said in Matthew 25 that we wouldn't be saved by what we said but by what we did—specifically, by coming to the aid of the least of our brethren, feeding them when they are hungry, clothing them when they are naked, and finding shelter for them when they are homeless. Those who followed this Jesus became men and women for others, and, under the inspiration of the best of them—saints like Francis of Assisi and Mother Teresa of Calcutta—they evolved over time into a community that has made huge institutional commitments to health and education—by, for example, founding and staffing hundreds of Catholic hospitals and thousands of Catholic schools. In a changing world, these saints (canonized and uncanonized) keep learning to do more, and now many of them are turning their attention to new, real-world issues—like technology's worsening of our environment. When Catholics and other Christians number two billion, they represent a potential force that a pope named Francis wants to enlist in helping to make a better world.

He said so eloquently in "Joy of the Gospel," giving voice to the Jesus message, that Jesus had come so we could have life and have it more abundantly. If anyone *had* gotten to the pope, as Rush Limbaugh charged, it was Jesus—the Jesus who showed us that he loves us, and that we can show our love for him by making a better world, by reaching out first to all those people on the face of the earth who are suffering from ignorance and poverty and disease.

As a Jesuit, conditioned to push the frontiers of change, Francis evidently thought it worth a try to see whether, in his humility, he could insert himself into the central conversations of our time—about wealth and poverty, fairness and justice, transparency, globalization, the nature of leadership, and the meaning of family.

As it turned out, he could. In his first year as a compassionate pope of and for the poor, he has made good on his stated desire to light a fire in the heart of the world. In July 2013, more than three million turned out to greet him at World Youth Day (really six days) in Rio de Janeiro; ecstatic crowds keep filling Saint Peter's Square; and by mid-December 2013, he had 11 million followers on Twitter—growing at a rate of 3,650 every day. (Pope Benedict hit a high of 2.5 million.) His bold, outspoken interview with the nonbelieving editor of a great Italian newspaper, offering his blessing to everyone of faith and no faith who wanted to make the world a better place, led the broadcasts of every radio and television station in the world. According to a January 2014 story in the *New York Times*, even the Democrats in Congress who were angling to raise the living wage were reminding themselves that "the pope is on our side."

In "The Joy of the Gospel" Francis was humble enough (and bold enough) to admit that the Church itself had to make a number of changes in its way of proceeding:

> We cannot leave things as they are. Let us be in a permanent state of mission. Let us transform everything, suitably channeled for the evangelization of today's world rather than for the Church's self-preservation. Let's abandon our complacent attitude, saying, "We've always done it this way." Let's not speak more about law than about grace, more about the Church than about Christ, more about the pope than about God's word. Before all else, the Gospel invites us to respond to the God of love who saves us, to see God in others, and to go forth from ourselves to seek the good of others. All of the virtues are at the service of this response of love. If this invitation does not radiate forcefully and attractively, the edifice of the Church's moral teaching risks becoming a house of cards.

In more ways than one, Francis has said he wants to see more freedom in the Church, particularly more freedom of speech. Bishops
should ask their people to stake out new paths; they should listen to
everyone and not simply those who would tell them what they would
like to hear. Under John Paul II and Benedict XVI there was only one
theology—Roman theology. Theologians all over the world who hadn't
trained in Rome's more traditional seminaries chafed at that. Now
Francis has signaled a new freedom for the world's theologians:

> Differing currents of thought in philosophy, theology and pastoral
> practice, if open to being reconciled by the Spirit in respect and love,
> can enable the Church to grow, since all of them help to express
> more clearly the immense riches of God's word. For those who long
> for a monolithic body of doctrine guarded by all and leaving no room
> for nuance, this might appear as undesirable and leading to confu-
> sion. But in fact such variety serves to bring out and develop differ-
> ent facets of the inexhaustible riches of the Gospel.

Church conservatives had feared that, in some of Francis's off-the-
cuff homilies, he was pushing for a watered-down faith. Now, in *Evangelii Gaudium*, conservatives saw that Francis was not correcting his
seemingly impromptu remarks (which were hardly about "faith," but
rather about "morals"). In this more considered exhortation, the pope
was only amplifying his off-the-cuff remarks on the Church's moral
teaching—and doing so in the key of mercy:

> I want to remind priests that the confessional must not be a torture
> chamber but rather an encounter with the Lord's mercy that spurs us
> on to do our best. A small step, in the midst of great human limita-
> tions, can be more pleasing to God than a life that appears outwardly
> in order but moves through the day without confronting great diffi-
> culties. Everyone needs to be touched by the comfort and attraction
> of God's saving love, which is mysteriously at work in each person,
> above and beyond their faults and failings.
>   The Church is called to be the house of the Father, with doors
> always wide open, so that if someone, moved by the Spirit, comes
> there looking for God, he or she will not find a closed door . . . nor
> should the doors of the sacraments be closed for simply any reason.
> This is especially true of the sacrament baptism, which is itself "the
> door." The Eucharist, although it is the fullness of sacramental life, is

not a prize for the perfect but a powerful medicine and nourishment for the weak. The Church is not a tollhouse; it is the house of the Father, where there is a place for everyone, with all their problems.

I prefer a Church that is bruised, hurting and dirty because it has been out on the streets, rather than a Church that is unhealthy from being confined and from clinging to its own security. I do not want a Church concerned with being at the center and that then ends by being caught up in a web of obsessions and procedures. If something should rightly disturb us and trouble our consciences, it is the fact that so many of our brothers and sisters are living without the strength, light, and consolation born of friendship with Jesus Christ, without a community of faith to support them, without meaning and a goal in life. More than by fear of going astray, my hope is that we will be moved by the fear of remaining shut up within structures that give us a false sense of security, within rules that make us harsh judges, within habits that make us feel safe, while at our door people are starving and Jesus does not tire of saying to us: "Give them something to eat."

In "The Joy of the Gospel" Francis also talked about "a conversion of the papacy" and said he wanted to assure the bishops of the world they would no longer be treated as the pope's errand boys:

The papal magisterium should not be expected to offer a definitive or complete word on every question that affects the Church and the world. It is not advisable for the pope to take the place of local bishops in the discernment of every issue that arises in their territory. The papacy and the central structures of the universal Church also need to hear the call to pastoral conversion. The Second Vatican Council stated that, like the ancient patriarchal Churches, episcopal conferences are in a position "to contribute in many and fruitful ways to the concrete realization of the collegial spirit." Excessive centralization, rather than proving helpful, complicates the Church's life and her missionary outreach.

According to John W. O'Malley—the American Jesuit whose *What Happened at Vatican II* is the best recent history of the council—Vatican II set a new style for the Church unique in the history of the councils. It came up with a new language, abandoning for the most part the juridical and other punitive language of previous councils: "Believe this, or be anathema! Behave this way, or be damned." Writes O'Malley,

> Such a striking shift in language, the adoption of a new language game, shall we say, always indicates a profound shift in awareness and personality and cannot be dismissed as "merely" a change in style. We know, moreover, that content and mode of expression are inextricably intertwined, that there is no thought without expression, that expression is what style is all about. . . . What made Michelange-lo a great painter was not what he painted but how he painted, his style. Style makes me who I am. If I am loved, I'm loved for my how; and if I get to heaven, I will get there because of my how.

Papa Bergoglio came breezing into the papacy determined to focus on his own unique how—impelled by the Holy Spirit and his Jesuit DNA to, as he put it, "lay the foundations for real, effective change," not by making any old-fashioned pronouncements, but rather by striking a new style.

This is the style that Pope Francis has made his own: the style of Vatican II and the bold, confident, missionary style of the Jesuit Or-der—always oriented to change for the greater glory. This style, this new way of thinking, explains how and why our new pope is changing a Church that was for a good many centuries considered unchangeable. "We see then," wrote Francis,

> that the task of evangelization . . . constantly seeks to communicate more effectively the truth of the Gospel in a specific context, without renouncing the truth, the goodness, and the light it can bring when-ever perfection is not possible. A missionary heart is aware of these limits and makes itself "weak with the weak . . . everything for every-one." It never closes itself off, never retreats into its own security, never opts for rigidity and defensiveness. It realizes that it has to grow in its own understanding of the Gospel and in discerning the paths of the Spirit, and so it always does what good it can, even if, in the process, its shoes get soiled by the mud of the street.
>
> More than by fear of going astray, my hope is that we will be moved by the fear of remaining shut up within structures that give us a false sense of security, within rules that make us harsh judges,

within habits that make us feel safe, while at our door people are starving and Jesus does not tire of saying to us: "Give them something to eat."

Francis knew that making such a radical change would not be easy, and he tried to tell everyone he needed their support and their prayers. On October 27, 2013, before a huge gathering that filled Saint Peter's Square and spilled into the Via della Conciliazione and adjacent streets, Pope Francis celebrated Mass and gave a simple homily about Saint Paul, a man who, he said, "kept the faith by giving it away." He seemed to be telling the throng why he admired Saint Paul, but he was— perhaps unconsciously—giving everyone some clues about the struggle he was going through as the 266th successor of Saint Peter.

Saint Paul wasn't just defending the faith, said Francis, but proclaiming it, spreading it, taking it to distant lands, in a battle with all those who wanted "to embalm the message of Christ within the limits of Palestine. He made courageous decisions, he went into hostile territory, he let himself be challenged by distant peoples and different cultures, he spoke frankly and fearlessly. He went out to the fringes and didn't dig himself into defensive positions."

I could not help feeling that, in this homily, Francis was talking more about himself and his own hopes and fears than he was talking about Saint Paul. It wasn't Palestine that was trying to embalm Christ's message but Rome. It wasn't Paul who had to speak frankly and fearlessly now but Francis. It wasn't Paul who found himself in hostile territory but Francis. The hostile territory wasn't Paul's Athens but Francis's papal court, where one or another of his courtiers might want to do him in. (Contemporary Romans who know their history say Francis dines in the Casa Santa Marta cafeteria, along with fifty other clerics, which means that if someone wanted to poison the pope's dinner, he would have to poison fifty other dinners as well.)

It isn't only the citizens of Rome who worry for the pope's safety. On December 16, 2013, columnist Liz O'Donnell told readers of the *Irish Independent*, "His reforms will inevitably upset many conservatives, and his celebrity status could make him a target for assassination. Unique people like Pope Francis come along once in a generation, and they can be taken away in a second of madness or evil. What a tragedy if his safety was compromised by any relaxation in his security detail."

The day before he gave his self-revealing homily on Saint Paul, Francis also took time to meet with a group of Jesuit alumni from Uruguay, feeling comfortable enough with them to reveal his hopes and his fears in a more direct way. He said, "I ask a favor of you: pray for me. People here are very good, my companions are good, and everyone works together, but there is much work to be done, and it is difficult to keep up. Pray for me, and for my collaborators, so that we can carry on. Many thanks!"

I marveled that he had the humility to confess that he needs help. In fact, he is getting a great deal of help. He has his Jesuit DNA, his drive to do ever more, to keep him going, and the power of the Holy Spirit, the moral support of 17,106 of his brother Jesuits, and the prayers of most of the world's 1.2 billion Catholics. (I say "most" because I am not too sure about the sourpuss Catholics who are asking, "Is the pope Catholic?")

On the evidence of Pope Francis's first months in office—with each winning action (so modest, so unassuming, so unpontifical), with each new homily, address, interview, general audience, message, phone call, letter, and Tweet, and, finally, his apostolic exhortation "The Joy of the Gospel," we see a man who understands that the time is right for him to lead the Church, the pilgrim people of God, on a new path. We can either be a part of this history (like God the Son, who became flesh and dwelt among us) or let history pass us by. We can decide to be human and real and down to earth or assume a posture of "let's pretend we are holy." We can prefer to be part of a people's Church, "bruised, and hurting, and dirty" because we have "been out on the streets," or we can affect the airs of executives ensconced safely in a corporate tower or a boardroom—or a palace.

As I have tried to show my readers here, Pope Francis hardly had a choice. His Jesuit DNA has driven him to rediscover, redefine, and set out on new frontiers and new boundaries with a holy boldness. For this, he would need time and freedom. In the *America/Civiltà* interview with the Jesuit editors, Francis said, "Time initiates processes, and space crystallizes them. God is in history, in the processes. We must not focus on occupying spaces where power is exercised but, rather, on starting long-run, historical processes." Dynamic versus static. Freedom versus power. Change versus no change. Pope Francis's style—which is the style of Vatican II—is itself the change.

These moves were more than the personal whim of a crazy pope that could be reversed by the next pope; they were the result of Papa Bergoglio's deep understanding of the (delayed) revolution that was Vatican II, something that a future pope is unlikely to veto. Perhaps the only thing that can stop Francis is a fear of failure. So far, he has shown no signs of fear, and my guess is that he will keep acting boldly, AMDG— for the greater good of the people of God. I base my guess on the pope's self-revealing homily on October 27, 2013, about Saint Paul's fearlessness and on his already-expressed admiration for Jesuit father John Navone's seminal work, A *Theology of Failure*. In an e-mail note to me on October 19, 2013, Navone wrote:

> Fear of failure too often condemns us to mediocrity. It is suicidal for an incipient hero. The motto of such fear is "Better a live jackass than a dead lion." Such crippling fear is often motivated by cowardice. Hans Christian Andersen tells of people who are afraid to tell the monarch he is naked. Paradoxically, fear of failure is often succumbing to failure itself. Would there have been the Resurrection had Jesus feared human failure? I believe most great human achievements have been made by persons who successfully overcame the fear of human failure.

For the world's sake, Pope Francis must not fear. But there are forces in the Church, on both the right and the left, that want him to stumble. Check out the so-called conservative bloggers on the Internet, and prepare to be shocked by the obscenities they aim at Francis. I am not at all sure that one of them (it only takes one nut) will not try to assassinate him.

Some skeptics on the extreme left keep up a drumbeat of criticism no matter what the pope says or does now, citing some conservative things he did in Argentina before he became pope as a reason to conclude they cannot trust him to stay his reforming course. They do not comprehend the depth of his conversion. One skeptic with the handle "commiepinkofag" commented on Marian Tupy's December 2013 article for the *Atlantic*:

> Call me when Frankie ordains a woman, marries a same-sex couple, says something remotely responsible about human reproduction, releases the child torture and rape files J2P2 and Benny the Rat locked

in the basement, or devotes the RCC's vast wealth to continuing
Christ's mission to the poor.

Liberals should cut Pope Francis some slack. If they are adult Christians with consciences, they do not need the pope to "say something
responsible about human reproduction." If birth control is a sin, Daddy
cannot give them permission to practice it. And if it isn't, he doesn't
need to. Liberals should grow up and find ways to support Francis in
the Church's most pressing piece of unfinished business—reversing
more than a thousand years of male chauvinism by giving women a
voice, a vote, and first-class citizenship in the Church. Until the Church
does that, Francis's words about "a Church of the poor" are pure rhetoric. The poorest people in the Church are the women of the Church.

How can one man, even if he is a pope, change that? He can't—not
by himself. He trusts that the Holy Spirit (whom Francis mentioned
ninety times in his exhortation) will enlighten our minds and enkindle
our hearts to help us make the Church not a Church *of* the poor but a
Church *for* the poor.

This is Jesuit stuff: to seek the good of others is AMDG, for the
greater good of the people of God. To see God in others is straight out
of the last meditation in Ignatius's exercises: "to see God in all things
and all things in God."

Francis is a self-professed sinner who knows his own limitations. But
he also has the necessary qualities of a captain to steer the Barque of
Peter through the storms of our time and trust that the People of God
will not jump ship. In the face of strong curial headwinds, he will probably have to take a zigzag course. But we hope he will steer his ship by
the Gospel and maintain a clear course in the direction of renewal,
ecumenism, and openness to new ideas. In *Evangelii Gaudium* Pope
Francis gave us a glimpse of the chart he is using on that voyage.

One way to start: by helping the poor be all they can be. The history
of the Church is full of the stories of all those saints who did that in
countless, creative ways, especially in their schools across the world. In
the United States, the Jesuits have founded twenty-eight universities
and forty-seven prep schools (and a growing number of lower schools
designed for the poor), teaching young men to think (and, lately, young
women as well). In the United States alone, more than a million men
and women call themselves Jesuit alumni. In this work, I have profiled

some Jesuits who have found uncommon ways of helping the poor—doing what no one else had thought of before—to illustrate the point I have been trying to make: that there is something special about the Jesuits—their DNA, their desire to try the untried. But a great many other priests and religious brothers and sisters, and millions of laypeople (including men and women of all the other great religions of the world, especially the generous American Jews I have known), have been helping the poor, too. So, in singling out the Jesuits, I do not want to denigrate the efforts of all the others.

I see a Jesuit pope who, because of his Jesuit DNA, has hit on a new way of teaching, not by spouting off pieties or preaching tirades against "the culture of death," but by giving good examples of his own poverty of spirit. Francis eats simply, he sleeps simply, he speaks simply. He trades in his Mercedes for a Ford. He makes us want to think about ways that we can live simpler, more authentic lives. Out of the box? Yes. Because of his Jesuit DNA? Yes. How many of the past eleven non-Jesuit popes have tried to come down from their thrones? How many of them have said, "I am the Church"? How few have said, "We are the Church"?

I think it would help if we put aside those old liberal-conservative categories and take a closer look at how Pope Francis carries himself these days, not as a standard-bearer for any ideology (a word he uses to describe people who are so stuck on an idea that they cannot see the reality of the world they live in). He smiled a few months back when an Italian journalist asked him how he felt when an American radio host accused him of being a Marxist. He answered her by shifting from the abstract to the concrete: "The Marxist ideology is wrong. But I have met many Marxists in my life who are good people, so I don't feel offended."

If you need to put Francis in your own little box to understand him, you could probably do no better than say he is a follower of Jesus or, even better, that he is a Jesuit on a mission, a Jesus mission to help make a better world.

After Bergoglio took over from Antonio Quarracino as archbishop of Buenos Aires, he became a different kind of prelate. He took a two-room apartment within two blocks of the cathedral, kept the archbishop's limo in the garage, and, when he had to go anywhere, rode a bus or a subway. He started contributing more of his time to the bishops' conference of Argentina and CELAM, the Latin American Episcopal Conference, where he was soon elected president. At CELAM's meeting in Brazil in May 2012, he delivered a paper that summed up what the Church in Latin America had to do to make a more just society there. He was a serious prelate. At this stage in his life, few ever saw him smile.

As soon as he emerged from the March 13 conclave as pope in 2013, he started smiling, and now we rarely see him in public when he isn't smiling. Possessed by the discovery that God loves him (and everyone else on the face of the earth), he reminds me of another modern mythic character: Sidney Stratton, the shy research chemist played by Alec Guinness in the 1951 movie *The Man in the White Suit*. Stratton couldn't stop smiling once he'd come up with a secret formula to produce a new miracle fiber. Once a shining white suit was made from the woven miracle fibers, the suit never tore, never got dirty (and if it did, a damp cloth was all you needed to make it look like new), and never needed pressing. Its only drawback? The miracle fabric couldn't take dye, so tailors could only offer it in three colors: white, white, and white. But luminous, because it was slightly radioactive. Sidney Stratton was smiling that inimitable Guinness smile because he had this big secret that would save the world—or at least solve one of humankind's three most pressing needs: food, clothing, and shelter.

The picture, made in Britain's Ealing Studios, became a classic; it still plays with regularity on the Turner Classic Movies channel. I wonder if there is a film buff alive who hasn't seen this comedy seven times. It ends with this whole mill town in Lancashire hating Sidney Stratton. If a man can get by with one suit of clothes, you see, textile workers could only look forward to the day when no one needed their labor any longer. Ditto for the mill managers. And the rich men who owned the mills, well, they would have to eat their losses and find someone else to rip off. The owners try to buy out Sidney Stratton, but he won't sell his idea, because he's a mad scientist who cannot let go of his own discovery. Everyone ends up chasing him down the street—just as the magic fiber begins to disintegrate on his back and he realizes the truth of the old adage: if it seems too good to be true, it probably isn't true.

But then, at the very end of the movie, Stratton is recalculating his formula on a scratch pad. Wide-eyed, he looks up and exclaims, "I see!" We don't have to be told: Stratton will soon be back at work over his test tubes, producing a fiber that does not fall apart.

Now, in real time, we are looking at another Man in a White Suit. His name is Francis, and he also has an invention that will change the world. It is the story of Jesus: come that we may have life and have it more abundantly, now and forever. Like Stratton's story, this invention is also too good to be true. Or is it? Over the last two thousand years, millions of people have believed it, and lived by it, abundantly or not so abundantly, in this life. That may be good enough. As for the next life, we look forward to that by faith, hoping there is life after death (and if there isn't, we won't have lost very much, right?).

If Pope Francis has anything to say about it, we will continue to tell the story of God sending us his only begotten son, starting out as a babe in a manger, and then a little Jewish kid who asked good questions of the temple elders. Francis has these two billion Christians out there, you see, potential missionaries, who will carry the Good News out to the world's edges. We followers? We have our own figurative white suits. If they get stained, God will always wipe them clean. That is what Francis keeps telling everyone: "God understands us, he waits for us, he does not weary of forgiving us in his mercy."

Millions of us are content to believe that, and that may be the secret of this pope's popularity—and of his rise to becoming *Time*'s Man of the Year. There will always be skeptics (Francis has called them "sourpusses") who choose not to believe in the story that is Too Good to Be True. How long, they ask, before the fabric of our belief begins to fall apart and they end up chasing Francis down the street? Or, more likely, how soon before they just give up on the Jesus presented to us by this compassionate, smiling pope and disappear up the beach, saying to one another, "We had hoped"?

Call me a Pollyanna, but I think Francis will always be our Man in the White Suit. He hasn't created a new fabric. He just keeps reminding us who Jesus was, a merciful guy who went around telling us how we could be happy by, for instance, being poor in spirit.

What may happen under Francis's leadership, however, remains to be seen, and that is the great drama that lies ahead. He is just one man—a charming man, to be sure, and a bold man who thinks that his

Jesuit motto, *magis gloriam*, is a sure guide to reforming the People of God. Francis is also a man who has missed the mark many times in the past, and he may well do so again. How? By relying, perforce, on other equally fallible men (sadly, few, if any, women) who are not brilliant enough or politically savvy enough to set up the machinery for the democratic, decentralizing reforms the Church needs if it is to make God's kingdom come—on earth.

In the meantime, Francis has urged us by his example not to judge others. "Who am I to judge?" may have sounded like the most uncon-sidered remark of all time. But it was tone-perfect for a pope who had just come off a triumphant six-day tour in Brazil, where he'd given a dozen talks—about Jesus, if you please!—that drew 24/7 coverage on the television networks of the whole world. That might have puffed him up. But it only seemed to make him more humble, confessing that he had no special expertise at reading human hearts.

Francis has been a *tantum quantum* Jesuit at every turn: whatever works. His message to the young people in Brazil in July was tailored for them: Jesus wants you to become his friend. But the medium added to the message: Jesus isn't a then but a now. Jesus is up to date. And so is his messenger, Pope Francis. For World Youth Day he descended on Copacabana Beach in a chopper, like a rock star,[1] under flashing pink and blue lights that flooded an enormous stage dominated by a giant cross—without a Christ's body on it. Back at the Vatican, he—the prac-tical Jesuit—got busy modernizing the Church's central administration by signing contracts with four of the world's most prestigious manage-ment consultants: McKinsey & Company, the Promontory Consulting Group, Ernst & Young, and KMPG. McKinsey and Promontory are both based in the United States; Ernst & Young is headquartered in London; and KPMG's home office is in the Netherlands. German busi-nessman Ernst von Freyberg, new president of the Vatican Bank, an-nounced he had also hired the U.S.-based law firm Cleary Gottlieb Steen & Hamilton to help with regulatory compliance issues, along with his own PR team from CNC, a communications firm based in Munich. All are global firms, but none have Italian roots, and most of the person-nel being brought into Rome these days to carry out their projects aren't Italian either (and layfolk to boot).

Why is the pope doing this? According to my reporter friends in Rome, it is to break the clerical (and mostly Italian) stranglehold on the place that reflects ancient ways of doing business in the court culture of the Vatican. His Jesuit DNA—his determination to reach for the *magis*—makes him want to replace the kingly style of his predecessors on the papal throne with something more like the leader of a democracy, a man of and for the people.

You need not take my word for it. I pass on the words of Óscar Andrés Rodríguez Maradiaga, the leader of the pope's Commission of Eight cardinals working for reform of the Church. In an interview with a German newspaper on February 6, 2014, he said, "I am totally convinced: We are at the beginning of a new era. Like 50 years ago, when Pope John XXIII opened the windows of the Church to let in fresh air, Francis wants to take the Church in the direction he himself is being driven by the Holy Spirit: closer to the people, not ruling in splendor from above but a living part of them."

We could well meditate on these words, uttered the aftermath of another story coming out of Germany at the moment Cardinal Rodríguez was giving his interview. In November, the secretary of the Extraordinary Synod of Bishops had sent a questionnaire out to all the world's bishops, asking them dozens of questions about how their people felt about many of the Church's teachings on the family. (Many of the questions zeroed in on the Church's traditional prohibitions on premarital sex, remarriage in the Church after divorce, birth control, and even same-sex marriage.)

Imagine the world's surprise when the German bishops, ignoring a Vatican request that the survey results should remain a secret, revealed in February that huge percentages of the people (as many as 97 percent on some questions) had been ignoring the Church's traditional teachings in these areas.

The meaning of this event—the survey and the worldwide response to the survey (which is sure to be the same almost everywhere as it was in Germany)—has just begun to dawn on me. For the first time in history, a pope was turning to the people of God to find out what they thought about the Church's positions on sex. I believed that Francis was making a mischievous move. By even consulting the faithful (as Cardinal Newman had suggested the Church ought to be doing in the middle of the nineteenth century), he was admitting that the people's actions were more of a theological jumping-off place than the abstract, centuries-old reasonings of a bunch of clerics. I daresay he already knew how the survey would turn out. From his own experience with the people in the slums of Buenos Aires, he knew how little they were following the Church's rules. By their actions, by simply not "receiving" the Church's moral teachings on sex, they were, in effect, putting their veto on them.

I believe Francis launched the survey to demonstrate to the world's bishops what he already knew—that the people had long ago rejected the reasoning of the Church's male, celibate clerics (who by their training, take a view on sex that has been conditioned by a long-standing opinion that sex was God's only mistake).

I would guess that Papa Bergoglio, who was possibly once in love himself, would like to put his blessing on what the people at large do, rather than on what his sex-fearing theologians have reasoned out with their "natural law." Is it possible that the Church's moral theologians relied on this sex-fearing strategy to help them deal with their own mandated celibacy? The marvel is that the strategy worked for them—up to a point. The double marvel is that it took the people at large so long to reject a way of being that was appropriate for men vowed to celibacy, but one not so appropriate for them, real people, living normal lives in the real world. I wonder if Pope Francis isn't thinking that the time has come at last for those moral theologians in the clerical Church to realize how inhuman (and unholy) it was for them to impose their clerical views on the people at large.

I know how the people will receive the results of the papal survey—with joyful thanks to Pope Francis for finding a way of doing what Cardinal Newman advised so long ago: consulting them on matters of doctrine. What the faithful have at last learned (from one another) is that sex was not God's only mistake, but rather one of his greatest gifts. I only hope the world's bishops see this, too, for when they start analyzing the results of their own survey, they will have a way of confirming what the pope already knows—that they can trust Christ's faithful. As Pope Francis said in his *America/Civiltà* interview, released in September:

> All the faithful, considered as a whole, are infallible in matters of belief, and the people display this *infallibilitas in credendo*, this infallibility in believing, through a supernatural sense of the faith of all the people walking together. The Church sometimes has locked itself up in small things, small-minded rules. The most important thing is

the first proclamation: Jesus Christ has saved you. And the ministers
of the Church must be ministers of mercy above all.

I love Cardinal Rodríguez for pointing out (for he knows the pope well
and I am only guessing), "Francis wants to take the Church in the
direction he himself is being driven by the Holy Spirit: closer to the
people, not ruling in splendor from above but a living part of them."

NOTES

PREFACE

1. Roberts and I got along so well because we both agreed that the Church should terminate the Congregation for the Doctrine of the Faith (which I will call by its former name, one that is still used in the Vatican itself—the Holy Office). As Roberts could testify from his own personal experience, the Holy Office had continued pursuing a policy of heresy hunting that paid as little attention to due process as the Roman Inquisition that condemned Galileo. In its history, the Orthodox Church has had nothing like the Holy Office's ministry of truth, and Orthodox Christians have kept the faith quite well, thank you very much.

I. A JESUIT POPE

1. Just before the conclave of 2005 began, Cardinal Óscar Andrés Rodríguez heard the story during dinner one night—that Bergoglio only had one lung. Suspecting this was a little pre-conclave propaganda, he hopped up, found Bergoglio, and told him, point blank, "They're saying you only have one lung and that you're in a weakened condition." Bergoglio laughed. "Forget it," he said. "I once had a cyst on my lung. They removed it, and that was that." His suspicions confirmed, Rodríguez was soon circulating around the other tables. "Listen!" he said. "Those of you saying that Bergoglio only has one lung are wrong." In February, he told a German newspaperman that someone in what he called "the inner circle" was out to damage Bergoglio's chances.

2. WHAT TO EXPECT OF A JESUIT POPE?

1. In 2009, after subjecting American Jesuit Roger Haight to nine years of investigation for his *Jesus, Symbol of God* (1999), the Holy Office condemned his work and told him he could not teach theology anywhere or publish any further in his field of Christology. Obediently, he hunkered down at *America* magazine's headquarters in New York, producing two books on the Spiritual Exercises of Saint Ignatius of Loyola—*Christian Spirituality for Seekers* (2012) and *Spirituality Seeking Theology* (2014). He also got a job to pay his keep at *America*, directing the PhD program at Union Theological Seminary.

2. In his blog on February 24, 2013, after Benedict's resignation, Leonardo Boff, Ratzinger's principal target among Latin America's liberation theologians, wrote,

> Whoever understands the logic of a closed and authoritarian system, not very open to the world, that does not cultivate dialogue and exchange (living systems are alive to the degree that they open up and interexchange) knows that someone like me, who does not plainly get in line with that system, will be watched over, controlled, and eventually punished. It is similar to the security systems that we have known in Latin America under the military regimes of Brazil, Argentina, Chile, and Uruguay. Within this logic, the then-prefect of the Congregation for the Doctrine of the Faith (former Holy Office, former Inquisition), Cardinal Joseph Ratzinger, condemned, silenced, removed from their teaching chairs or transferred out more than one hundred theologians.

3. In addition, it seems that Pope Francis is a fan of G. K. Chesterton, the English journalist who was also a popular theologian and the creator of the still widely read Father Brown mysteries. In 2005, Cardinal Bergoglio, who was on the honorary committee of Argentina's Chesterton Society, approved the wording of a prayer for Chesterton's canonization.

4. THE JESUIT DNA

1. Years later, long after I'd left the Jesuits, I was walking up Columbus Circle in Manhattan on my way to a movie with my girlfriend. When I saw a panhandler in my path, I whispered to Lily through clenched teeth, "I am *not* gonna tumble to this guy." I passed him by, trying not to look at him. And then,

from behind me, his voice rang out, "In the name of Jesus Christ of Nazareth, won't you help me?" I froze and said to Lily, "He said the right words." I fished a dollar out of my pants pocket and turned back to him. What the hell? I had an extra dollar, and he was only human. And so was I.

2. Today I wouldn't send Jim Maher to the dungeon of the pots, as I did then. With old age comes wisdom, and with wisdom, mercy. So much of what we did then in the novitiate seems inhuman today. And, since Vatican II, "being human" is one of the virtues that many Jesuits (including, it seems, Pope Francis) value most.

3. Bud Schallert explained, "We live in an absolute monarchy attenuated only by the insubordination of its subjects and the stupidity of its superiors." In retrospect, I would have to say the General Congregation's ban on smoking was not stupid—just an idea that was several decades ahead of its time. Now we know: smoking kills us.

7. OTHER RELIGIONS

1. I am adapting here a profile I did on Dall'Oglio in my 2006 book, *A Church in Search of Itself*.

2. I first profiled Jacques Dupuis in *A Church in Search of Itself*.

3. This quote is taken from a New Delhi publication called *JNANADEE-PA*, vol. 1, no. 2 (July 1998). Readers can find it online at http://sedosmission. org/old/eng/Rayan.html. (This is part of an online treasure trove of articles bearing on the Church's missionary outreach sponsored by SEDOS [Service on Documentation and Study on Mission], a missionary consortium based in Rome.)

4. In his *America/Civiltà* interview, this is what I think Pope Francis was talking about when he said, "If the Christian is a restorationist, a legalist, if he wants everything clear and safe, then he will find nothing. Tradition and memory of the past must help us to have the courage to open up new areas to God. Those who today always look for disciplinarian solutions, those who long for an exaggerated doctrinal 'security,' those who stubbornly try to recover a past that no longer exists—they have a static and inward-directed view of things. In this way, faith becomes an ideology among other ideologies."

8. LIBERATION THEOLOGY

1. Nicholas Cafardi, dean emeritus and professor of law at Duquesne University, and a former chair of the U.S. Conference of Catholic Bishops' National Review Board for the Protection of Children and Young People, proposed in a February 2014 bulletin of *U.S. Catholic* that laypeople have more of a say in the selection of bishops. In answer to an objection that this would bring politics into the process, Cafardi wrote, "Priests already do campaign to become bishops; the laity just do not know about it. Priests campaign with their bishop friends to get on the provincial list. They campaign with the papal nuncio to get on the list of three names sent to Rome, usually with the help of affluent donors who have direct access to the nuncio. There are even stories of the head of a wealthy Catholic fraternal organization carrying the names of priest friends to Rome for advancement." Future historians will be derelict if they do not pore through reports on Bergoglio by the Buenos Aires nuncios, Pio Laghi and his successor Ubaldo Calabresi, to see why they promoted Bergoglio inside the Vatican.

9. PIONEERS

1. The following narration is taken from my original piece, published in the *Tablet* in September 2002.
2. People everywhere are complicit in their own suicide. Residents of Los Angeles have an average of almost three cars per family and almost no rapid rail transit, but their smog problem has lessened in the last two decades because the State of California has imposed expensive, rigid controls on carbon emissions from their cars. Many of the eight million people in Mexico City living under a laissez-faire, if not corrupt, government drive clunkers—many of which are cast-offs from Los Angeles—that fill their mountain basin with lethal pollutants.

11. STILL JESUITS

1. Eugene Bianchi's latest publications can be found at http://www.bianchibooks.com.
2. Among those shocked: Tom Roberts, an editor of the *National Catholic Reporter*, who recruited Dear to write a regular column for *NCR*. In a Febru-

ary 3 column, addressing Dear's charge that the Jesuit order "no longer advocates for justice or works of justice," Roberts wrote:

> It is a shame, because recent Jesuit newsletters are filled with examples of justice work being done by individual Jesuits and Jesuit institutions throughout New York, New England and Maryland. From the Jesuit Refugee Services to advocacy for a just minimum wage to support for immigration reform to university service programs to the Ignatian Solidarity Network to a call for help in promoting juvenile justice reform, the evidence would suggest that the Jesuits have hardly given up on promoting justice.
>
> I know my comments may appear to some as a liberal heresy. But for me, the overriding issue is journalistic—either the record matters or it doesn't. Serious questions abound about the efficacy of working in or around the military, taking on its uniform as officers (and that's not only a question for Jesuits), legitimate questions exist about military programs on campus and support of wars that popes have condemned. However, the clear intent of Dear's statement, to establish that he stands singularly among Jesuits as a voice raising questions about such practices, is more than mild exaggeration. I have no interest in getting into the details of internal conflicts among Jesuit brothers. However, I think that in assessing the charges Dear levels, as in hearing of the breakup of any long-standing relationship, one must be wary of the explanation that places the entire blame on one side. I have a much greater interest in the truth of the record regarding Jesuits and the promotion of justice, in what is clearly documented and verifiable as a counter to the claims John made in his parting statement. Those matters are publicly important.

12. THE MAN IN THE WHITE SUIT

1. In fact, in February 2014, he landed on the cover of *Rolling Stone*, as if he were a Mick Jagger or a Bruce Springsteen or a Britney Spears.

BIBLIOGRAPHY

Baum, Gregory. *Amazing Church: A Catholic Theologian Remembers a Half-Century of Change*. Maryknoll, NY: Orbis, 2005.

Berry, Jason. *Lead Us Not Into Temptation*. New York: Doubleday, 1992.

Berry, Jason, and Gerald Renner. *Vows of Silence*. New York: Free Press. 2004.

Bianchi, Eugene C., and Rosemary Radford Ruether. *A Democratic Catholic Church: The Reconstruction of Roman Catholicism*. New York: Crossroad, 1992.

Briggs, Kenneth. *Double Crossed: Uncovering the Catholic Church's Betrayal of American Nuns*. New York: Doubleday, 2006.

Brou, Alexandre. *The Ignatian Way to God*. Milwaukee: Bruce, 1952.

Cahill, Lisa Sowle, John Garvey, and T. Frank Kennedy, eds. *Sexuality and the U.S. Catholic Church: Crisis and Renewal*. New York: Crossroad, 2006.

Carroll, James. *Practicing Catholic*. New York: Houghton, Mifflin, Harcourt, 2009.

———. *Toward a New Catholic Church*. Boston: Houghton Mifflin, 2002.

Collins, Paul. *Papal Power*. London: HarperCollins, 1997.

Congar, Yves. *My Journal of the Council*. Collegeville, MN: Liturgical Press, 2012.

Cozzens, Donald. *The Changing Face of the Priesthood*. Collegeville, MN: Liturgical Press, 2000.

———. *Faith That Dares to Speak*. Collegeville, MN: Liturgical Press, 2004.

———. *Freeing Celibacy*. Collegeville, MN: Liturgical Press, 2006.

———. *Sacred Silence: Denial and Crisis in the Church*. Collegeville, MN: Liturgical Press, 2002.

de Guibert, Joseph. *The Jesuits: Their Spiritual Doctrine and Practice, A Historical Study*. Chicago: Institute of Jesuit Sources, 1964.

Dupuis, Jacques. *Toward a Christian Theology of Religious Pluralism*. Maryknoll, NY: Orbis, 1997.

Divarkar, Parmanda R., trans. *A Pilgrim's Testament: The Memoirs of Ignatius Loyola*. St. Louis: Institute of Jesuit Sources, 1995.

Dunne, George H. *Generation of Giants*. Notre Dame, IN: University of Notre Dame Press, 1962.

———. *King's Pawn: The Memoirs of George H. Dunne, S.J.* Chicago: Loyola University Press, 1990.

Faggioli, Massimo. *True Reform: Liturgy and Ecclesiology in Sacrosanctum Concilium*. Collegeville, MN: Liturgical Press, 2012.

———. *Vatican II: The Battle for Meaning*. New York: Paulist Press, 2012.

Farley, Margaret. *Just Love: A Framework for Christian Sexual Ethics*. New York: Continuum, 2008.

Fiedler, Maureen, and Linda Rabben, eds. *Rome Has Spoken: A Guide to Forgotten Papal Statements, and How They Have Changed Through the Centuries*. New York: Crossroad, 1998.

Fox, Matthew. *The Pope's War: Why Ratzinger's Secret Crusade Has Imperiled the Church and How It Can Be Saved*. New York: Sterling Ethos, 2011.

Fox, Thomas C. *Sexuality and Catholicism*. New York: George Braziller, 1995.

France, David. *Our Fathers*. New York: Broadway Books, 2004.

Ganss, George E., ed. *The Constitutions of the Society of Jesus*. St. Louis: Institute of Jesuit Sources, 1970.

———. *Ignatius of Loyola: The Spiritual Exercises and Selected Works*. New York: Paulist Press, 1991.

Gibson, David. *The Coming Catholic Church*. San Francisco: HarperCollins, 2003.

Granfield, Patrick. *The Limits of the Papacy*. New York: Crossroad, 1987.

Kaiser, Robert Blair. *A Church in Search of Itself*. New York: Knopf, 2006.

———. *Clerical Error: A True Story*. New York: Continuum, 2002.

———. *The Politics of Sex and Religion*. Kansas City: Leaven Press, 1985.

Keen, Sam. *The Passionate Life: Stages of Loving*. San Francisco: Harper & Row, 1983.

Kendall, Daniel, and Gerald O'Collins, eds. *In Many and Diverse Ways: In Honor of Jacques Dupuis*. Maryknoll, NY: Orbis, 2003.

Kennedy, Eugene. *Tomorrow's Catholics: Yesterday's Church. The Two Cultures of American Catholicism*. Ligouri, MO: Triumph Books, 1988.

———. *The Unhealed Wound: The Church, the Priesthood, and the Question of Sexuality*. New York: St. Martins, 2001.

Küng, Hans. *The Catholic Church: A Short History*. New York: Modern Library, 2001.

Lacouture, Jean. *Jesuits: A Multibiography*. Washington, DC: Counterpoint, 1995.

Lakeland, Paul. *The Liberation of the Laity*. New York: Continuum, 2004.

Letson, Douglas, and Michael Higgins. *The Jesuit Mystique*. Chicago: Loyola Press, 1995.

Lobdell, William. *Losing My Religion*. New York: HarperCollins, 2009.

Lowney, Chris. *Heroic Leadership: Best Practices from a 450-Year Old Company That Changed the World*. Chicago: Loyola Press, 2003.

———. *Pope Francis: Why He Leads the Way He Leads*. Chicago: Loyola University Press, 2013.

Macy, Gary. *The Hidden History of Women's Ordination: Female Clergy in the Medieval West*. New York: Oxford University Press, 2008.

Mahoney, Jack. *Christianity in Evolution: An Exploration*. Washington, DC: Georgetown University Press, 2011.

Manning, Joanna. *Take Back the Truth: Confronting Papal Power and the Religious Right*. New York: Crossroads, 2002.

Marty, Martin. *The One and the Many: America's Struggle for the Common Good*. Cambridge, MA: Harvard University Press, 1997.

McBrien, Richard P. *Lives of the Popes: The Pontiffs from St. Peter to John Paul II*. San Francisco: HarperCollins, 1997.

Meissner, W. W. *Ignatius Loyola: The Psychology of a Saint*. New Haven, CT: Yale University Press, 1992.

Martin, Robert Bernard. *Gerard Manley Hopkins: A Very Private Life*. New York: Putnam, 1991.

Morwood, Michael. *Tomorrow's Catholic: Understanding God and Jesus in a New Millennium*. Mystic, CT: Twenty-Third Publications, 2000.

Navone, John. *A Theology of Failure*. New York: Paulist Press, 1974.

Noonan, John T., Jr. *A Church That Can and Cannot Change: The Development of Catholic Moral Teaching*. Notre Dame, IN: Notre Dame University Press, 2005.

O'Callaghan, Joseph F. *Electing Our Bishops: How the Catholic Church Should Choose Its Leaders*. Lanham, MD: Rowman & Littlefield, 2007.

O'Malley, John W. *The First Jesuits*. Cambridge, MA: Harvard University Press, 1993.

———. *What Happened at Vatican II*. Cambridge, MA: Harvard University Press, 2008.

O'Collins, Gerald. *Living Vatican II: The 21st Council for the 21st Century*. New York: Paulist Press, 2006.

Orsy, Ladislas. *Receiving the Council: Theological and Canonical Insights and Debates*. Collegeville, MN: Liturgical Press, 2011.

Piqué, Elisabetta. *Francesco: Vita e rivoluzione*. Torino: Lindau, 2013.

Quinn, John R. *Ever Ancient, Ever New: Structures of Communion in the Church*. New York: Paulist Press, 2013.

Radcliffe, Timothy. *What Is the Point of Being a Christian?* London: Burns & Oates, 2005.

Ratzinger, Joseph. *Salt of the Earth: The Church at the End of the Millennium: An Interview with Peter Seewald*. San Francisco: Ignatius Press, 1997.

Reese, Thomas J. *Inside the Vatican: The Politics and Organization of the Catholic Church*. Cambridge, MA: Harvard University Press, 1996.

Rigert, Joe. *An Irish Tragedy: How Sexual Abuse by Irish Priests Helped Cripple the Catholic Church*. Baltimore: Crossland Press, 2008.

Robinson, Geoffrey. *Confronting Power and Sex in the Catholic Church*. Mulgrave, Victoria, Australia: John Garrett, 2007.

———. *For Christ's Sake: End Sexual Abuse in the Catholic Church for Good*. Mulgrave, Victoria, Australia: John Garrett, 2013.

Roberts, Thomas d'Esterre. *Black Popes*. New York: Sheed and Ward, 1954.

Roberts, Tom. *The Emerging Catholic Church: A Community's Search for Itself*. Maryknoll, NY: Orbis, 2011.

Rohr, Richard. *Falling Upward*. San Francisco: Jossey-Bass, 2011.

Rubin, Sergio, and Francesca Ambrogetti. *Papa Francesco: Il Nuovo Papa Si Racconta*. Milan, Italy: Salani Editore, 2013.

Russell, Mary Doria. *The Sparrow*. New York: Ballantine, 1997.

Rynne, Xavier. *Letters from Vatican City*. New York: Farrar Straus, 1963–1966.

Savart, Louis M. *The New Spiritual Exercises: In the Spirit of Teilhard de Chardin*. New York: Paulist Press, 2010.

Schultenover, David G. *A View from Rome: On the Eve of the Modernist Crisis*. New York: Fordham University Press, 1999.

Selling, Joseph. *The Reaction to Humanae Vitae*. Ann Arbor, MI: University Microfilms, 1979.

Shaw, Russell. *American Church: The Remarkable Rise, Meteoric Fall and Uncertain Future of Catholicism in America*. San Francisco: Ignatius Press, 2013.

Schillebeeckx, Edward. *The Real Achievement of Vatican II*. New York: Herder and Herder, 1967.

Schoof, Mark. *A Survey of Catholic Theology, 1830–1970*. New York: Paulist Newman Press, 1970.

Spence, Jonathan D. *The Memory Palace of Matteo Ricci*. New York: Penguin, 1985.

Steinfels, Peter. *A People Adrift*. New York: Simon and Schuster, 2003.

Suhard, Emmanuel. *Growth or Decline?* South Bend, IN: Fides, 1948.

Swidler, Leonard. *Making the Church Our Own*. Lanham, MD: Sheed and Ward, 2007.

———. *Toward a Catholic Constitution*. New York: Crossroad, 1996.

Thavis, John. *The Vatican Diaries*. New York: Viking, 2013.

Tillard, Jean-M.R. *The Bishop of Rome*. Wilmington, DE: Michael Glazier, 1983.

Vallely, Paul. *Pope Francis: Untying the Knots*. London: Bloomsbury Academic, 2013.

Weber, Nick. *The Circus That Ran Away with a Jesuit Priest: Memoir of a Delible Character*. Indianapolis: Dog Ear Publishing, 2005.

Willis, Robert J. *The Democracy of God: An American Catholicism*. New York: iUniverse, 2006.

Wilson, George. *Clericalism: The Death of Priesthood*. Collegeville, MN: Liturgical Press, 2008.

Wills, Garry. *Papal Sin*. New York: Doubleday, 2000.

Wiltgen, Ralph. *The Rhine Flows into the Tiber*. New York: Hawthorn, 1967.

Wright, Jonathan. *The Jesuits: Missions, Myths and Histories*. New York: HarperCollins, 2004.

INDEX

accountability, in Church, 186
Adam and Eve, 44
Ad Gentes, 87
ad majorem Dei gloriam (AMDG), 14, 63, 64, 124, 126, 131, 135, 195, 196
Africa, Czerny in, 133, 137–139
African Jesuit AIDS Network (AJAN), 133, 138–139
AIDS, 133, 137, 138–139
Alinsky, Saul, 154, 155, 159–160
ambition, of Francis, 73, 124
AMDG. *See ad majorem Dei gloriam*
America, 41, 128, 206n1; arranging interview with Francis, 16; editors of, 9, 11, 15, 17, 18
America/Civiltà interview, 67–69, 71, 72, 74, 111–112, 117, 119, 194, 202–203, 207n4
Americanism, 23, 24
American Jesuits, 155–156
American Jewish Committee, 30
Anglican Church, 24
Annuario Pontificio, 10
anti-Semitism, 80
Apostles' Creed, 82
Apostolic Palace, 5, 182
Aquinas, Thomas, 4, 171–172
Argentina: "disappeared" in, 113–114; Jesuits in, 113–115
Argentina Province, 26
Arizona, Meyers in, 173–175

Arrupe, Pedro, 25, 45, 88, 136, 137, 155–157, 177, 183
Asia, Church in, 88, 92–93
Asian Jesuits, 88
Asian theology, 93
An Asian Theology of Liberation (Pieris), 92

Bauman, John: Alinsky and, 159–160; at Boston College, 166; Central America and, 165–166; in Chicago, 160; faith of, 161, 165; in Oakland, 153–154, 161–163; ordination of, 161; PICO founded by, 147, 153–154, 158; as revolutionary, 147
Bea (cardinal), 78, 84
Benedict XIV, 129
Benedict XVI: on homosexuality, 183; red Prada shoes of, 5; resignation of, 1, 206n2; secularism and, 73, 85; theologians and, 10, 13, 14, 190. *See also* Ratzinger, Joseph (cardinal)
Bergoglio, Jorge, 33, 205n1; as bishop of slums, 115–116, 118, 121; as Buenos Aires archbishop, 1, 3–4, 10, 113, 115, 116, 197–198; in Córdoba, 68, 118; critics of, 113, 114; defenders of, 113; errors made by, 117; liberation theology of, 113, 116, 119–120, 137; as pragmatist, 116; as provincial in Argentina, 25–26, 68, 113, 114, 117,

123, 137; at Saint George (Germany), 117, 184. *See also* Francis

Berman, Paul, 91

Berrigan, Daniel, 45, 175–176

Bianchi, Eugene, 173

Bible, 37, 80

birth control, 24, 182, 196

bishop of Rome, Francis as, 182

bishops, survey of, 201–202

The Bishop of Rome (Tillard), 183

Blake, Eugene Carson, 132–133

Blanshard, Paul, 128

Blessed Virgin Mary, 19, 70, 94, 97, 181

Boff, Leonardo, 119, 120–121, 122, 206n2

Boston Shakespeare Company, 140

Brazil, Francis in, 13, 189, 200

Brophy, Frank Cullen, 130

Brown, Edmund G. (Jerry), Jr.: Buddhism studied by, 168; as California governor, 167–168, 169; as Jesuit at heart, 169; Mother Teresa and, 168; as pioneer, 167–169; presidential bid of, 168; in Society of Jesus, 167

Bruni, Frank, 71–72

Buddha, 93, 96

Buddhism, Brown and, 168

Buddhists, 92, 96, 98–99, 100; Buenos Aires archbishop, Bergoglio as, 1, 3–4, 10, 113, 115, 116, 197–198

Cafardi, Nicholas, 208n1

Cain, Bill: Jesuit DNA of, 139; with network TV, 140; as New York Jesuit, 139, 143; Oldham's interview with, 143–145; as pioneer, 139–146; in theater, 140, 141–143; Treanor's interview with, 145–146

California Democratic Party, Holstein in, 170–171

California governor, Brown as, 167–168, 169

California Province, 127, 128, 131

la campaña (the Company), 19

Campbell-Johnston, Michael, 113–114

capitalism, 24, 185, 187–188

carbon emissions, 134, 208n2

Carroll, James, 6, 70

Carroll, John, 22

cartoneros, 116

Casa Santa Marta, 5, 17, 183

Castel Sant'Angelo, 10

Casti Connubii, 24

Catherine the Great, 22

CatholicCulture.org, 74

Catholic League for Religious and Civil Rights, 74, 140

Catholic News Service, 74

Catholic Theological Society of America, 105

Catholic Worker movement, 81

CDF. *See* Congregation for the Doctrine of the Faith

CELAM. *See* Latin American Episcopal Conference

celibacy, 61, 141, 185, 202

Central America, PICO in, 165–166

centralized infrastructures, 134–135

Chambers, Whittaker, 49–50

charter, of Vatican II, 87

Chesterton, G. K., 206n3

Chicago, Helfrich and Baumann in, 160

China, 128–129; Saso in, 171, 173

Chinese Christians, 129

The Christhood of Jesus and the Discipleship of Mary: An Asian Perspective (Pieris), 101–102

Church: accountability in, 186; Anglican, 24; in Asia, 88, 92–93; change in, 85; conservatives of, 74–75, 190; freedom in, 190; as happy, 82; interview about, 68, 72, 110–111; in Latin America, 119–120, 121; as learning Church, 78; moral teachings of, 69, 190–191; obituary of, 77; open spirit of, 124; redefining of, 69, 73, 79; sense of citizenship in, 124; sex scandal in, 141, 185; as teaching Church, 78; view of, 77–78

Church, Charism, and Power (Boff), 120

Church in Search of Itself, 1

citizenship, sense of, 124

Civiltà Cattolica, 16, 17, 106

Clement XIV, 10, 22, 47

Clemmitt, Marcia, 12

clericalism, 73, 185

Coelho, Ralph, 76

Colbert, Stephen, 16

commission, of John XXIII, 182

Commission of Eight, 73, 201
Common Rules, 37
Commonweal, 76, 126, 128
Communism, 80, 120
Company of Jesus, 19–20, 22
compassion, 37, 206n1
conclave of 2013, 2, 4
Confucius, 96, 129
Congregation for the Doctrine of the Faith (CDF), 97. *See also* Holy Office
Congregation for the Evangelization of Peoples, 105
Congressional Quarterly, 12
conservatives, and Francis, 74–75, 190
Contemplation for Obtaining Love, 35–36
contraceptives. *See* birth control
Conwell, Joseph, 63, 65
Cooper, Gloria: background of, 150–151; education of, 151; empowerment of, 147; excitement of, 149; PICO and, 149–150, 151, 152; representatives and, 148; San Diego Unified School District, 152; SDOP and, 151–152; Six-to-Six program supported by, 152, 158; solution and, 149; speeches of, 148–149, 152; Cortesi, Arnaldo, 79–80
Córdoba, Bergoglio in, 68, 118
Council of Chalcedon, 93, 94, 102
Council of Trent, 82
Counter-Reformation, 79
CQ Researcher, 12
Cross, Ratzinger and, 121
culture of encounter, 11
Czerny, Michael: AJAN helped by, 133, 138–139; at Jesuit Curia's Social Justice and Ecology Secretariat, 133; in Johannesburg, 133–134, 135–136; in Nairobi, 138; as pioneer, 133–139; in Rome, 139

Dall'Oglio, Paolo, 88–92
Daniélou, Jean, 79, 131
Dante, 141
Day, Dorothy, 81
Dear, John: Berrigan and, 175–176; as ex-Jesuit, 178; Jesuit DNA of, 177, 178; as Maryland Province Jesuit, 175, 176–177; with Pace e Bene, 179; as pioneer, 175–179; Shea and, 176–177;

in Society of Jesus, 175
de Foucauld, Charles, 89
de Goes, Benedetto, 28, 29
Degollado, Marcial Maciel, 2
Deir Mar Musa, 89, 90
de Lubac, Henri, 79
A Democratic Catholic Church: The Reconstruction of Roman Catholicism (Bianchi and Ruether), 173
Dick, John A., 11–13
Digitatis Humanae (Murray), 130
"disappeared," in Argentina, 113–114
disordered affection, 33
Divine Comedy (Dante), 141
Divine Milieu (Teilhard), 125
dogma, 82
Dolan, Timothy, 72
Dominicans, 10, 19, 78, 129
Dominus Iesus, 6, 103
Donohue, William, 74, 75, 140
Dunne, George, 50, 132–133; in California Province, 126, 127, 128, 131; in China, 128, 129; Daniélou and, 131; in Geneva, 132; at Georgetown University, 132; at Harvard, 128; Hollywood craft unions and, 127; Jesuit DNA of, 132; Luce and, 129–130; memoir of, 129–132; at Phelan Park, 127; in Phoenix, 126, 127, 129, 131; as pioneer, 126–133; racism crusade of, 126–127, 137; responsibility of, 132; in St. Louis, 126, 127
Dupuis, Jacques: book published, 105–106; concrete experience of, 104; education of, 103; history and, 104; in India, 103, 104; notification regarding, 107; Ratzinger and, 106–107, 109; in Rome, 104, 105, 108–109

Earth Summit, 134
El Salvador, executions in, 114
Emeritus College, Bianchi's founding of, 173
empowerment, 147
enculturation, 87, 88
environmentalists, 134–135
Equivocation (Cain), 142, 146
Esquire, 14

European Jesuits, 21, 47
Evangelii Gaudium. See "The Joy of the Gospel"
evangelization, 187
examen, 36–37, 40, 61
excommunication, 23, 80, 101, 165
executions, in El Salvador, 114
exercises. *See* Spiritual Exercises of Saint Ignatius
Exercitium Caritatis, 40–42, 61
exhortation, of Francis. *See* "The Joy of the Gospel"
ex-Jesuits, 167–179. *See also specific individuals*
Ex Quo Singulari, 129
Extraordinary Synod of Bishops, 201

faith traditions, of PICO members, 157–158, 164
Federation of Asian Bishops, 87–88
fides sperans salutem (faith hoping for liberation), 94
The First Jesuits (O'Malley), 21
First Vatican Council. *See* Vatican I
Fort Benning, Holstein at, 170
Francis: ambition of, 73, 124; as bishop of Rome, 182; in Brazil, 13, 189, 200; business and, 200–201; in Casa Santa Marta, 5, 17, 183; clothes of, 5; conservatives and, 74–75, 190; on conversion of papacy, 191; critics of, 195–196; culture of encounter of, 11; election of, 2–4; on freedom in Church, 190; homilies of, 5, 15, 85, 193; on homosexuality, 183–184; humility of, 73, 124, 189, 194; Jesuit DNA of, xii, xiii, 15, 27, 45–46, 52, 65, 71, 85, 123, 124, 185, 192, 194, 197, 201; as Jesuit, xiii, 3, 6, 10; on Jesus, 184, 186, 187, 188, 200; "The Joy of the Gospel," 75, 186–188, 189–191, 194, 196; leadership of, 83, 187; liberals and, 196; liberation theory and, 122; as listening pope, 71; as Man of Year, 81, 184, 199; message of, 4–5, 6, 13; name of, 9; normalcy of, 6–7; popularity of, 189, 199; Roman Curia reform and, 27; as sinner, 68, 118, 119, 184, 196; smile of, 198; as soccer fan,

15; style of, 192, 194; theologians and, 14; at World Youth Day, 189, 200. *See also* Bergoglio, Jorge; interviews, with Francis
Franciscans, 10, 19
Francis: Life and Revolution (Piqué), 118
Francis of Assisi, 9, 188
French Jesuits, 21

Gaillardetz, Richard, 75
Gaudium et Spes, 20, 25, 79, 81, 87, 121
gay priests, 183
General Congregations, of Jesuits, 25, 62, 63, 136
"Generation of Giants" (Dunne), 128–129
The Genesis of an Asian Theology of Liberation: An Autobiographical Essay on the Art of Theologizing in Asia (Pieris), 102
Geneva, Dunne in, 132
Germany, Bergoglio in, 117, 184
Giddings, Luther, 163
global warnings, 134, 208n2
God, 36, 56, 69; Vatican II and, 80, 82
God talk, 93
Goodstein, Laurie, 73
Gorman, Thomas K. (bishop), 79
Gospels, 13, 25, 32, 47, 48, 87, 97, 110, 128, 155, 161
Gregorian University, 11, 24, 104, 106, 109
Gregory XVI, 22–23
Growth or Decline? (Suhard), 24, 47
Guinness, Alec, 198
Gunpowder Plot, 142
Gutiérrez, Gustavo, 122

Haight, Roger, 206n1
Harvard, 128
Hasler, Bernard, 23
health care, for poor, 155
Hélder Câmara, Dom (archbishop), 81, 119–120
Helfrich, Jerry: Alinsky and, 159–160; in Chicago, 160; death of, 165; in Oakland, 153–154, 161–163; ordination of, 161; PICO founded by, 153–154
hell, 38, 81, 182

Heroic Leadership: Best Practices from a 450-Year-Old Company that Changed the World (Lowney), 29
Heyndrickx, Jeroom, 9
Hindus, 88, 104
HIV/AIDS, 138
Hollywood craft unions, Dunne and, 127
Holstein, Robert Mills: board service of, 170; in California Democratic Party, 170–171; death of, 169, 171; at Fort Benning, 170; as pioneer, 169–171; in prison, 170; in Society of Jesus, 169
Holy Office, 100, 106, 107, 108, 120, 122, 125, 129, 205n1
Holy Spirit, 63, 65, 85, 88, 111, 177, 185, 192, 194, 196, 201, 203
homilies, of Francis, 5, 15, 85, 193
homosexuality, 183–184
"Hope in Islam" (Dall'Oglio), 89
Hopkins, Gerard Manley, 21, 58
How the Pope Became Infallible (Hasler), 23
How to Write a New Book for the Bible (Cain), 142–144
humility, of Francis, 73, 124, 189, 194
Hunt, Mary, 70–71, 73–74

Ignatius-Juana model, 64
The Imitation of Christ (à Kempis), 37
Impelling Spirit (Conwell), 63
the Incarnation, 34
India, Dupuis in, 103, 104
Industrial Areas Foundation, 160
Institute of Social Order, 127
Internet, xiii, 67, 76, 195
interviews, with Francis: *America/Civiltà*, 67–69, 71, 72, 74, 111–112, 117, 119, 194, 202–203, 207n4; about Church, 68, 72, 110–111; on clericalism, 73; comments on, 74–76; on Curia, 73; about God, 69; on new way of thinking, 69; by Scalfari, 72–73, 123, 124; on women, 71, 73
Irish Independent, 193

Jalics, Franz, 26
Janssens, Jean-Baptiste, 25
Jesuit approach, of Loyola, 21, 28
Jesuit colleges, 20

Jesuit Curia's Social Justice and Ecology Secretariat, 133
Jesuit DNA, 3, 14, 28, 147; acquisition of, 31–45, 46–52, 53–61; of Cain, 139; of Dall'Oglio, 92; of Dear, 177, 178; of Dunne, 132; of Francis, xii, xiii, 15, 27, 45–46, 52, 65, 71, 85, 123, 124, 185, 192, 194, 197, 201; of Malone, 16; of Teilhard, 125
Jesuit education: classical schooling, 48–49; philosophy, 48, 49–50; regency, 49, 53; theology, 48, 49, 53
Jesuit missionaries, 46–47
Jesuit Muslim. *See* Dall'Oglio, Paolo
Jesuit pope. *See* Francis
Jesuit Reductions, 21
Jesuits: *ad majorem Dei gloriam*, 14, 63, 64, 124, 126, 131, 135, 195, 196; in Argentina, 113–115; Brown as, 169; Cain as, 139, 143; coadjutors, 20; daily office of, 20–21; decline of, 61–62; *Exercitium Caritatis*, 40–42, 61; denying of, 39; escapades of, 29–30; Francis as, xiii, 3, 6, 10; hell and, 38; justice and, 135, 136; as learned clergy, 21; love and, 27; Loyola as founder of, 19; mission statement of, 15; practicing virtues, 39–40; professed, 20; risk-taking of, 29, 32, 45; in Russia, 22; scholastics, 20; self-discipline of, 38; social action and, 137–139; Spiritual Exercises of, 32, 33–34, 61, 63; temporal coadjutors, 20; "the Kingdom" advanced by, 25; training of, 32–33; at Vatican II, 78–79. *See also specific Jesuits*
Jesuits: A Multibiography (Lacouture), 20
Jesuit theologians, 10, 93
Jesus, 15, 68, 82; Chinese face of, 129; exercise relating to, 34; followers of, 80, 82–83, 90; Francis on, 184, 186, 187, 188, 200; trekking with, 35; view of, 93, 94; words of, 81. *See also* Company of Jesus; Society of Jesus
"Jesus Lost in the Temple," 96–97
Jews, 80, 182
Johannesburg, UN summit meeting at, 133–134, 135–136

John XXIII, xiii, 15, 30, 181–182, 183,
    201; commission appointed by, 182;
    Communism and, 80; as Man of Year,
    78; Vatican II launched by, 77, 78, 182
John Paul II, 2, 85, 120, 183; liberation
    theology opposed by, 120; sex scandal
    and, 1; theologians and, 10, 14, 63, 190
"The Joy of the Gospel" (*Evangelii
    Gaudium*), 75, 186–188, 189–191, 194,
    196
juniorate, 46, 47
justice, 25, 47, 81, 115, 126, 132, 157, 161,
    165, 207n2; Jesuits and, 135, 136;
    social action/justice, 80, 102–103,
    137–139, 162, 177

Kingdom advancement, 25, 126
King's Pawn (Dunne), 129, 132
Kolvenbach, Peter Hans, 104, 106,
    107–108, 133, 169, 177
Koran, 90

Lacouture, Jean, 20
Laghi, Pio, 114, 115
Latin, 39, 48
Latin America, Church in, 119–120, 121
Latin American Episcopal Conference
    (CELAM), 116, 198
Latin Mass, 182
Law, Bernard (cardinal), 1
learning Church, 78
Legionaries of Christ, 2, 11
Leonard, Robert, 54, 55
Leo XII, 22
Leo XIII, 23, 24
Lex dubia non obligat, 39
liberals, and Francis, 196
liberation theology, 25–26, 93, 102–103,
    122; of Bergoglio, 113, 116, 119–120,
    137; John Paul II's opposition of, 120,
    190
Limbaugh, Rush, 188
Lombardi, Federico, 16, 17, 75–76
López de Loyola, Íñigo. *See* Loyola,
    Ignatius
L'Osservatore Romano, 6
love, Jesuits and, 27
Lowny, Christopher, 28–29, 43

Loyola, Ignatius, 11, 14, 64; Berrigan and,
    45; company set up by, 19–20; Jesuit
    approach of, 21, 28; as Jesuit founder,
    19; Rules for the Discernment of
    Spirits, 43, 44; Spiritual Exercises of,
    32, 33, 61, 63; on Three Divine
    Persons, 34; Xavier and, 43
Loyola University, 127, 176
Luce, Clare Boothe, 129–130
Lumen Gentium, 87

magis gloriam, 16, 46, 127, 147, 200
Maher, Jim, 41–43, 207n2
Maher, Zachaeus, 131, 132
Malley, Pat, 55–56
Malone, Matt, 15, 16, 17, 18
Man of Year: Francis as, 81, 184, 199;
    John XXIII as, 78
The Man in the White Suit, 198–199
Manning, Timothy, 132
Marcó, Guillermo, 115
Marconi, Guglielmo, 11
marginalization, 10, 24, 38; of women, 62,
    63–64, 65
marriage, 84
Martin, James, 15–16, 17, 18, 160
Martín, Luis, 23
Martin, Malachi, 30
martyrdom, 45, 119, 121
Marx, Karl, 116
Marxism, 120, 188, 197
Mary. *See* Blessed Virgin Mary
Maryland Province Jesuit, Dear as, 175,
    176–177
Mass: in China, 128; Latin, 182; with
    Pieris, 99–100
Massignon, Louis, 89
Matthew 25, 188
McDonough, Peter, 173
McGuire, Donald, 29–30
McIntyre, James Francis, 127
mercy, 4, 69, 190, 203
Merton, Thomas, 81, 118, 183
Messori, Vittorio, 121
Mickens, Robert, 5, 6–7
Middle Ages, 20
Middle East, 91
Mills, C. Wright, 77
Mirus, Jeff, 74

Modernism, 23
Mohammed, 90. *See also* Muslims
Mombé, Paterne, 139
morality, 116
Mother Teresa, 30, 168, 188
Mount Saint Michael's, 49–50, 51, 52
Mueller, Gerhard Ludwig (archbishop), 122
Mugica, Carlos, 116
Murray, John Courtney, 79, 130
Muslims, 31, 88–89, 90, 91
Myers, David: in Arizona, 173–175; awards of, 174; dismissed by Olmsted, 174–175; as Oregon Province Jesuit, 173; as pioneer, 173–175; as quintessential Jesuit, 175; Yaquis supported by, 173–174
Mystic, Shaman, Oracle, Priest (Saso), 172

Nairobi, Czerny in, 138
Nasrec, 135
National Catholic Reporter, 9, 75, 76, 178
national lobby, PICO as, 166
Navone, John, 117, 195
Negro, 155–156
network TV, Cain with, 140
New York Times, 12, 71, 73, 79–80, 189
NGOs. *See* nongovernmental organizations
Nine Circles (Cain), 141–142
No Bars to Manhood (Berrigan), 45
nongovernmental organizations (NGOs), 135
Nothing Sacred (Cain), 140, 141, 144, 145

Oakland, 153–154, 161–163
Oakland Tribune, 154
Obama, Barack, 160–161
O'Collins, Gerald, 108
O'Donnell, Liz, 193
O'Farrell, Ricardo, 26
Oldham, Madeleine, 143–145
Olmsted, Thomas (bishop), 174–175
O'Malley, John W., 21, 83, 191–192
"On the Sin of Segregation" (Dunne), 126–127
Opus Dei, 11
Oregon Province Jesuit, Meyers as, 173

Oregon Shakespeare Festival, 142
original sin, 44
Ottaviani (cardinal), 78, 83, 84, 125

Pace e Bene, 179
Pacific Institute for Community Organizing (PICO): in Central America, 165–166; Cooper and, 149–150, 151, 152; faith traditions of members of, 157–158, 164; foundation of, 153–154; history of, 153–155; human growth and, 158; as national lobby, 166; network of, 157; new course of, 164–166; Washington impacted by, 148
pain, 37, 38
Palin, Sarah, 161
papal infallibility, 23, 83–84, 181
Pascendi Dominici Gregis, 23, 24
Passionate Uncertainty (Bianchi and McDonough), 173
Pastor Aeternus, 181, 182
Patriarch of Constantinople, 171
Patriarch of Rome, 171
Paul III, 20
Paul VI, 30, 84, 97, 182
Peace Corps, 132
Pell, George (cardinal archbishop), 3
Phelan Park, Dunne at, 127
The Phenomenon of Man (Teilhard), 125
philosophy. *See* Jesuit education, philosophy
Phoenix, Dunne in, 126, 127, 129, 131
PICO. *See* Pacific Institute for Community Organizing
Pieris, Aloysius: art with, 96–97; books of, 92–93, 101–102; Buddhists and, 92, 96, 98–99, 100; faith of, 100; Mass with, 99–100; as scholar, 98; school run by, 101; in Sri Lanka, 92, 93, 96, 97, 98, 100; theology of, 92–95, 97; Tulana Research Centre founded by, 92, 93, 95, 98; visit with, 95–97
pilgrim people, 81, 111
pioneers: Bianchi, 173; Brown, 167–169; Cain, 139–146; Czerny, 133–139; Dear, 175–179; Dunne, 126–133; Holstein, 169–171; Myers, 173–175; Saso, 171–173; Teilhard, 125–126

Piqué, Elisabetta, 118
Pius IX, 23, 24, 181
Pius X, 23, 24, 181
Pius XI, 24, 84, 181
Pius XII, 6, 22, 24, 47, 102, 111, 181
Pontifical Council for Interreligious
    Dialogue, 105
poor, 119–120, 135, 196–197;
    empowerment of, 147; health care for,
    155; justice for, 115; Vatican II and, 81
Pope Francis: Untying the Knots (Vallely),
    115, 122
Portier, William, 76
Portuguese Jesuits, 28
prison, Holstein in, 170
probabiliorism, 38
Protestants, 79, 80
*Providential Timeliness of Vatican II: A
    Long-Overdue Halt to a Scandalous
    Millennium* (Pieris), 102
Purgatory, 181

Quarracino, Antonio (archbishop), 197
quintessential Jesuit, Meyers as, 175

Raab, Scott, 14–15
racism crusade, of Dunne, 126–127, 137
Rahner, Karl, 79, 98, 118, 184
Rotunno, Nicola, 99–100
Ratzinger, Joseph (cardinal), 2, 10–11, 18,
    82, 102, 103; Boff and, 120–121; Cross
    and, 121; Dupuis and, 106–107, 109;
    Vatican II and, 121. *See also* Benedict
    XVI
Rayan, Samuel, 87, 103, 104–105
redefining, of Church, 69, 73, 79
redemption, 44
Reed, Tom, 60–61
Reese, Thomas J., 9–10, 18, 76, 119
regency. *See* Jesuit education, regency
Religion and American Democracy
    (Dunne), 128
Religion News Service, 122
religions, non-Christian, 87–112
Renaissance, 20
La Repubblica, 72, 123
Rerum Novarum, 23
Reveille for Radicals (Alinsky), 154
revolutionary, Bauman as, 147

Ricci, Matteo, 88, 128
Rinser, Luise, 118
Roberts, Tom, 208n2
Rocca, Francis X., 74–75
Rodríguez Maradiaga, Óscar Andrés, 201,
    203, 205n1
Rohr, Richard, 69–70
Roman Curia, 1–2, 27, 45, 65, 68, 73, 79,
    120, 124
Roman theology, 190
Rome: Czerny in, 139; Dupuis in, 104,
    105, 108–109
Romero, Oscar, 114
Roncalli, Angelo Giuseppe. *See* John
    XXIII
Rosica, Thomas, 6
Ruether, Rosemary Radford, 173
Rules for the Discernment of Spirits, 43,
    44
Russell, Mary Doria, 12
Russia, Jesuits in, 22

Saint George (Germany), Bergoglio at,
    117, 184
Saint Paul, 97, 150, 193, 195
Saint Peter's Square, 4, 5
Salesians, 10
salvation, 36, 80, 81, 94, 95; of souls, 20
San Diego Organizing Project (SDOP),
    151–152
San Diego Unified School District, 152
Saso, Michael: background of, 171; in
    China, 171, 173; in Honolulu, 172; in
    Japan, 172; as pioneer, 171–173; in
    Tibet, 173; as wordless prayer believer,
    171
Scalfari, Eugenio, 72–73, 123, 124
Schallart, Eugene, 57–58, 207n3
Schotte, Jan (cardinal), 17
Scola, Angelo (cardinal archbishop), 2
SDOP. *See* San Diego Organizing Project
Second Vatican Council. *See* Vatican II
Secretariat for Promoting Christian Unity,
    78
secularism, 73, 85
sex scandal: in Church, 141, 185; John
    Paul II and, 1
Shakespeare, William, 142
Shea, James, 176–177

Sheehan, Michael (archbishop), 177
sinners, 80, 81; Francis as, 68, 118, 119,
    184, 196
Sistine Chapel, 2
Six-to-Six program, 152, 158
smoking, 59, 207n3
social action/justice, 80, 102–103,
    137–138, 162, 177
social sin, 127
Society for Development and Peace
    (SODEPAX), 132–133
Society of Jesus, 31, 63, 118, 155;
    Bergoglio and, 26; Bianchi in, 173;
    Brown in, 167; changes in, 124, 156;
    chauvinism of, 64; Conwell and, 63;
    Dear in, 175; founding of, 19–20;
    Holstein in, 169; purpose of, 25;
    restoration of, 22; suppression of, 10,
    22
SODEPAX. See Society for Development
    and Peace
solar panels, 135
soteriologically inconsequential, 94–95
Spadaro, Antonio, 16–17, 67, 117
Spanish Jesuits, 21
The Sparrow (Russell), 12
Spiritual Exercises of Saint Ignatius, 32,
    33–34, 61, 63
Sri Lanka, Pieris in, 92, 93, 96, 97, 98, 100
St. Louis, Dunne in, 126, 127
Stand-Up Tragedy, 140
stray dog problem, 163
Suhard, Emmanuel Célestin (cardinal),
    24, 47–48
Summa Theologica (Aquinas), 172
survey, of bishops, 201–202
sustainable development, 135
Synod of Bishops, 17
Syria, 89, 91–92
Syriac Catholic Rite, 89

Tablet, 5, 6, 105, 133
Taking a Long Road Home (Bianchi), 173
tantum quantum, 33, 65, 200
teaching Church, 78
teachings, of Church, 69, 190–191
Teilhard de Chardin, Marie Joseph
    Pierre, 167; education of, 125; Jesuit
    DNA of, 125; as pioneer, 125–126

theater, Cain in, 140, 141–143
Thelen, Bert, 62
theologians, 206n2; Benedict XVI and, 10,
    13, 14, 190; Francis and, 14; Jesuit, 10,
    93; John Paul II and, 10, 14, 63, 190
theology: Asian, 93; in Jesuit education,
    48, 49, 53; of Pieris, 92–95, 97; Roman,
    190. See also liberation theology
The Theology of Failure (Navone), 117
Thomas à Kempis, 37, 50
Three Divine Persons, 34
Tibet, Saso in, 173
Tillard, Jean-Marie Roger, 183
Toward a Christian Theology of Religious
    Pluralism (Dupuis), 105
Treanor, Tim, 145–146
Trial by Fire (Dunne), 50, 127
The Trial of the Catonsville Nine
    (Berrigan), 45
"The Trouble with Francis" (Hunt),
    70–71
"'The Truth Will Make You Free': The
    Theology of Religious Pluralism
    Revisited" (Dupuis), 109
Tucci, Roberto, 79
Tulana Research Centre, 92, 93, 95, 98
Tyrrell, George, 23

University of Louvain, 11
University of Paris, 19
UN summit meeting (Johannesburg),
    133–134, 135–136; analysis of, 136;
    NGOs at, 135

Vallely, Paul, 26–27, 115, 116, 122
Vatican Bank, 2
Vatican I, 23, 181
Vatican II, 11, 15, 25, 69, 73, 76, 102, 123,
    164, 195; changes in, 78, 80–85, 186;
    charter of, 87; Communism and, 80,
    120; God and, 80, 82; Jesuits at, 78–79;
    Jews and, 80; John XXIII's launching
    of, 77, 78, 182; marriage and, 84; new
    attitudes at, 82; papal infallibility and,
    83–84; pilgrim people and, 81; poor
    and, 81; Protestants and, 79, 80;
    Ratzinger and, 121
Vatican Press Office, 2, 16, 17, 182
Vatican Radio, 11

Vehementer Nos, 23

Washington, PICO and, 148
WATER. *See* Women's Alliance for
    Theology, Ethics and Ritual
Weigel, Gustave, 79
West Coast Compañeros, 28
What Happened at Vatican II (O'Malley),
    83, 191
Wijesysingha, Shirley, 101
windmills, 135
Witness (Chambers), 49–50
women: interviews about, 71, 73;
    marginalization of, 62, 63–64, 65

Women's Alliance for Theology, Ethics
    and Ritual (WATER), 70
wordless prayer, 171
World Trade Organization, 134
World Youth Day, Francis at, 189, 200
Wright, Jonathan, 31

Xavier, Francis, 43

Yaquis, Meyers and, 173–175
Yorio, Orlando, 26

Zimmers, Eugene, 57
Zorzin, Victor, 117–118